Sold My Soul for a Student Loan

Sold My Soul for a Student Loan

Higher Education and the Political Economy of the Future

Daniel T. Kirsch

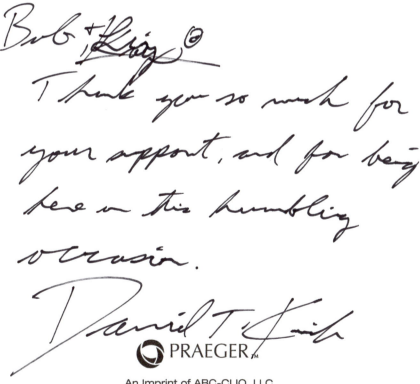

Bob + Krig 😊
Thank you so much for your support, and for being here on this humbling occasion.

Daniel T. Kirsch

PRAEGER™

An Imprint of ABC-CLIO, LLC
Santa Barbara, California • Denver, Colorado

Library of Congress Cataloging-in-Publication Data

Names: Kirsch, Daniel (Daniel T.), author.
Title: Sold my soul for a student loan : higher education and the political economy of the future / Daniel T. Kirsch.
Description: Santa Barbara, CA : Praeger, [2019] | Includes bibliographical references and index.
Identifiers: LCCN 2018055205 (print) | LCCN 2019000783 (ebook) |
  ISBN 9781440850721 (ebook) | ISBN 9781440850714 (cloth : alk. paper)
Subjects: LCSH: Student loans—United States. | College costs—United States. |
  College graduates—United States—Finance, Personal. | Debt—United States.
Classification: LCC LB2340.2 (ebook) | LCC LB2340.2 .K57 2019 (print) |
  DDC 378.3/620973—dc23
LC record available at https://lccn.loc.gov/2018055205

ISBN: 978-1-4408-5071-4 (print)
     978-1-4408-5072-1 (ebook)

23 22 21 20 19   1 2 3 4 5

This book is also available as an eBook.

Praeger
An Imprint of ABC-CLIO, LLC

ABC-CLIO, LLC
147 Castilian Drive
Santa Barbara, California 93117
www.abc-clio.com

This book is printed on acid-free paper ∞

Manufactured in the United States of America

To the next generation of students of humanity. Keep questioning, keep studying, keep arguing, and keep struggling. Your work matters.

Contents

Preface   ix

Acknowledgments   xi

Introduction   1

Chapter 1   The American Debtor as Worker, Consumer,
                 and Citizen   23

Chapter 2   The Ideology of Homeowner Democracy and
                 Trust in Government   35

Chapter 3   The Government's Creation and Destruction of the
                 American University   67

Chapter 4   Responses to the Crisis: The New Debtor Movements   91

Chapter 5   The Sin of Debt and the Hope of Forgiveness in the
                 Twenty-First Century   121

Notes   147

Index   173

Preface

Every author takes pains to articulate just how many people have assisted in the creation of the final published work. What is not always explained is the personal motivation behind the exploration of a book's topic, especially in the realm of social science.

Through a series of regrettable personal and financial decisions from ages 21 to 28, I accumulated over $90,000 in student debt, which then compounded. After taking several more years to complete my doctoral dissertation in 2014, I resolved to put away that topic (coded racial campaign rhetoric for statewide offices in New England) for a time and try to focus on something that had substantive and even material importance for me and others like me. It took some serious thought to define just what that topic would be, partly because I had trouble situating myself in a community: Political science academics? Millennials? Generation X? None of these seemed to be quite right. My thought process was directed toward my six-figure student debt payments that would soon come due for the first time in over a decade of postsecondary education, and the need to reconcile my employment and financial realities with those balances and accounts.

I began to read about student loan borrowers' experiences online in a series of message boards that were created to facilitate people sharing their stories, especially in the wake of Occupy Wall Street in 2011, in which I was never involved. I began to see that grassroots political groups had formed in relation to the issue. More traditional political institutions, such as labor unions and political parties, were facilitating the advancement of an agenda in the halls of Congress and state legislatures that would advocate for those who, like me, had not sought fame and fortune in their education, but had found their vocation and had made some poor financial decisions in attempting to fulfill it.

Having long since abandoned the idea of a career in political activism and advocacy, I thought I would rather make a career of political analysis than engage in the rough and tumble of political life. I decided to tell the story of some of these borrowers whose stories were found on message boards on the Internet, and contextualize it within a framework of alienation from both political and academic life, both familiar themes in my own way of thinking. I submitted a paper to a conference that, for the first time, was completely unrelated to my dissertation topic. It was a risk, but it was one worth taking to see if I could marry my two passions, political and academic, under the auspices of a relevant issue in which I had somewhat of a literal investment. I received two types of feedback about the paper: that it spoke powerfully to a silent part of the population, those with student debt; and that my work was aligned too much with borrowers' plight and that I should be wary of any people who had any part of or sympathy with the Occupy movement.

I was approached by a savvy acquisitions editor who believed I had caught on to something that was sure to carry weight in the conversation in the coming years. Through a series of drafts and consultations with some of the most gifted writers and editors I know, I crafted a book proposal that gained acceptance from the publisher, and I set to work. Now I just had to write the book.

There were plenty of economic studies of student debt from the National Bureau of Economic Research and the Federal Reserve Bank of New York. There were also people talking about student debt and alienation, and about student debt as indentured servitude, and mining the stories, as my paper had, from some of the websites that began to sound more and more familiar. I decided that I would go deeper, and after situating the exploration of the issue politically, I would seek people who have dealt with various aspects of this issue: not just student-borrowers, but college admissions officers, attorneys, politicians, organizers, activists, and university administrators, and fully engage with their different perspectives, probing how they think and talk about this issue and the political possibilities it presents. I took several risks and reached out to people who are arguably celebrities in the world we're about to traverse, and many of them responded affirmatively to my invitation to speak. Some chose to remain anonymous, but their insights are no less valuable. I am in every way grateful to them for speaking with me, and I hope that the fruits of all of these conversations are enjoyable to readers. I came through this intellectual journey with new positions and new understandings of what must be done in student debt. I am grateful to readers for making the journey a shared adventure.

Acknowledgments

Victory has a thousand parents. Using that criteria, this book is unquestionably victorious. In the course of writing this book, I consulted with some of the most gifted writers and editors I know. The following people have proven themselves to be valuable and steadfast colleagues, and have more than earned my friendship. I hope their mention here is a small step toward my earning theirs. These exceptional individuals are Tom Durwood, Sarah Marusek, Jose Marichal, Vanessa Torrado, Tatishe Nteta, Alana Jeydel, Andrew McLean, Lonce Bailey, John Hinshaw, Carol Ruxton, Dean Robinson, David Bateman, Jamila Michener, Paul Buhle, Eli Meyerhoff, Jeffrey Broxmeyer, Mark Brown, Monicka Tutschka, and Jessica Lawless. Thank you to the University of Massachusetts Amherst, Cengage Learning, Valley Forge Military College, the Western Political Science Association, the Caucus for a New Political Science, the American Political Science Association, and the State of Wisconsin for facilitating my introduction to such generous and gifted people.

I will also thank the staff of the three libraries where I conducted my research: the W.E.B. Du Bois Library at the University of Massachusetts Amherst, the May Baker Memorial Library at Valley Forge Military Academy and College, and the Sacramento State University Library.

Thank you also to the Pennsylvania state chapter of the American Association of University Professors, who were always supportive and understanding, and to the Philadelphia chapter of the Democratic Socialists of America (and its alumni) for demonstrating how powerful an issue this can be, and how much the voice of borrowers needs to be heard.

To my colleagues and friends who helped put me in touch with interviewees and research angles, thank you for your kindness and your help. It has not been forgotten.

Thank you to my students, who have always inspired me and renewed my faith in the power of higher education. Thank you especially to my student research assistants, who were extremely helpful, especially in the initial research stages, Alex Hammond and Benjamin Kaufman, both of whom have gone on to bigger and brighter adventures since advancing the substance of the manuscript.

My wonderful colleagues in the California Faculty Association, the Department of Political Science at Sacramento State, the Los Rios College Federation of Teachers, and the Division of Behavioral Sciences at Sacramento City College, where my work teaching young members of California's Capital Region funded my ongoing research and writing. I am particularly grateful to Jim Shoch, Nancy Lapp, Judy Beachler, and Rosamaria Tanghetti.

My interview subjects, first the anonymous interviewees, who were gracious with their time, attention, and insights; this book could not have been written without their contributions. To the named contributors, including Elizabeth Henderson, Benjamin Anderson, Chris Hicks, Adolph L. Reed Jr., Jake Virden, Jason Rosenstock, David Halperin, and Cory Mason. All of these capable professionals have done more than I could ever hope to do alone in making this conversation matter. Finally, another person in this category who defies categorization is Miranda Merklein, who sadly passed away before the project went to press. It is my fervent hope to honor her memory with the publication of this book and the issues she raised while we talked, and that she never stopped talking about.

My extraordinarily capable and supportive editor, Jessica Gribble, who saw the project from its inception to its completion.

To my family, especially my parents, thank you for teaching me what I needed to frame the world through a lens that values and prioritizes the dignity and respect of others. In particular, thank you for teaching me to value education, which you always did in word and deed.

My wife, Morgan, is a constant support, an enlightening presence, and a source of inspiration.

Finally, it is with great sincerity that I remind the reader that any and all shortcomings and errors rest entirely with the author alone, and that anything outstanding is purely due to the wisdom the author displayed in leaning on greater minds than his own.

Introduction

"The personal is political." The second-wave feminist adage coined by Carol Hanisch in 1970 conveyed that the social structures defining gender roles were arrived at through ages of political decisions, and thus can only be addressed politically, not individually.[1] This understanding informs the conversation surrounding student debt in every corner of the political realm. If anything personal in the United States is political, debt is. From an individual perspective, every person makes a decision to borrow to finance anything—a home, a car, and increasingly, postsecondary college and university education. This is truer now than ever, when roughly one in four American adults hold some student debt.[2] The average debt among graduates increases every year, now at $30,000 for new graduates, and student debt now ranks as the highest nonmortgage consumer debt in the United States, surpassing auto loans and credit card debt in 2013.[3] What is most worthy of study is how much of the current political structure has facilitated this circumstance, how effective the various policy measures that have sought to address the crisis have been, and what should still be done to address their effectiveness.

The student debt crisis is perhaps the latest symptom of the slow death of the "American Dream," which is best understood as a universal ideological narrative of social mobility and stability that we need not celebrate in order to criticize the erosion of its widespread viability and availability.[4] While public higher education funding is being slashed, the archetypal and still predominant liberal arts curriculum in higher education itself is being devalued as a punchline, and the entire education sector of the economy is scrambling to secure a future for its very purpose while it is in higher demand than at any other period. While the value of a STEM (science, technology, engineering, and math) education is at an all-time high in public opinion, civic education—education aimed at reproducing the means of citizenship in a democracy—in the form of history, social studies, and the arts is being slashed nationwide.[5] Students often encounter civic education for the first time in college.[6]

The current political moment is one of vastly increased household debt disproportionately held by young people, stagnating household wages, and a precarious and competitive job market for 18- to 34-year-olds that demands academic certifications as a prerequisite to entry. Homebuying and health care costs are increasingly out of reach, and the life expectancy rate in the United States is for the first time on the decline.[7] There was a record low turnout among many constituencies in the 2016 elections, and a growing tendency to disparage any perspective of public or collective identity or commensurate responsibility.[8] An entire generation, in a situation where a public utility is more in demand but less accessible, has made a "rational" calculation: borrow as much as possible, whether from the federal government directly or from private loans guaranteed by the federal government, or in any way possible.[9] This is to try to "get ahead" even in the form of loans that require no credit check and are virtually impossible to discharge in bankruptcy. They "did everything right," a phrase used often by borrowers and analysts.

Borrowers placed their trust in their agreement with their creditors, their own government, that if there is a systemic failure, the implicit social contract would demand that there is an escape clause. Breakdown of this contract, being suffered exclusively by the borrowers with zero risk to the creditors, is causing social frustration and popular demands for public policy shifts, and an absence of credible established forces that increasingly safeguard apparently inadequate, minimalist solutions. A populace that can only continually express its disdain for outcomes without receiving an official response that reflects their motivations is the very antithesis of, and is toxic to, democracy.

At a time when the need for citizen empowerment is perhaps greatest, the need for a foundation of democratic citizenship in a popularly available and widely achieved higher education curriculum centered on liberal arts carries less weight in the social conversation than ever before. The lack of universally accessible voting procedures and procedural civic education are symptoms of a disease that, at its root, does not assign a collective urgency to participation in the political system within the educational system. The current crisis and the lack of an effective public policy response to it is a recipe for massive alienation among an aggrieved and law-abiding population of borrowers who "did the right thing" to better themselves through the hard work of education without fully realizing the magnitude of debt they were taking on while in deferment during their student status, alternately breeding radicalism and reaction when the loans come due as a material reality. Student debt is, of course, a drag on the economy, harming our society in both the short and long term by damaging the credit of a huge portion of society that should be buying homes and starting careers. Politically, student debt ultimately alienates borrowers from American democracy by sabotaging the American Dream of homeownership and social mobility, harming the credibility of democracy itself in the United States. As will be demonstrated throughout the chapters that follow, any policy solution must at a bare minimum address the three largest sites of culpability and misery in the ongoing student debt crisis: (1) the federal government holding and/or guaranteeing a majority of existing student debt it is also legally empowered to completely forgive, but which right now encourages tuition increases at every college and university, and effectively makes the majority of student loans nondischargeable, even in bankruptcy, surpassing home mortgage, auto, and credit card debt in level of security to the creditor and risk to the borrower; (2) state legislatures that have drastically cut public funding, encouraging public universities and colleges to raise tuition and student fees that largely finance tuition payments; (3) finally, for-profit colleges and universities, almost all of their revenue coming from federal loans, preying upon students that cannot afford their tuition, and failing to graduate 84 percent of their students.

In this book, the discourse surrounding student debt will make plain how the political process has shaped the phenomenon of student debt, and how the crisis, as a consequence, has affected the political system. Methodologically, some choices had to be made as to how to investigate these questions. There is voluminous data on the scale of the student debt crisis available from sources such as the Federal Reserve Bank of New York and the National Bureau of Economic Research. Each of these studies plays an important role in contextualizing the circumstances of the crisis and the impacts it has on the economy. There are also many studies that demonstrate how the system of student loans has somewhat served as a stand-in for the story of borrowing, particularly in the late twentieth and early twenty-first centuries. Several books do this ably as well, exploring the more technical aspects of what has been called "The Student Loan Mess," "The Student Loan Scam," and "The Student Loan Swindle."[10]

What has been missing is a narrative of how different important actors see this issue, using an interpretive method that hinges on a culturally contextualized read of the situation, an ethnography of the world of student debt enabled through interviews and participant observation. The author has most certainly been a participant-observer in this culture or world of student debt, and the burden falls here to interpret that world. In addition, college admissions officers, attorneys, politicians, organizers, activists, and university administrators have been interviewed for the purpose of engaging fully with their different perspectives, probing how they think and talk about this issue, and discussing the political possibilities presented by the intersection of where many of them arrive in their ideas for solutions that may change that world.

The United States has already entered the "world" of the student loan crisis, and it is finally time to stop, take a look around, and talk to the world's inhabitants by engaging in some deep ethnography. In fact, this entire generation of borrowers sees themselves as victims of this American Dream ideological narrative, caught in a web of promises that were not fulfilled despite their good-faith participation. From interviews conducted for this book as well as online testimonies of hundreds of borrowers in several forums, it's clear that they see themselves as victims of the broken promise of the American Dream of mortgage-based homeownership, stability of employment, and a comfortable retirement through reliance on governmental institutions and middle-class-geared programs like student loans; they are saddled collectively with more of a financial burden at the start of their career through a public policy–facilitated borrowing scheme that exceeded personal consumer risk than any precedent in U.S. history. The American Dream itself is an ideological narrative that social science has long critiqued. This work does not mean to celebrate or champion this narrative, only to note its existence as the ideological underpinning and foundation of social goods upon which the U.S. political-economic system has been built. The system has, in a sense, been mortgaged with promises to future generations, and if it has not yet defaulted, it is certainly in danger of foreclosure.[11]

This book is an exploration of how to best understand the growing reality of student loan debt in the modern political and social context of the United States, and its effects on the political outlook of borrowers and their relationship to the American Dream of social mobility and its fallback, stability. In the following pages, the causes and consequences of debt are discussed in the traditional relationship Americans have had with those debts in the post-2008 era. Debt, particularly student debt, affects the decisions people make and the resulting cultural consequences that act in concert with the political and economic structures of our society. Through a textual analysis of political theory, public policy, popular culture, and interviews that draw upon the expertise of policymakers, financial analysts, social activists, university administrators, faculty, and borrowers themselves, we take an ethnographic, 360-degree view of this issue. The alienation and the disempowerment of citizens affected by the crisis overlaps significantly with the youngest generations of voters.

The Roots of Student Debt Discourse in the United States

To explore this topic, it is useful to look at some of the ways in which most people have been discussing student debt by way of linguistic analogy and simile. Analogies of the "company store" and "indentured servitude" have been invoked by many of the 43 million people in the United States who have accrued student debt. Clearly, most of these have been meant as a way of expressing a historical parallel that illustrates the principles at work in the logic of student loans. The parallel of heavily indebted student borrowers today with the coal miners' "company towns" in the last half of the nineteenth and first half of the twentieth centuries is intriguing and feels familiar.[12] The song "Sixteen Tons," popularized by baritone Tennessee Ernie Ford in 1956 is most known for its chorus, in which the singer bemoans being "another day older and deeper in debt" as a result of workplace ties and obligations.[13]

The popular song itself is cultural shorthand for workplace exploitation, evidenced by the fact that it is commonly referenced today in political discourse among politically active and aware citizens.[14] The song itself was about the "truck system" among Kentucky coal miners, a form of debt bondage, itself a form of labor trafficking (a subset of human trafficking), which is now explicitly illegal in the United States.[15]

To explore the history and discourse of student debt in the United States is a complex task. It is inseparable from the modern history and discourse of work itself in this country. Consumer debt, more broadly, is born of a very particular and definitely crucial moment in the history and development of modern political economy. Consumer debt has been facilitated and indeed, even dispensed, by the federal government itself, from mortgages to student loans. A central problem is the address of the cost or benefit, social and material, to the quality of democracy in the execution of these policies by legitimated governmental structures. Another complication is the attachment of direct financial and legal subservience of the education industry and those ensconced within it to the financial institutions that already influence much of society and formal governmental structures, with their decision-making (political) power and influence.

It is now no longer shocking to read the latest statistic of $1.5 trillion of student debt held nationwide.[16] It seems consistent with a high government debt and high national indebtedness generally.[17] That this debt is four times larger than it was in 2005, the majority of it was accumulated after the financial crisis of 2008 hit, and that one in ten of those dollars are in a state of default is not necessarily shocking.[18] What is less often the focus is where and how this type of debt is held, who holds it, how and why it was accumulated, and the effects it has on their lives, as citizens and as people in a very particular stage of life.

Nearly two in five of everyone between the ages of 18 and 29 have student debt, and one in five between ages 30 and 44.[19] The average amount of debt for the 23 million households with student debt is $49,000.[20] Both the average amount of debt held by new college and university graduates and the proportion of graduates with student debt increases every year.[21] In the most highly educated generation in U.S. history, student loan borrowers now constitute the clear majority of graduates.[22] In a representative democracy, elites usually come from the ranks of the highly educated and reflect their constituents' values. Student debt, which has already begun to affect employment, homeownership rates, and even health outcomes, is in the top ranking of concerns among citizens under 30.[23]

Student debt is certainly the dominant financial concern among this new generation, and how it will be handled politically will have lasting consequences for the political climate of the United States.[24] Decision-makers in the political and financial realm have crafted myriad and sometimes confusing and even contradictory solutions to this emerging crisis, and still students are demanding some type of loan forgiveness, though it is not being heard.[25] Many are treating it more as a chronic illness to manage than a financial reality. After a certain grace period of nonrepayment after graduation, more and more students are searching for forgiveness programs through either the government, their employer, or their private loan servicer.[26] Such programs may be long-term and not immediate, but they provide an alternative route to financial solvency.[27] Some political groups have chosen to utilize students' feelings of alienation for political mobilization and even an attempt at a "debt jubilee," which would mean a massive forgiveness of debt.[28] Many young borrowers are now expressing regret at their own education and wishing they had heeded that old warning "neither a borrower nor a lender be."[29]

"Grace period." "Forgiveness program." "Debt jubilee." "Neither a borrower nor a lender be." Among most student loan borrowers who have "sold their soul" there is an element of contrition and ultimately a humble request for some type of forgiveness.[30] A religious quality of conversation pervades the student debt policy discussion, and it is perhaps time for a "Come to Jesus" moment among those who see the borrowers themselves as the source of the problem.[31] Indeed, because students lacked agency in the origination of their debt, there is alienation from some of the pillars of our society:

1. The financial institutions that lend to them and have direct oversight of their material well-being and worthiness, and thus act as their site of perhaps principal anguish and conflict;

2. The federal government that encouraged and assisted them in borrowing high amounts without a credit record, essentially co-signing (aka "guaranteeing") the loan, and the pervasive ideology of the necessity of upward class mobility that supports such policies;

3. The institutions of higher education that compelled and/or persuaded them to borrow sums they could not afford;

4. The workplaces that do not pay them enough to make their payments without significant hardship and wrangling;

5. The supposedly representative democracy that is not responding to their plight, or doing anything to prevent this harm from recurring to others.

Politics in a So-Called Democracy

Defaulting is the end of the line. It's the recognition that someone is incapable of paying a previously recognized debt, and usually results in nonpayment of that debt by the borrower. The creditor must "write off" that loan. The negative consequence for the borrower, of course, is a lasting stain on a person's or financial institution's creditworthiness record. By some accounts, the default itself is an illustration of the kind of frustration that alienates the citizens of the student loan world. There is little agreement surrounding the very concept of "default." There are classifications of "default" by some financial institutions, but traditionally, defaults can be discharged in bankruptcy.[32] There is no accompanying discharge of defaulted loans by the federal government in its lending capacity on a normalized basis. The exact circumstance in which the government will allow borrowers to default is still being debated in the courts.[33] The issue is not being debated as a priority in state legislatures, nor in the halls of Congress.[34] This circumstance is a perfect example of the kind of disconnection and alienation these borrowers are experiencing.

Policies that directly affect borrowers in material ways are completely out of their reach. One reason is the Malthusian logic of American democracy:[35] Despite the increasing population, the number of representatives remains the same, increasing the distance between most of the people and their elected officials.[36] Elected officials might be as responsive as they have always been, but ultimately the quality of representation suffers as time goes on. This is also a fiction, however, because as the competition for elected office grows fiercer and more resource-hungry, officials must satisfy large donors to their election campaigns.[37] In response, people must act collectively in order to have any hope of transcending the financial constraints that place them below the tier of donors to which officials must report to maintain their position. Borrowers, however, have a particular difficulty in taking collective action and/or mobilization uniquely linked to their status.

To gain leverage over the powerful few, collective action can be taken in any number of contexts by average citizens. Workers in a traditional workplace may, for example, organize into a labor union that may instigate a work stoppage to force fair terms in contract negotiations or disputes. Neighbors in a community largely of renters may organize a tenants' association that may perpetrate a rent strike in the face of subpar living conditions or rising rents and force the landlord to respond to their demands. Voting residents of a community may organize to take over a school board or city council that has raised taxes too high or is threatening to cut the arts or music, for example.[38] In each of these instances people are collectively organizing in order to realize a common goal, at some personal cost.

For the most part, there are very real and immediate, and potentially permanent, material losses that may result in financial instability in the short and long terms if borrowers refuse to pay debts. Of course, creditors may have to minimize negative consequences if there is a widespread public outcry in conjunction with a massive debt strike, but both of those circumstances seem difficult to imagine, and they are probably unlikely to occur absent an accompanying sequel to the Great Recession. Further, there is a physical space that neighbors in a school district share, and this is also the case with the aforementioned labor unions, which have seen a precipitous decline. Their success lies in their ability to take action in a concentrated way with the positive goal of improving their collective and thus individual working conditions. It is in the hope for improvement among people with whom one has existing relationships that can determine collective action. For debtors, particularly student debtors, none of these circumstances exist.

Student loan debtors have not yet experienced law enforcement retribution on a mass scale, but such options are open to the federal government and private lenders to secure repayment.[39] Beyond a purposeful online search, the vast majority of debtors have no obvious way of finding other debtors who may share their circumstances in their day-to-day lives, and thus they have no effective collective voice to speak to political forces. They are silenced.

Borrowers cannot exercise any sort of civil right to participate in a deliberative process. Even if they are not inclined to defer, they must. Rather than focus on their wages or improving their collective condition, they are compelled by necessity to focus their extracurricular energy outside of work and home concerns into contending with their debt. With each passing year, there is an increase in that giant $1.5 trillion number. This is a process that no one takes the blame for, and an ongoing transformation of a generation of students into a generation of debtors. This process begins the process of reification—the attribution of (misplaced) material priority to an abstract concept, or just making the immaterial into the material, and thus the unimportant into the important—of debt that is occurring, which further comes at the expense of participation in democracy.[40] The avenues of individual appeal and a semblance of solvency are not legally closed, of course. Those avenues are, rather, largely out of reach. A cumbersome and even overly restrictive voting process effectively closes those avenues for most people and has a chilling effect on voting and participation. In a similar sense, keeping a focus on debt payment compels people to keep jobs they do not want to make payments and focus on the proper way to pay rather than become involved in politics to assert their rights and protections.[41] Such a pattern dismisses as irrelevant even people's communities, harming the democratic process by keeping their voices out of the political arena. What perhaps demonstrates best how difficult entry into homeownership has become is the success story for those few young people (less than half the rate of the previous generation), one in three of whom have leveraged their retirement funds in order to secure a mortgage loan.[42]

The Causes of the Crisis

Many borrowers see themselves as essentially defrauded through the disbursement of easy credit, or in the words of anthropologist David Graeber, one of the organizers of Occupy Wall Street in 2011 and the author of *Debt: The First 5,000 Years*, "scammed."[43] If one were to adopt the narrative most highly indebted student borrowers have, it is certainly a morality play narrative reminiscent of Faust's selling of his soul to the devil, or Aladdin's three wishes from the Genie in *Arabian Nights*. Former students feel as if they have unwittingly sold their soul and/or their future for a short-term gain.

There is no one direction of causality, but the model of government-funded higher education prevalent in the post–World War II era has gradually shifted to one heavily funded by consumer debt. The student loan structure itself was explicitly altered in 2010. The federal government had acted as the guarantor of private loans to firms such as Sallie Mae. Under the terms of the Affordable Care Act, all federally guaranteed private loans were abolished, and all new federal student loans were disbursed by the federal government directly. The structure of federal loans themselves, both before and after this change, has always favored loans with no credit check and debts that are undischargeable for the vast majority of borrowers, even in bankruptcy.[44] This became increasingly relevant to millions of students with the rise of for-profit colleges and universities such as the University of Phoenix and the Corinthian Colleges, beginning in the 1990s, which are permitted to take 90 percent of their revenue from federal student loans (and up to a remaining 10 percent from veterans' loans under the new GI Bill).[45]

Higher education credentialing (that is, the attainment of a degree in higher education purely for professional advancement) gained import after the flight of manufacturing from the United States, by virtue of outsourcing, removing 33 percent of manufacturing jobs from 2000 to 2010 alone.[46] Job seekers from colleges and universities experienced an intense bottleneck, perversely encouraging the growth of part-time work for desperate young workers at the expense of the health insurance and pension benefits of full-time work.[47] Employers knew they could get that job filled with part-time work from a highly educated workforce. There was a new industrial reserve army, and to be in it, one needed a four-year degree.[48] The latest figures have been approaching 65 percent of jobs requiring some college education.[49] As of 2017, four-year college graduates enter the job market with excess of $37,000 in debt and find a plethora of low-wage part-time jobs waiting. Real median wages (adjusted for inflation) have only increased marginally, from $18/hour to $19/hour in the past forty years, while the cost of essentials (such as housing) has increased exponentially over the same period, despite rising productivity in the American labor market and a rising college graduation rate. This matters because the implicit social contract of taking risks to increase one's marketability should see a commensurate increase in the average wage. This is not the case, so that means that people will (and do) see exponentially higher debt loads and payments as a share of income despite the risks they took to better themselves. Coupled with the declining importance of civic education in the form of liberal arts, these borrowers/wage earners are less equipped than ever before to participate in their governmental process.

Traditional liberal arts–based college education, the foundation of democratic citizenship—the idea that a citizenry must be able to think critically, communicate effectively, and be culturally and historically literate in order to consciously advance society's interests in a thoughtful and meaningful way, perhaps exemplified by fields such as English, history, and philosophy—itself has now become socially devalued.[50] Take the case of the University of Wisconsin–Stevens Point administration that laid off liberal arts faculty and ended thirteen programs of study that were not financially viable for this public institution to maintain.[51] Former president Barack Obama made a joke about "art history" essentially being a useless field to study, in favor of studying engineering.[52] Governor Scott Walker of Wisconsin sought to legislatively change the state's historic mission of the "Wisconsin Idea" from one that linked higher education to citizenship, to one that linked it explicitly to job training.[53] These emphases on a "return on investment" philosophy of higher education are responses to the unfortunate consequence of operating in a countercyclical field during an economic upturn.[54] There is now a shrinking pool of students, even in nearly—and in some cases completely—cost-free community colleges (e.g., Tennessee, Minnesota, and Oregon), and many private colleges (e.g., Sweet Briar College, which has a $77 million endowment) are thinking of closing in order to escape the financial tailspin of sinking tuition revenues and rising marketing costs to keep students interested. The State University of New York is at least somewhat returning to a tuition-free model, although only for students coming from parent households making an income of less than $125,000 a year.[55] Many institutions are cutting their tuition in half, or eliminating tuition for working-class and poor students, and many colleges are offering financial aid packages that explicitly do not include loans.[56] Even the Federal Reserve Bank of New York has recently remarked that student loans are weighing down the housing, auto, and consumer credit market for consumers entering the economy.[57] The debts themselves behave unlike other debt and are nondischargeable.[58] This occurred despite the plea in 2007 to abandon such a structure from Milton Friedman, a conservative economist and adviser to Nixon and Reagan.[59] Such widespread ideological agreement for a solution makes the continued suffering of this generation of borrowers inexplicable unless government actors have instead become subservient to the financial interests of creditors, a causal variable that is no longer in serious question by social scientists.

Student loans are now linked materially and metaphorically (and generationally as a corollary) to home mortgages and thus to the subprime mortgage crisis. Traditional measures of economic health had failed to take into account that housing, far from an indicator that demonstrated the strength of the credit market, had operated as a source of credit, and the housing market was itself driving its own inflationary bubble.[60] As the evidence in this book will demonstrate, there is a widespread consensus that people who should now be buying homes are not, and that there still exists an incentive to work and buy a home, but no incentive to earn a broad-based, liberal arts–oriented college education that supports citizenship in a democracy.[61]

There is also a consensus that the student loan crisis is analogous to the subprime mortgage crisis, that it is in effect a higher education "bubble" that will burst at some point. Borrowers lament that as a result of this situation, they went to a college they could not afford and now—even more so— cannot afford to buy a home. Many borrowers' total loan balance is more than they make in a year, and certainly their balance is not one that, mathematically, they will ever repay in their lifetimes.[62] Borrowers will likely never transcend the debtor/creditor relationship, and by extension will not escape the class distinction, particularly palpable in the United States, of the homeowner/renter citizenship dichotomy and bifurcated class structure. The United States is truly set up as a Lockean property-based citizenship society; at times it was made explicitly so.[63] The inability to participate in such a system as the result of two different credit markets (housing and education) failing to serve borrowers leaves out a large number of people from meaningful citizenship. While in the postwar period workers received a "mortgage" and "union card" after high school or military service, today neither seems available to the median college graduate.

As we have seen, public universities, once rhetorically reckoned as a "public good," now have the rhetorical ring of a "failed experiment."[64] States such as Arizona have cut their funds to public higher education by over 58 percent since 2008, or over $3,500 per student. Arizona itself then subsequently increased tuition revenue by nearly $5,000 per student.[65] With increased demand for funds in the form of student tuition and fees, there is an increased demand for student loans. Among students, alumni, and parents as consumers and donors, there is a resentful perception of college as a credentialing process; a suspicious look at strange costs, such as the so-called administrative bloat that has seen an over 300 percent increase in nonacademic staff at colleges and universities since the 1980s; and fewer students now agreeing that developing a "meaningful philosophy of life" is as important as "being very well-off financially."[66] This is one of the powerful indicators that as a result of a morass of disconnected public policy choices, the foundation of citizenship and trust among the next generation has been eroded due to the necessity of survival. Using the framework of Maslow's hierarchy of needs, it would appear that students are much too immersed in satisfying the bottom rungs of "physical" and "security" needs to be mindful of the more broad-thinking "social" or even "ego" needs, let alone the top rung of "self-actualization" that would be more widely available in an idealized society.[67] By saddling students with debt they take on in order to finance an education from beleaguered institutions that finance themselves with tuition and largesse from "generous" alumni and donors, the value they might otherwise have derived from a liberal arts education modeled on public civic participation will be lost.

The Policy Response to the Crisis

The historical face of private higher education is once again potentially emerging, demonstrated somewhat by the close relationship elite universities enjoy with hedge funds, that is, as investment locations for their endowments and as alumni employment generators and sources of donor revenue.[68] This is particularly the case—once again in Arizona—where the Charles Koch foundation donated $3 million to help found the Center for the Study of Economic Liberty at Arizona State University Business School.[69] Charles Koch is part of the brotherly duo that has become the most prominent and activist conservative donors to Republican campaigns and causes in the last thirty years.

Public institutions are dealing with declining enrollments and revenues in several ways. Some are moving toward 100 percent online courses, and many are marketing clichéd bonus features to potential students, often called the "rock walls and lazy rivers" lifestyle phenomenon of making college more of a lifestyle choice and luxury option rather than an intense education. Many are seeking more out-of-state students to charge more for tuition, contrary to their original mission of educating the residents of the state or community they serve.[70] There are social actions and political actions, particularly among labor unions and consumer rights organizations, partially inspired by Occupy Wall Street, to resist these trends and to force the political system to deal with the results of this socially self-destructive slide. But for many activists who were borrowers themselves, the choice is to either struggle to restore education as a public good that supports the humanities and social sciences or agree that they should "regret" their education as "useless" or even "stupid."[71] Such thinking is no doubt supported by the investment analysis of credit rating agencies such as Moody's, which downgraded higher education as a sector in 2013 along with the bond ratings of several of its largest entities, such as the University of California.[72] Moody's also, after seeing that graduate student teaching assistants would be permitted to establish labor unions under the National Labor Relations Act, cautioned that such a decision would have negative consequences for private universities.[73] Their logic suggests that low-cost, high-revenue institutions should seek to lower labor costs wherever possible and charge higher tuition to as many students as possible without reliance on public subsidy. These students, by and large, are then faced with chronic debt. The society-wide recognition of student debt as a $1.5 trillion phenomenon that affects one-third of households has also spawned a cottage industry of books (read: this one), art, music, journalism, and of course, attorneys. Many attorneys have built legal practices around finding clients with student debt, particularly those who attended for-profit institutions of higher education, but others have gone to work for nonprofit organizations whose mission is shielding borrowers from "predatory" lenders.[74]

The public policy response to the question of large numbers of borrowers who have what may fairly be termed "chronic" levels of student debt that will simply not be repaid by the original borrowers over the course of their life-time has been substantial. The two perhaps most prominent policies signed into law by Presidents George W. Bush and Barack Obama respectively are known popularly as income-based repayment (IBR) and public service loan forgiveness (PSLF).[75] There are bills sponsored in Congress and many of the state legislatures that would allow borrowers to refinance student loans if they are delinquent or in default. The status quo is that loans may only be refinanced once, the terms of which are binding for the entire life of the loan and the borrower.

Income-based repayment is a cousin to another public policy solution favored by the business community and some Republicans called income-share agreements (ISAs) that seek to allow high levels of borrowing with the understanding that a lifelong tax will be levied on borrowers' earnings as a result. Public higher education administrators and faculty are critical because of its status essentially as a regressive tax on students who cannot afford to pay the full tuition during their enrollment, but such an arrangement may well become law.[76]

Citizens Respond: Democracy Arrives at the Crisis

Many activists have fought back against this tide, asking "Whose university?" is the modern American institution.[77] Traditional social organizing on the issue as one of many involved in community, labor, or identity-based organizing, not around debt itself, seems to be the only alternative to sub-mission to the current state of affairs. Organizers interviewed for this book all seem to believe that organizing as debtors is, perhaps for several reasons, a dead end. It could be because of the invisibility of the issue, or it could be simply because the issue is one that is more dependent than other issues on the material fundamentals of finance: the ability to repay debts incurred. At their core, the most active programs that are focused on granting the most resources to the student debt crisis are StudentDebtCrisis.org, spontaneous nonprofits that grew out of the Occupy movement; the Institute for College

Access & Success, a foundation funded by the Gates, Ford, and Lumina foundations; and Higher Ed, Not Debt, a joint campaign by the largest public employee labor unions. There does not seem to be a consensus among or within any of these organizations that a large-scale forgiveness must occur, but it is certainly a conversation that is being had, albeit outside of legislative chambers. Such organizing has also pressured presidential candidates to come up with plans to address the issue for future students and for current borrowers and debtors.

Some of the people interviewed for this book, including formers students, activists and organizers, attorneys, journalists, and academics and administrators, tie the student debt crisis directly to citizenship. Several borrowers alluded to attempting to be "respectable citizens" by paying the next payment on their loans. Is that what it takes? What does citizenship mean in an era that encourages for-profit higher educational institutions to recruit military veterans (to maximize the veterans' federal loan benefit) to their institutions but that only graduate 4 percent of first-time, full-time enrollees?[78] What does citizenship mean when borrowers vote overwhelmingly for a presidential candidate who promises to address their concerns (i.e., Bernie Sanders) and then ultimately are shut out of the electoral debate when he loses at an early stage of the election process?[79]

It is worth discussing the negative, stimulative effect on the economy that a weakened consumer base will eventually have.[80] In terms of public policy consequences, Social Security benefits are being garnished to cover student loan payments for beneficiaries and for their children. Many borrowers are being forced to use the SNAP program ("food stamps"), which is itself under threat.[81]

Parents are also shamed when the loan comes due and their children don't have a job. The parents and their college-age children "did everything right" and obtained a college education.[82] This is perhaps the most popular maxim among borrowers, activists, and policy influencers. Borrowers took out "good debt" in order to further their education and obtain skills to participate in the economy, and while enrolled, they did what they were told, as well.[83] There are so many mixed messages, however, that they soon learned that "doing everything right" meant little.

There are now social supports for debtors, such as Debtors Anonymous, and there is a political bureau dedicated to protection of their interests, the Consumer Financial Protection Bureau, which is not seen by most observers as an ally of financial institutions, but explicitly of consumers.[84] There are activist organizations, such as Strike Debt and the Debt Collective, that are both supportive of borrowers and sites of grassroots political resistance to the crisis.[85] The institutional mechanism of support, called Higher Ed, Not Debt, is perhaps the most mainstream political establishment project aimed at solutions both for existing debtors and future students.[86] Under the political leadership of politicians such as Elizabeth Warren, they have called for an end to the use of student loan interest payments to the federal government as a revenue enhancement and are beginning to try to overturn laws with negative impacts on young workers.[87]

In the meantime, big banks will continue to own the profits of for-profit institutions.[88] They encourage the structure of predatory loans, high tuition and fees, and balloon payments of tuition, and then blame the students for taking on too much debt to survive in such an economic system where education is compulsory. Federal policy has facilitated this system, effectively making borrowers subject to a regressive tax system that taxes the working class more heavily than the wealthy. The working-class political movements attempting to combat this trend have been largely unsuccessful, though they have been persistent in their efforts.

The Method

Within each of the social sciences, there are more popular methods of data collection and data analysis. In this book, the method of study is one usually referred to as political ethnography, an interpretive method that collects data primarily through interviews and participant observation, and seeks to use interpretive, often linguistic, logic to draw inferences and suggestions for future research and future political action. Ethnography is a more popular method of research in anthropology and sociology, and less often used in political science scholarship.

The more predominant method in political science research is quantitative, large-N (large sample size), survey-based research that often relies on mathematical linear regressions. In sociology and anthropology, there is not often such readily available data, and especially in anthropology, the researcher is often tasked with breaking new ground by discovering the existence and interaction of the worlds being studied. In political science, the researcher is usually only the latest to research a question or isolate a previously or lately neglected independent variable, such as age cohort, gender, race, years in office, political party, source of campaign contributions, and so on.

The fairly well-traversed path in political science is certainly laid with statistical aptitude and readily available quantitative data. There is a subset of political scientists, however, chiefly championed by Peregrine Schwartz-Shea and Dvora Yanow, co-authors of two of the definitive textbooks on the subject.[89] Their textbooks and Methods Cafe, a project of conversations between seasoned and novice scholars providing mentoring in aspects of interpretivist research, are organized at several annual meetings in the political science discipline.[90] Schwartz-Shea and Yanow also lead symposia in leading journals and a network of similarly inclined scholars, which provide an alternative perspective of scholarly research into politics. In the latest symposium,

Schwartz-Shea (2017), writing with Samantha Majic rather than her fellow co-founder Dvora Yanow, defines interpretive methodology:

> what unites the works in this symposium is these scholars' *intentional immersion* in the lifeworlds of those studied (as opposed, e.g., to the artificiality of an experimental lab) in order to access individual and community meanings (what Geertz, 1983, called "experience-near concepts"). For all our contributors, this has meant conducting field research (domestically or overseas) that involved varying degrees of interactions with and observations of those studied. It is the *getting close* to research participants *and* events that produces the evidence that is distinctive from interviews alone and, especially, from more decontextualized forms of evidence-generation such as policy documents, quantitative data sets, and experiments.[91]

Schwartz-Shea and Yanow assert that interpretive research holds "philosophical rigor" of "logic and argumentation—rather than procedural rigor." Interpretive research requires researchers to constantly identify relevant documents, interview subjects, and settings, and to select, gather, and analyze them in print.[92] Such a perspective is particularly attractive in a first foray into the relatively new political phenomenon of the politics of student debt. An open-minded interpretation is warranted when seeking to understand the dynamics and discourse for a powerfully significant issue for what will soon be the dominant generation in politics in the United States. A study of alienation from citizenship based on this issue would be difficult to quantify. Antebellum statesman Henry Clay of Kentucky is likely erroneously quoted as opining: "Statistics are no substitute for judgment." The insight is no less salient for its lack of authenticity.

James M. Curry, a modern researcher in league with Drs. Yanow and Schwartz-Shea, who has written persuasively for a diversity of social science approaches in research into American politics, says:

> Perhaps as important, in-depth qualitative approaches enhance the ability to speak to political practitioners about our research. These forms of research occur "on the ground" among the elites and practitioners that we are studying, helping us to gain a sensibility about their world and its cultural particularities, its rhythms and jargon, and—ultimately—that which is important to them.[93]

It is the hope of this author that Dr. Curry's entreaty is followed here in the interviews and interactions with some politicians that have been positive on both sides of the conversation and will enhance the "goodwill" that Curry also calls for. This is also true of the interactions with organizers, activists, administrators, attorneys, journalists, faculty, and other borrowers. In fact, a hopeful note from the outcome of the study is the degree to which many of these constituencies already share a vocabulary and a historical sense about student debt, and perhaps the interactions each of these contributors have had with an academic on this topic will enable constructive thought and discourse moving forward.

Matthew Lange, a methodologist, aptly defines ethnography as "[a] type of social scientific method that gains insight into social relations through participant observation, interviews, and the analysis of art, texts, and oral histories." He further explains the strengths of ethnographic research:

> its ability to offer descriptive insight into the characteristics of a phenomenon and its ability to analyze complex phenomena. Most notable, ethnographic methods are usually the best means of gaining insight into motivation, perspectives, values, rituals, and other factors commonly considered as a subcomponent of culture.[94]

Lange also enumerates the need among ethnographers for being skilled at recognizing "patterns" in the data, and that such research is commonly held to be important in "ideographic" (read: idiosyncratic, individual) explanations of the particular case under study, but not necessarily generalizable to a universe of cases. In a field such as the universe of how people experience student debt and the nature of its relationship to the political system, there is no real "universe" of cases.

In addition to familiarity with the general framework of student debt as an issue and its discourse among existing borrowers, there was a need to flesh out the dynamics of the issue among those who held and acted upon very different motivations and perspectives. The most efficient way of gathering that data was through interviews with representatives of the aforementioned constituencies of actors. For example, Joe Soss, a political scientist who conducts the "Interviewing" conversation during Schwartz-Shea and Yanow's Methods Cafe, demonstrates the technique of the researcher becoming immersed in the world of the political or social phenomenon being studied, by interviewing those administrators grappling with the apparent manipulation of social welfare by private enterprise in the wake of the "welfare reform" of the 1990s. Here is a sample of the narration possible as a result of their interviewing process:

> Providers had financial incentives to cook their numbers and confronted few barriers to spending funds in questionable ways. As a senior ACS manager told us in an interview: "There is always the incentive there to, uh, not make your numbers but to make up your numbers." The full scope of unreported problems cannot be known, but the most publicized scandals paint a damning portrait.[95]

Soss and his co-authors here represent a high standard of interview-based ethnography into this political phenomenon, and researchers would be wise to mimic such powerful insights into the dynamics of student loan borrowing and its political ramifications for borrowers and for the overall political process.

The nature of this research is indeed investigative and exploratory, and as such, should appropriately borrow from the best research techniques. By necessity, all of the interviews for this book were conducted by phone. A journalism text by Writer's Digest editor John Brady outlines some practical advice for interviewers, much of which can be discerned as clearly best practices. Many of these interview tips were logical, concise, and illustrative. Brady relates advice on how to ask questions, preferring "open-ended" rather than "closed-ended" questions: "The wide-open question not only gives the interviewee room to breathe; it gives the interviewer room to grapple."

Brady notes that Alex Haley, co-author of *The Autobiography of Malcolm X*, says of his interviewees, "I want to meet him, form an impression of him—which I hope will be fair, honest, and accurate—and try to communicate this to the reader. I have never known anybody beforehand." The Average Reader was certainly on the mind of the author in those interviews.

On follow-up questions, Brady offers a human touch that proved extremely appropriate for the type of dynamic conversations staged by the open-ended questions recommended above: "Follow-up questions do more than secure specifics—they brace rapport. They indicate you are genuinely curious about the subject's life and charred times."[96] In the presence of professionals, the author made it plain the interviewees were educating both the author and readers, rather than the other way around. There was also a need for anonymity in the sensitive nature of the employment of some of these experts. It was their candor and insight, not their brand names, that the author was seeking. It is a minor inconvenience that some of the subjects remained anonymous, as their narratives, anecdotes, and expertise advances the knowledge of our subject matter, which is precisely the point. In order to allow the reader to see a more complete picture of each interviewee, large sections of the interviews were left in interview form. The reader will hear from over a dozen people with different perspectives who, in the end, share many of the same concerns about the student debt crisis. Without honest, open, and comprehensive conversations about the impact of this new issue on our politics that are accessible to a general audience that is affected by them, we will keep repeating depressing statistics about trillions of dollars and economic drags and half-true idioms and stereotypes about parents' basements. With such a conversation, we can begin to understand how we got here, and where we are going, and how the political system may hold more possibility than we have considered before.

The Book

Chapter 1 of this book explains the theories behind the current student loan crisis and the method of case studies and interviews. The chapter outlines the basis of social critique and discourse framing the student loan crisis, and clarifies the context in which student debt is part of the wider story of the changing cultural narrative of work and finance for the vast majority of the citizens of the United States.

Chapter 2 draws corollaries from the student debt crisis to the mortgage crisis of 2008, beginning with interviews with experts and policymakers familiar with the issue. The ideology surrounding American homeownership and the political support structure needed to fulfill its central tenets is explored in light of the crisis underpinning the default of the American Dream. The American economy and state, with the aid of the real estate industry, created a nation of citizens whose most prized asset was their mortgage debt and their union card; now the discussion turns to the current generation that still waits for both envelopes to arrive in the mail.

Chapter 3 opens a window into the psyche of the borrower. The political economy of student debt itself is explored through statistics and interviews with financial professionals, administrators, attorneys, activists, public officials, and borrowers. The chapter narrates student loans as a problem, with an eye toward just how the crisis came to be a crisis. The borrowers here deliberate between considering themselves victims and considering themselves culpable. Some of the interviews are with people involved in the administration of higher education, who can explain the perspective of institutions that need student revenue to function, from public to private institutions, including elite universities and historically black colleges and universities. There is a tendency to downplay the risks of student debt to potential students, as well as to alumni and close observers who would not wish to see the financial health of their alma mater subject to such shaky foundations.

Chapter 4 provides insight into the health and welfare of higher education in the United States, as well as the health of the body politic. The future is examined from the critical perspective of the status of antidebt activism and the hope for the reestablishment of public citizenship through education. A particular dichotomy that is interesting to observe is the debate between pragmatic policymaking solutions and social collective action organizing as a response. It is the hope of this author that this work can serve as somewhat of a springboard toward a conversation between both approaches, in order to begin to achieve a discursive vocabulary that can one day lead to consensus and implementation of solutions that will address all of the historical and future concerns of this potentially explosive issue. There are more and more ways borrowers are becoming organized and are organizing themselves politically, as part-time workers beginning to organize into unions, to unions themselves pumping resources into campaigns that specifically address the needs of their members that have widespread student debt, and with a renewed focus on the welfare state (including the system of higher education) that this crisis has wrought. This crisis is potentially demonstrating the importance of politics to a generation of citizens with regard to their options as debtors. Alternatively, it could serve to further alienate this generation of borrowers from work, from higher education, from the financial sector, from the economy, and ultimately from their own membership in a democracy.

Chapter 5 addresses the possibility of perhaps the most radical solution to this crisis, that of student loan forgiveness by federal policymakers. As noted above, a plurality of millennials now favor this policy solution. Widespread loan forgiveness is in no way being discussed in Washington as a policy solution to the debt crisis. Forgiveness itself, however, has every precedent and potential for a real and substantive policy discourse. Only in the context of the half-measures of income-based repayment and public service loan forgiveness, both of which are now on the chopping block as too expensive for the government, does it exist, and so overall forgiveness seems completely off the table. The chapter assesses the effects on citizenship of the current crisis as well as whether ideologies of the American Dream can prevail in a democratic system of governance, or if a critical mass of the people will insist on some form of official legal forgiveness, as they have so many times in the American past.

There are significant calls for a more wide-ranging level of student loan forgiveness, but again, none yet by elected officials in positions of authority.[97] The idea of immediate forgiveness has great precedent in U.S. government policies (and debt forgiveness specifically has a much longer history).[98] Virtually every president since Johnson has introduced or signed legislation or taken executive action that included loan forgiveness to particular sectors to stimulate housing, as part of a package of disaster relief or trade agreements, and even as humanitarian foreign aid packages. In the chapter, we will explore those cases.

The issue of student debt itself was a clear presence in the U.S. election of 2016. Each contender for the nomination of the two major parties to the presidency unveiled a plan to significantly address existing student debt, and some unveiled large-scale proposals to curb the future of student debt. Some plans are largely in line with the existing state of affairs, which encourages a state of chronic or, as some authors call it, "endless" debt.[99] Nevertheless, the partisan divide recurs, with one lobbyist interviewed for this project plainly asserting that loan forgiveness programs are popular with "Democrats" and unpopular with "Republicans," who "think we're subsidizing large swaths of the population." This conception is despite the fact that only about 500,000 borrowers are enrolled in the public service loan forgiveness program out of 41,000,000 with student debt in the United States.[100]

Donald Trump, a Republican, ultimately won the U.S. presidential election in 2016, and his loan forgiveness proposal (unveiled partially in a speech shortly before the election and detailed in his proposed budget) arguably went farther than most Democrats in at least one way, and was even reminiscent of a plan put forth by major left-wing groups in 2014 and 2015, forgiving all debt for student loans after fifteen years (though only for undergraduate debt—graduate debt is thirty years). It is fair to say the Trump plan questions the value of and implicitly threatens the existence of loan forgiveness for public employees, such as teachers, civil servants, and nonprofit workers.[101]

The Trump administration's Education Department has come under fire recently in several *New York Times* stories that report thousands of claimants for public service loan forgiveness have had their status revoked while involved in the ten-year public service commitment.[102] Further, the education secretary, Betsy DeVos, has revoked a rule that granted a 60-day grace period to student loan borrowers who have defaulted on their loans.[103] DeVos has also announced that the Department of Education will be expending fewer resources on such borrower protection programs, potentially creating even more alienation than currently exists.[104] It does not necessarily take a visit to the resource of MappingStudentDebt.org to realize the intuitive truth: such actions harm mostly those students with low balances who have not paid them back as a result of bad employment prospects in poorer regions, while those least likely to default are those with high balances living in highly developed urban and suburban wealthy ZIP codes.[105]

The initial hypothesis underlying the research for this project pointed to a possibility that the initial contact with the federal government would have made borrowers associate the federal government *qua* lender with private lenders, such as Sallie Mae or Great Lakes. Such an association would cast a negative pall on the relationship of borrowers to the federal government. Scholars have found that initial exposure to the political system during one's "coming of age" (the time one ascends to voting age, or the first time one votes) and the prevailing generational political tendency of the time period can have a significant influence on lifetime partisanship.[106] As a corollary, it would seem that such a negative initial exposure to the federal government, that of creditor to debtor, would, for a lifetime, influence potentially an entire generation of borrowers to nurse a strong distaste for the federal government.

Actually, the opposite has proven to be true, based on interviews and data culled from commentaries online by borrowers. The more contact borrowers have with agents at the U.S. Department of Education, the more they comment that they appreciate being treated "as a person" rather than screamed at and harassed by representatives of private lenders. It seems that the system put in place by the Bush and Obama administrations was making lemons into lemonade by turning the crisis into an opportunity for young voter borrowers to experience a positive interaction with government programs and agencies that would instill confidence in the democratic nature of the political system and the possibilities of a soluble social welfare system.

This alienation is from not only a democracy, but an entire political and economic system. The kind of alienation from civic effectiveness as well as economic bootstrap capitalism is one that will see consumer confidence suffer. In an economy where the 100 largest corporations in the world effectively traffic mostly in new cars, new phones, and new wars (and fuel, raw materials, and infrastructure to facilitate the manufacture of those products), it would seem that such consumer confidence is vital to keep consumption and thus economic growth functioning.[107] Instead, there is a tendency to simply do more of the same, that is, allow as much borrowing as possible with unlimited risk to the borrower and zero risk to the creditor. Students are mostly unaware that inability to pay their student loans later could get them disqualified from the professions that their educations have paid for, especially in the cases of attorneys and nurses.[108] There is a unique, totalizing, octopus-like reach to student loans that is of a unique historical nature. The nondischargability of student loans in a bankruptcy marks perhaps a new moral low in securitization, which is significant in the age of the moral hazard, encouraging financial institutions to lend at will with the promise or guarantee of an eventual federal taxpayer bailout.[109] That promise carries with it the full faith and credit of the United States, as do the majority of student loans.

CHAPTER ONE

The American Debtor as Worker, Consumer, and Citizen

There is a point at which the autonomy of the citizen in a democratized polity becomes compromised by the obligations she carries. Further, if those obligations are somehow universalized within the polity, then the central authority in the polity is no longer authentically democratized. Those obligations must be understood and defined politically as citizenship or as servitude, but they cannot be oversimplified by unhelpful analogy to French Revolution citizenship and American antebellum slavery. It is the task of the researcher to define instead what the abstract nature of each concept means today in the context of American life.

Citizenship itself is popularly understood as a positive concept, one in which the citizen takes great pride in the contribution she makes to the overarching, perhaps imagined, community, from which she also derives material benefits.[1] The positivity of the concept is not without complication, however; that pride may also be understood as a nationalistic, and inherently an authoritarian, ideology. Still, ideologically tinged democracy is substantively distinct from servitude. Servitude is the theft of agency, will, and/or social dignity from a human being in service to another. The loss of this agency is the antithesis of democratic citizenship and humanity, and so the question of its loss is an urgent one. It is striking the degree to which the modern generation of student loan debtors have adopted the vocabulary of servitude both implicitly and explicitly to describe their material conditions.[2] Is it perhaps not worth making a claim that borrowers are either free citizens or some kind of indentured servants or wondering if there is a balance that is more empirically accurate.

Citizenship and servitude are concepts that must be explored for clarity about the magnitude of student debt to the political system. "Working hard" and "getting ahead" are familiar (and definitively related) tropes in the discourse and ideology of the American Dream writ large. Tropes antithetical to American Dream ideology, that is, "laziness" and "dishonesty," are assigned en masse to immigrants, minorities, and the poor generally, in order to justify wealth and income inequality among racialized groups and the undeserving.

Ideology is the structure of ideas, concepts, and values in a society that ultimately serves the material interests of the ruling class.[3] If a society is, for example, beset by an ideology of commercialized consumer individualism, the very best exemplars of commercialized consumer individualists would constitute the ruling class. One's status as a "debtor" in such a society would be a clear indication that such a person cannot, or at least implicitly does not, belong to the ruling class, and further does not "deserve" to have any impact on the polity through the idealized notion of citizenship. Ideology obscures the present with its structured inequalities by making them appear to be part of the natural order, and subsequently creates its own direction for the future.[4]

The American Debtor as Worker

The rags-to-riches discourse is still very active and alive, while clearly undercut in the popular imagination recently by the work of Thomas Piketty and others, who demonstrate with clear data that the most likely predictor of individual lifetime wealth creation is parental wealth ownership.[5] Thus, political institutions employ a multiplicity of ideological devices in order to perpetuate their preferred narrative. The reality of the nature of work is not as important as the popular manner in which it has been comprehended and engaged by workers *qua* workers and further, workers *qua* consumers or citizens. With the lack of importance of the concept of citizenship in modern discourse, workers tend to adopt a more consumerist ideology. This is perhaps not surprising, as it could fairly be interpreted as a refusal, encouraged by popular culture, to see themselves in the identity of "worker," given the negative caricature of the work narrative.

When contemplating the work relationship, purveyors of popular culture and ideology often essentialize the employer-employee relationship into a somewhat romantic, perhaps overdramatized and simplistic version, one of exploiter and exploited. There is perhaps no better imaginary for this than the visualization of coal mining and professions like it, wherein miners work endlessly in a small, dark, hot space underground that is genealogically tied to the Western religious ideal of the underworld/afterlife. Indeed, it is perhaps the grim unreality of the work that allowed mine workers to gain popular support for their labor organizing efforts to the degree that they did in their heyday.

Coal mining is often portrayed as the most arduous, most dangerous, and physically most taxing work occupation. It is indeed difficult work, and it has had a long history of maltreatment of workers. It spawned the creation of the United Mine Workers (UMW), one of the most enduring and successful labor unions in the United States, which had at its height during the New Deal era as many as 800,000 members, and is chiefly responsible for the institution of the eight-hour workday. "Company towns" arose often in manufacturing plants or coal mines in the late nineteenth century, the sole employer also acting as landlord and bank to workers. "Company stores" thrived, where employees took on store credit (debt) that became a wage garnishment, a source of worker intimidation and alienation, and a profit center for the company. The company store was a popular focus of frustration, even hatred, as it was perhaps the workers' primary interaction with their employer outside of normal work hours, and one that ironically and inextricably tied them closer to their workplace with each new interaction. It may be said that the company store contributed directly to the negative perception of the company by the workers and their families, and ultimately persuaded them to unionize.

What does it mean for the federal government to be acting as a "company store" to a generation of citizens? There are few mutual endorsements of the public good for society and citizen clearer or more substantial than a higher education degree, which celebrates the literacy, communication, and culture of the polity that accredits and bestows the degree. Degree-seekers incur tuition costs that very often compel them to make a calculation that they must literally go "deeper in debt." They "owe their soul to the company store," now carrying a meaning of additional matriculation in degree programs or obtaining more loans from their government in order to recover from their debt. This is an application of a concept often referred to as the "sunk-cost fallacy" in economics, though like many modern economics concepts, there is a dispute, and this one involves whether the principle of sunk cost is a "fallacy."[6] Whether it is or is not a fallacy, there has certainly been a widespread modern tendency to keep in pursuit of education in the absence of obvious alternatives, such as gainful employment.[7] Such a confusing state of affairs can no doubt lead to the alienation of citizens.

The reference to the plight of the mine worker who has sold his soul must resonate with people who have continuously been employing all of these strategies while simply going "deeper in debt." "Inequality" has become the buzzword of the political and social system, but vague exhortations against the abstract notions of inequality fail to critically examine any material consequences of that inequality.[8] They fail to take seriously the long-term consequences of such an economic model that sees no alternative to the supply side of giving back more and more resources to the capitalist class in the form of tax cuts, government subsidies, lax regulations, and monetary largesse financed by the central bank. The resulting deprivation of the majority of people goes unnoticed until, and even when, the economic well-being of the overall population suffers. The wealthy can only purchase so many goods and services before they begin to save and are generating no new spending.[9]

In general, the present story of American workers is not a pleasant one. Wages have stagnated since the 1970s, incomes have flatlined, and workers are being asked constantly to "do more with less" even when such a painfully obvious directive from The Boss is impossible.[10] Worker productivity in the United States has been increasing since the 1970s, and yet they are not realizing those gains. Instead, to supplement those wages, households have adopted several long-term strategies: borrowing on various lines of revolving credit (debt), buying low-quality food and goods made abroad by laborers making a fraction of what Americans do, and seeking more education and credentials in order to finance a higher income and thus a higher "standard of living." The vast majority of Americans have used a combination of all of these strategies to maintain their middle-class status, one that is not easily maintained.[11] Debt is a symptom of the inability of debtors to maintain their status as consumers with their existing wages. Debtors are merely the working class being doubly taxed.

The question must be asked who or what the new company store, that is, the guarantor of last-resort security in a precarious era, actually is. If the company store is the site of the worker's oppression outside the workplace that itself is owned by the owners of the workplace, then that is the logical place to begin. The majority of college students and graduate students in the United States also at least have part-time jobs, and many work full-time.[12] They anticipate graduating, quitting their minimum wage job, and going to work as a health or business-oriented professional. Thus, they identify more as "students" than as "borrowers" (or "workers") and certainly not as "debtors." The indebted status and the self-identification as a debtor is not realized until the loans come due.[13] It is at that point, where education ends and work begins, that the greatest inequalities make themselves known. It is when significant income comes in, the start of their American Dream, when the majority of students realize that they now must pay an unanticipated sum of money to a lender monthly. The consequence is little savings and late payments that damage their credit history. For a small minority of graduate students (physicians, attorneys, accountants), those for whom the idea of student debt was created, they actually plunge into high-income careers, and they may see their student loan payments as a rite of passage in their relative youth. There is some work to suggest this is a stand-in for what used to be called a progressive income tax.[14]

"Debtors," then, may not be a particularly useful identification for material political and social commonality that can plausibly generate a political solution. Not all debtors are in crisis, or in need of a policy solution. Many are employed, many own property, and many are making payments. Examining the characteristics of the debtor population may shed some light on their shared material interests. Roughly one-third of student-loan debtors who have graduated or left college are behind in payments or in default on their loans.[15] The regions with the highest rates of default are those areas with high unemployment and high poverty. Graduates who are employed are much more likely to pay down their debts than those who are unemployed or impoverished. Another class of debtors, perhaps as many as one third, are enrolled in so-called income-based repayment (IBR) plans.[16] These are debtors who would be in default if they were held to the terms of their original agreement, which saw them paying a higher percentage toward the principal loan amount monthly. Given that only one-third of debtors are able to fulfill their original agreement, IBR is a policy solution that allowed debtors to pay a maximum percentage of their monthly income toward their overall debt without regard to the principal loan, for up to twenty-five years. The plan allows debtors who might default to avoid credit risks and even financial ruin. A plurality of newly realized debtors are enrolling in the programs, both the public and private options, to the extent that they exist; however, the rates of default are not declining and so the policy is not entirely successful.[17]

As filmmaker Michael Moore made clear in his 2009 post–financial crisis documentary, *Capitalism: A Love Story*, it is not likely that a worker will feel free to quit her job if she is compelled to pay her loans as her primary legal obligation.[18] It hearkens back to what Marx and Engels called the "industrial reserve army" of workers desperate enough to take any wage on offer.[19] A docile workforce is ideal for an employer who wishes to cut costs by simply underpaying or in other ways undervaluing or mistreating the workforce. "Debtor" status is in part merely an exacerbation of the condition of work, a kind of unmanageable tax on poor workers. The question thus becomes how the Faustian selling of one's poor soul occurred.[20]

The American Student Loan Debtor as Consumer

Perhaps one of the most searing narratives of the American consumer society, albeit focused primarily on its environmental impact, is one that is plainly accessible to nonacademic audiences.[21] A 2007 twenty-five-minute documentary, *The Story of Stuff*, by Greenpeace activist Annie Leonard, has developed into a video series, a foundation, and an accompanying book. In it, Leonard deftly and succinctly summarizes the market logic of consumption through the theories of the late World Bank economist Victor Lebow.

Lebow, writing in the post–World War II period, critically realized the necessity of consumption as a ritualized, even "religious" experience, due to its role as the central key to economic growth and prosperity. While Lebow himself was not necessarily influential, he was a regular contributor to *The Nation* magazine, and he certainly captured the essence of the so-called

Golden Age of Capitalism. As Lebow may have predicted, 99 percent of consumer goods in the United States are no longer in use six months after purchase.[22] If consumerism itself is valued higher than labor in the macro-economic model, then labor costs could be safely frozen and further under-valued, and therefore cut, so long as they do not impact the mandatory consumer spending. Borrowing to spend would become not only an option to keep spending up, but an absolute necessity once the threshold of other income supplements (enumerated above) has been maxed. The United States has reached this reality. The sacrament of consumerism by way of debtors has commenced in the form of credit cards, second mortgages, federally guaranteed student loans, and more.

Consumerism is compulsory in America. From an early age, children are socialized into consumerism itself. The toy trucks of boys and the dolls of girls translate into socially constructed and supported gender identities. By the time children are ready for college, spending is part of who they are. Being a consumer is being an American. The American consumer is, para-doxically, the engine of world capitalism and at its mercy. American demand for goods and services drives manufacturing of all types, from the automo-tive to the agricultural to the service industry. In order for capitalism to work, a steady consumer base must compel a large number of people to con-tinuously keep an ethic of acquisitiveness and hunger for The New. This is the basis for the existence of the advertising industry and the central func-tion of the Internet and social media. Without the socialized desire for goods consumption, there would be no reason for accounts or credit at the com-pany store, no reason to maintain a certain wage or income threshold, no economic reason necessitating college, and no reason to go into debt. Even a four-year degree has become little more than a credential enabling more access to consumer goods. Desperation sets in when people cannot afford their own daily lifestyle, and this is the case for an increasing number of average citizens, who have largely accepted that they have no political recourse, if the consistently low voting participation rate of the United States is any guide. Alienation from the American Dream ideal is a logical next step.

In the familiar narratives of religion, folk tales, classical literature, and country music, the desperation of selling one's soul is usually involved in the morality tale of a devil character.[23] In popular culture today, there are count-less versions of the "deal with the devil." People in folk tales typically have sold their soul in order to fulfill some lifelong wish, such as true love, free-dom from some type of imprisonment, and of course, some type of pecuniary wealth. The moral of such stories always includes unforeseen consequences. Today's students cannot anticipate the consequences of their loans. The mate-rial reality of college and university attendance today is socially compulsory, and credit so easy to obtain that no such risk is presented to students in vir-tually any quarter. There are some who would posit that they understood the consequences, but borrowing money for an education (often a value similar to the down payment on a first home) requires the kind of knowledge acquired in an education that the majority of students simply do not yet possess. The consequences vary with size of debt, employment status, and living expenses. However, 20 percent of borrowers hold more than $50,000 in student debt.[24]

The student-worker must now work to avoid financial ruin by endless obligation to her employer and to her lender of last resort, which may be the federal government itself. This is the place at which the autonomy of this individual must be questioned, as the obligations that the worker now carries significantly outweigh the virtues and obligations of citizenship. It can reasonably be asserted, however, that the degree to which this tension exists in the modern economy is omnipresent. It is this omnipresence that may have an impact on the manner in which people now interact with their government in the new phase of democracy and capitalism. It may present an opportunity for a positive engagement with government, or it may prove to extend the alienation that borrowers have from lenders; students may feel hostility to their system of government, alternately encouraging radicalism and reaction.

The Student Loan Debtor as Citizen

Any ostensibly democratic government must realize the consequences of policies that encourage the accumulation of consumer debt to the detriment of its own values. Charles Lindblom made this point in his book *The Market System* (2002), an extension of his earlier article "The Market as Prison."[25] If a community's politicians are aware that the voters have in essence ceded their vote to the company, and they have made the collective calculation that they must keep the business running in the town, then woe is the elected politician who holds office when the company decides to leave town. In such a scenario, the business holds dominion over local politicians in struggling communities, and arguably, all communities. The town must win the masochistic race to the bottom in order to keep itself chained to the last rung of the market ladder. Lindblom's 2001 work is notable because of the logical extrapolation of his argument to the national political economy. What are the duties and obligations of citizenship in a market economy, then? Can it even be meaningfully exercised?

Such questions cut to the heart of the question of political engagement and citizenship itself. If the locus of political power in a society can be established, the first step in a critical analysis is determining the nature of its power and whether or not it is democratic. If a society has a locus of power that does not spring from the organically expressed desire of the people, it simply is not authentically democratic. If the majority of society is "in debt," then it follows that a series of critical points must be addressed to establish the significance of those obligations and the centrality of them to the democratic project.

In democratic government, citizens celebrate and communicate their own worth, culture, and humanity, as well as that of other members of the polity.[26] These values have been embedded in the liberal arts model in American colleges and universities, which cannot be easily commodified.[27] The publicly funded liberal arts are a gateway to mass citizenship, in which those aspects of culture, communication, and reflection previously available only to wealthy elites are instead opened to all. The alternative educational model is one of vocational training, in which a stratified underclass is taught only the bare minimum that is necessary for their entry into the low-wage workforce, and even then under protest from elites who must fund the enterprise. The elites, meanwhile, still provide the well-rounded education and socialization process for their children, who will inherit their social place.

The relationship of student borrowers to the institutions and organizations (government, banks) that they interact with must be broken into its constituent parts to dissect the political process that is occurring. In fact, this may be the central question of the political moment, as student-borrowers are moving into a new relationship in the polity, namely one of stakeholder (debtor) rather than beneficiary (borrower). If one in three households in the United States now holds some form of education-based debt, this is a relationship that must figure in the political calculus of the polity itself.

For example, if an employer would rather not abide a regulation or program (i.e., a student loan income-based repayment program that relies on taxable revenue from the business sector) that benefits their workers, and lobbies the state or federal government to evade or abolish it because it impedes the employer's profit margin, the employer also lobbies the workers with hopes of benefiting directly from those profits. The employer calls this logical, but it clearly comes from an irrational basis and is enough to confuse the duties of citizenship. Should workers support a policy that indirectly may affect them or a policy of more direct benefit? This is the worker-voter dilemma, and now the borrower/voter dilemma in response to the crisis.

The Academy as Company Store

Finally, it is necessary to explore the metaphor of the academy as the company store. The company store was everywhere, as landlord, town developer, social benefactor. Increasing reports have emerged regarding the nexus between elite American private universities and financial institutions, showing a financially beneficial relationship. Elite universities with admission typically granted to less than 5 percent of applicants are certainly a talent pool from which financial institutions recruit, and such practices have become more and more prevalent in the last several decades. Amy Binder chronicled the recruitment of Ivy League graduates to the ranks of venture capital and investment banking in an article entitled "Why Are Harvard Grads Still Flocking to Wall Street?" At such institutions, it is common for financial industry employers to poach liberal arts majors anxious about the next step in their lives after graduation, simply because they are an effective group to market to, and the appeal of new associates from Harvard increases a financial firm's cachet.[28] The culture of literacy and communication is not dead, it seems, only relegated to employers who can recruit from elite institutions. From this relationship alone, elite universities have grown to depend on revenue and donations from wealthy alumni who are now principally employed by the financial services industry. Such alumni often become active and vocal alumni donors who use their power to withhold those donations if the university takes actions that displease them. At a minimum, the university is incentivized to be hospitable toward the employers of their donors, in hopes of large donations directly from their corporate foundations toward campus construction projects, an endowed chair at their Business School, or simply toward their endowment. They are disincentivized from allowing the campus to become a place of criticism toward either the industry itself or, certainly, the employer directly.[29]

In addition, Astra Taylor, the director of such films as *Zizek!* and *Examined Life*, wrote a piece for the *Nation* in which she called the Ivies "hedge funds with universities attached." She makes the case that elite university endowments have essentially become great stores of wealth owing to a combination of their nonprofit status, well-to-do alumni networks, and longevity. The endowments are heavily invested in hedge funds, mega-wealthy mutual funds that pride themselves on being a "hedge" against market volatility with "alternative investment strategies" that include militating against government action against inequality.[30]

The original educational mission of these institutions seems somehow quaint in the face of the material reality that they have primarily become pillars of the global financial and political order. Several public intellectuals have lately brought attention to the overall denigrated condition of higher education in American life, and have called for a renewal of the spirit that they claim made the institutions, and indeed America, great. William Deriesewiecz writes in *Excellent Sheep* about the increasing "neoliberalism" pervading private higher education, and its perversion of the very ideas inherent in the liberal arts themselves, encouraging conformity rather than freedom of thought and deed, balanced with fellow-feeling and citizenship. Jennifer Washburn in *University Inc.* writes about the "corruption" experienced as universities are increasingly influenced and even controlled by large corporations and financial institutions. In "Saving Our Public Universities," a piece in *Harper's* by novelist Marilynne Robinson, there is an eloquent defense of

"America's Best Idea," that is, the public university with a curriculum dedicated to the spread of the liberal arts:

> The dominant view today is that the legitimate function of a university is not to prepare people for citizenship in a democracy but to prepare them to be members of a skilled but docile working class. . . . there is a vast educational culture in this country, unlike anything else in the world. It emerged from a glorious sense of the possible and explored and enhanced the possible through the spread of learning. If it seems to be failing now, that may be because we have forgotten what the university is for, why the libraries are built like cathedrals and surrounded by meadows and flowers. They are a tribute and an invitation to the young, who can and should make the world new, out of the unmapped and unbounded resource of their minds.[31]

As elites in any field do, these institutions have set trends in higher education. Not only elite private institutions are in the business of cultivating large endowments and investing heavily in financial services, but second- and third-tier colleges and universities, public and private, have begun to cater increasingly to elites. They have curbed need-based financial aid in favor of increased loans to cover tuition for low-income and low-household-wealth students. They have increased merit-based aid to reward mostly upper-middle-class students for their high school achievements. They have increased the budgets of "rock walls and lazy rivers" in order to entice those with financial means and, of course, relied heavily on marketing both those lifestyle features and the alumni networks themselves to demonstrate a return on investment. This business orientation encourages parents, who see that their children will be able to secure gainful employment postgraduation.[32] Many institutions have done this in order to compete for the same pool of American rising freshmen, but it is also in part because public higher education subsidies have dropped dramatically, by 50 percent nationwide, at a time when a college degree is virtually a prerequisite for any employment at all. Even community college administrators are beginning to speculate about the outsized influence banks have over policy at their institutions when their bond rating goes down after borrowing to finance their deficits, even over the governing boards and prominent donors of the institutions.[33] So, while it is from a different perspective, public institutions are increasingly subservient to industry rather than in partnership.

The marketization of the broader field of higher education begs several questions:

1. How can institutions of higher education maintain their original mission of educating the citizens of our democracy without succumbing to the

predatory nature of the profit model of private industry, doing all it can to please the customer and/or the shareholders?

2. What are the entry costs in this market? If it is governed according the rules of the market, should the issuance of new credit not also be subject to stringent regulation and safeguards? And further, should traditional consumer debt protections such as bankruptcy still exist?

3. Can this marketizing trend be counteracted by public policy or collective action? And if so, how should citizens most constructively focus their energies to resist this marketization? How can those who have already been harmed by this trend be protected in new rounds of reform?

These questions will be addressed and the possibilities explored in the upcoming interviews with borrowers, activists, attorneys, administrators, and faculty.

CHAPTER TWO

The Ideology of Homeowner Democracy and Trust in Government

Men being, as has been said, by nature, all free, equal, and independent, no one can be put out of this estate, and subjected to the political power of another, without his own consent. The only way whereby any one divests himself of his natural liberty, and puts on the bonds of civil society, is by agreeing with other men to join and unite into a community for their comfortable, safe, and peaceable living one amongst another, in a secure enjoyment of their properties, and a greater security against any, that are not of it.

—*John Locke*

Credit, too, is an important form of social coercion; mortgaged workers are more pliable—less likely to strike or make political trouble.
—Doug Henwood, *Wall Street: How It Works and For Whom* (1997)

Homeowner Ideology and Trust in Government

Student debt is currently nearly half of all nonhousing consumer debt in the United States.[1] While the federal government is the guarantor of the majority of student loans, it is also the guarantor and/or facilitator of all mortgage debt. Despite its rapid appearance on the social and political scene, student debt is still a distant second place in terms of the share of personal debt to the home mortgage.[2] The American Dream of social stability and universal homeownership from which the new generation is becoming alienated is, coincidentally or not, in large part of English pre-Enlightenment social contract theorist John Locke's philosophy. John Locke made a simple argument: people want to protect themselves and their homes, and they formed communities as social mutual-aid societies to protect against invaders. Communities, thus formed, needed a government to continue to consult the people whose property inspired and continues to inspire the state. It is debated in his writings whether the people give the state legitimacy or their property does, and whether those with more property should have more of a voice in governance. From this Lockean understanding of government that prevailed in England and later the American colonies and the United States came Anglo-American liberal democracy.

More recently, modern economic journalist Doug Henwood wrote in 1997 that credit itself, and specifically the modern housing mortgage, prevents rather than encourages political participation among borrowers, since so much of their political and social standing rests in their mortgage remaining in good standing. It is perhaps a grand irony that the very policy explicitly shaped by Locke's ideas should also undercut and even make a mockery of his ideals. Such a possibility demonstrates how the way in which American democracy has become realized dialectically relates to the creation of the widespread debt that can alienate borrowers from both the government and the political system.

There is no more quintessentially American form of debt than the housing mortgage. As Jeffrey Hornstein chronicles, the mortgage in the twentieth century became the chief manner in which families bought their homes.[3] Hornstein's work is important because it underlines the self-consciously Lockean ideology that guided U.S. federal government housing policy in the past half-century. The ideology of homeownership became synonymous with the American Dream of social mobility.

Owning a home provided a dual incentive to homeowners: (1) to continue producing for their employers in order to keep paying their mortgage, and thus keep a home for themselves and their children, and (2) to ensure steady property values for their community, resulting in steady taxes for public services, and a solid investment. These are the twin primary incentives for democracy and capitalism, respectively. The first incentive provides for a stable workforce; the second incentive gives homeowners a stake in democracy. Locke asserts in the above quotation and throughout his philosophical treatises that the prime motivation to enter political society is to guard such "property."

Imagery that conjures the American Dream described in this way is perhaps most effectively evoked by the imagery of Norman Rockwell's 1943 *Four Freedoms* paintings, inspired by President Franklin D. Roosevelt's 1941 "Four Freedoms" speech.[4] The *Freedom of Speech* painting, which depicts a man standing up to speak his mind at what appears to be a New England–style town meeting, demonstrates a willingness to safeguard the other "freedoms" (and by extension, common ownership of the safety of their community) with that political action. Support for and trust in government is certainly a pillar of homeownership, or at least homeownership tends to make one more of a supporter of government in general in the modern era. There is certainly a relationship, borne out by statistical public opinion data. Based on the most widely recognized opinion dataset in political science, the University of Michigan voter survey in existence since 1946, we can see what that relationship is based on the answers to a few questions related to "trust in government" and the respondent's status as a homeowner. Whether by cognitive dissonance or by a true gratitude for the mortgage interest deduction, American homeowners historically show more trust in government than American renters. This is an indicator of the mutually supportive relationship between the American political structure and homeowners historically.[5]

This balance of interests has become unbalanced in the last twenty years, however, as homeownership has become a policy end in itself. According to the federal Department of Housing and Urban Development (HUD), "By 2001, the nation's homeownership rate had soared to an all-time high of 68.1 percent as of the third quarter that year." In wishing to take some credit for the furthering of this goal, HUD further notes, as of 2018 "The FHA and HUD have insured over 34 million home mortgages and 47,205 multifamily project mortgages since 1934. FHA currently has 4.8 million insured single family mortgages and 13,000 insured multifamily projects in its portfolio."[6] Speaking only of individuals, as of 2015, 44 percent of Americans have mortgage debt, and the median mortgage debt is $103,000.[7] According to the New York Federal Reserve, student debt is the only kind of household debt that continued to rise through the Great Recession, and it now has the second largest total balance after mortgage debt.[8]

Seemingly, wages have surely increased in an era when we see massive growth. For example, in 1964, average hourly wages for nonsupervisory employees on the nonfarm payroll was $2.50, in June 1980 it was $6.82, in June 2000 it was $13.99, and in June 2018 it was $22.62. However, in constant 2018 dollars, those values, respectively, are $20.39 (1964), $22.09 (1980), $20.45 (2000), and again, $22.62.[9] This is despite a massive increase in worker productivity. In fact, according to the Economic Policy Institute, "From 1948 to 1979, productivity rose 108.1 percent, and hourly compensation increased 93.4 percent. From 1979 to 2013, productivity rose 64.9 percent, and hourly compensation rose 8.2 percent."[10] In a world of wage stagnation relative to homebuying, it is a rational decision to borrow to increase your earning potential in an economy of perceived scarcity.

The modern consumer economy is arguably an economic model that is collapsing on itself, at least in the United States. Social mobility and mere social status maintenance, reflected in homeownership, has become out of reach because of the decision to assume higher education debt in combination with the failure to find postgraduate employment. There is little doubt that this grim state of affairs has produced an effect on the political attitudes of the affected generation. The political identity of generational cohorts have been demonstrated by quantitatively oriented public opinion scholars such as Gary Jacobson to have been primarily impacted by the political moment in which they first came of age and were socialized into the American governmental structure.[11] The first impressions baby boomers had of government were the widespread public university campus protests against the Vietnam War, FHA first-time homebuyer loans, and being the first generation to watch their parents and then themselves retire with Social Security. Generation X and millennials have seen wars with no sustained campus protests except perhaps for Occupy, filled out a federal financial aid/borrowing form likely because their parents or guidance counselors told them to, are much more shut out of the housing market, and Social Security is now being garnished for many people who borrowed to attend college or send their children. These social and political moments have produced mixed results in terms of the impression they give of the penetration of the state into the daily lives of its citizens.[12]

Society has yet to see what happens when an entire generation of Americans' first impression of their government is that it has encouraged many of their brethren to be mired, post-college, in a lifetime of debt with poor job prospects. To borrowers, it may make little difference at first who holds their loans, though the identity of their loan-holder may have greater import when it comes to questions of long-term debt forgiveness.[13] For nearly a century, the United States facilitated an American Dream whose centerpiece was home ownership.[14] It was debt that was central to the lives and even identity of the American middle class, so much so that homeownership dictated how people felt about education and even civil rights. In fact, the American Dream of homeownership for middle-class students was so commonplace that an entire generation of the children of Baby Boomers were encouraged to seek a "postmaterialist" life. In this postmaterialist life they do not seek material advancement as their primary consideration, but seek to pursue their passions in their profession and perhaps make the world a better place.[15] Of course, the framework of postmaterialism takes as a given the stability of housing and financial security, and an employment market flush with income opportunities at every skill level and differentiated ability.

This generation of both Generation X and millennials also has as its cradle baseline a communications and transportation infrastructure the world has never before seen. The new generation undoubtedly has different impressions of how debt is structured, the morality of debt, and the long-term social desirability of the maintenance of debt, in terms of what goals such a system serves and how they might be affected by it.

Wall Street on the Housing and College Financing Crises

There are clearly linkages and parallels between the 2008 subprime financial crisis and the student debt crisis. To wade into the waters of reactions to both instances of debt and the reaction it provoked among the youngest generation, here is one of the most prominent voices of the debt activist movement, Alexis Goldstein. Goldstein is a journalist and financial professional who has chosen to devote her working life to anticorporate activism as one of the most prominent figures in Occupy Wall Street. She has worked on Wall Street and is knowledgeable about its profit and incentive structure, as well as the effects of that structure on ordinary people. She especially has insight into some of the linkages between the subprime mortgage crisis and the student loan crisis. She explains several of the central causes of the crisis, including the proliferation of for-profit colleges and universities, the absence of student-borrower protections in the form of bankruptcy, and the decline of public funding. She also heavily delves into how the American Dream has been yanked out of reach for young borrowers.

> *Interviewer:* How is the student debt crisis like the subprime mortgage crisis, and how is it not?
>
> *Goldstein:* My first answer to that is quoting someone else, Rohit Chopra, who used to be at the Consumer Financial Protection Bureau, who is now at the Department of Education. He essentially described for-profit colleges, in particular, as "subprime goes to college." I agree with that very strongly. I think one of the biggest similarities between the student loan crisis and the subprime crisis is they're both crises that have originated out of people doing the, quote unquote, "right thing," people doing the thing that society has held up as an aspirational goal for everyone that's supposed to make your life better, and not make your life worse.
>
> In the subprime crisis, obviously, that means the American Dream of owning a home. The idea being: Well, you'll always have the value of the home. It doesn't matter if you have a mortgage or not, you live in your home, so it's not like everyone's mortgage is going to be worthless at the same time, so the value should always go up. It seems like this safe investment that would always be secure. Obviously, we learned the lesson the hard way that that is not the case, especially when you combine it with incredibly predatory, exploitative behavior on behalf of the financial system, as we saw in the subprime crisis, where people of color were disproportionately targeted for subprime loans.
>
> *Interviewer:* Is there a good example of this?
>
> *Goldstein:* This is one example: The Department of Justice found that Wells Fargo gave black and Latino borrowers subprime loans, even when they

had the same income levels and credit scores as white borrowers. They disproportionately gave subprime loans to people of color, essentially, who would have qualified for prime loans, just because they were black and brown. They settled with the Justice Department for $175 million over these allegations to resolve the lawsuit, essentially.

Wells Fargo in Baltimore, there was some reporting saying they found emails where they were referring to subprime loans as "ghetto loans," and they were referring to black people as "mud people." Those are in emails from Wells Fargo officials. You see it systemically, but you also see it in the microcosm, too.

The main similarity I see between the student debt crisis and the subprime crisis is: The fact that we hold something up that's supposed to always be a positive, that we tell everyone as a society to go out and get, right? A house, or an education. We say it will only be good for you, it will only better you, and instead, it turns into a nightmare for some folks. I think that that's been very true for the subprime crisis, and it's been very true for the student debt crisis for a lot of people.

There's also that similarity, especially when it comes to for-profit schools, that people of color and, especially, low-income people of color, are disproportionately targeted for the worst of whatever the financial product we're talking about. Either the subprime loan, or the most fraudulent for-profit school that has the least to actually offer its students. Then people are buried in this mountain of debt that they have a really difficult time getting out of.

What I'm trying to say is, with the mortgage market, it was this flood of securitization [*Editor's note: "Securitization" is best understood as the process of reducing lending risk to the creditor, i.e., increasing their "security" by increasing penalties for default to the borrower, or reducing the legal ability of borrowers to default.*], and that's part of what made the crisis so bad. It's made more complicated by the fact that the federal government has more of a direct role than they did in the mortgage crisis. That's another thing that's different. Although, obviously, they had a very big role in the mortgage market, too, right? As sort of the ultimate backer of a lot of these loans through FHA insurance and things like that. There's a lot of similarities, but I'm basically trying hard to find some differences.

Goldstein's insights help contextualize the environment in which student loans began to balloon into a crisis. Her focus on the mortgage crisis as disproportionately falling on marginalized communities is also a failure of the political system that encouraged these phenomena to occur when borrowing rose to historic highs. The collapse of 2008 was driven by one form of consumer debt, and the government ultimately de facto guaranteed the loans of those lenders who issued beyond their realistic expectations of making their investment profitable. The word "bailout" became a refrain and rallying cry for outrage among borrowers and the general population. Goldstein correctly points out that the federal government acts as a sort of backstop and ultimate guarantor of loans in the housing market, and that similarly, the government was such a backstop in the student loan market until 2010. However, a fundamental shift occurred in 2010: the federal government itself assumed the role of lender.

Goldstein notes that such loans are ultimately a revenue enhancement for the Treasury, but seemingly gives little analytical weight to this new role assumption. Certainly the same market principles apply, and borrowers are still borrowing from a financial entity in order to matriculate, and yet this altered relationship of government-as-lender is one that should give practitioners and analysts of democracy pause, as it is a completely alien relationship to new borrowers and students, and one that becomes crucial in their encounters with their government. The relationship certainly has potential for shaping the impression new borrowers perceive of the federal government itself.[16]

One central point is that the principles of borrowing and lending remain the same, as does the vocabulary: default, arrears, bankruptcy, credit, guaranteed. Student loans are still loans, and they can have an impact on the credit record of borrowers in much the same way as any other type of consumer loan: home, auto, or revolving credit. The structure of student loans themselves, particularly those that are federally guaranteed, is extremely different.

First, it is vital that we explore the definition of "guaranteed." To whom is the loan given by the federal government and taken by students guaranteed? It is guaranteed to the lender, who has become, in a plurality of cases, the federal government itself. How? By ensuring that student loans cannot be discharged in bankruptcy, unless borrowers can provide definitive evidence in court of an "undue hardship," a standard that has proven costly and impossible to meet.[17] The federal government itself has litigated some cases that make it clear it does not intend the "undue hardship" standard to garner widespread use for the purposes of student loan forgiveness. It is more difficult to discharge student loan debt than any other type of debt, and yet it is the only form of debt that does not require or even encourage an examination of the borrower's credit history.

One expert on financial markets interviewed in this chapter (named "Alan" for the purposes of this book), who had some particularly relevant insights on this point, has worked for government, finance, and lobbying organizations. He wished to remain anonymous because of the sensitive nature of the work he does. An attorney, Alan attended elite private institutions in both his undergraduate and law school education. His insights are particularly useful in examining the financial logic behind student loans to lenders as well as the impact of these loans on individuals' participation in the labor economy. Alan stresses at several points the nondischargeability of student loans. Making a related point to Goldstein, Alan explores effectively the rationale behind conceptually (though not, perhaps, legally) "securitizing" the earnings of college graduates for life, which will become self-evident, but also the hindrance that has on the borrower's economic participation. In a personal communication before the interview, Alan offered this assessment: "My basic view is that the student loan market or system is a total disaster. It's a massive credit market serving critical functions with respect to supporting economic productivity and redressing income inequality that is being inter-mediated without regard to ability to repay or the value of the thing being financed, and is therefore no surprise as producing terrible outcomes." A further message read:

> The non-dischargeability of student loans is one of the weirdest government policies out there. When you compare it to other non-dischargeable debts, it's akin to saying that your implicit moral obligation to repay a student loan is the same as your implicit moral obligation to pay taxes or support your children.

The interview began with broader views of the crisis, but progressed to Alan's specific conceptual view of student loans compared to historical lending practices in the Western world, as well as the crosscurrents of tension operating within and in concert with the student loan market. These comparisons are tremendously valuable in adding a broader historical context to the crisis.

Interviewer: If you would, please explain your basic view of the student loan market.

Alan: We're talking about the financing of an asset outside of any system in which borrowers or lenders actually think long and hard about what value that asset is. By comparison, if you look at the mortgage market, any other lending market, if you're going to lend somebody money to purchase something, and especially if you're not going to look at their ability to repay, you know, out of an income stream, you are almost always deeply concerned what's the value of what you're financing. Banks would never lend you $200,000 to buy a $10,000 house, right? We have the entire world of credit underwriting built on the loan to value ratio. If you were to ask me, "What's really going on?" if you look at all those people borrowing $200,000 to go to a nonaccredited law school, it's not the fact that they borrowed money, it's the fact what they purchased with that money is economically worth much less than what they paid for it.

Interviewer: Could that have been avoided?

Alan: Well, when you begin to look at it in the way I've described, it becomes much more of a consumer protection story. It's really, really weird to me. In 2009, Congress passed something called the CARD Act [*Editor's note: "CARD" is an acronym for the Credit Card Accountability Responsibility and Disclosure Act of 2009.*[18]]. The CARD Act was a response to the abuses in the credit card lending market. It did a bunch of different things, but one of the things it did is effectively made it illegal to make credit card loans to anyone under the age of 21 unless they had an adult co-signer or counselor. There's a sort of implicit notion embedded in that prohibition—it's an inherently unfair and deceptive act of practice to give someone under the age of 21 an unsecured line of credit. It's weird to think that in consumer protection matters, by law, you don't trust someone under the age of 21 to take out a $500 credit card line, but we're perfectly okay—in fact, we'll happily encourage—if they borrow $100,000 to purchase an asset, a college degree, which again, may or may not have that value. It just strikes me as completely and utterly ludicrous. These people are making enormous lifelong financial decisions without asking them anything like the kind of rigor, but if you want to take out a $500 credit card loan, forget it.

Interviewer: How can such a disconnect exist in law?

Alan: You still have to go to court and enforce it, but again, the nondischargeability is not unlike giving someone a kind of lifetime security interest in their income stream. There is an old common law distinction between courts of law and courts of equity. In courts of law, there's a bunch of rules written down, and you have to follow them. Courts of equity are less concerned with specific, explicit rules, and instead are more concerned with implicit rules of justice. So that, even if the law didn't require it, but basic principles of equity required it, common law courts would enforce it. Bankruptcy really has its roots in old equity law principles: even if it wasn't written down, as a matter of justice, you can't make someone effectively an indentured servant to a debt for their life. You have to have a notion of dischargeability of debt after a certain period of time.

To me, if you think of bankruptcy as effectively being about equity in this way, the nondischargeability of the debt is a total non sequitur. You could kind of theorize, I guess, why taxes might not be something you could discharge in bankruptcy. You also could certainly theorize why child support obligations are something you shouldn't be able to discharge in bankruptcy. Again, as a matter of equity.

Interviewer: So why doesn't the current student loan market function this way?

Alan: Clearly, I think, by making it nondischargeable, you lower the economic risk of the lender, or whichever party ultimately bears the default risk of that loan. In almost every case it's actually the federal government, whether it's the old system in which the federal government guaranteed loans or the new system in which they're direct government loans. Even in the old loan structure, nondischargeability was much more about protecting or limiting the economic risk to the federal government as the guarantor in default. In spite of all that, in law school it was not uncommon to get a true, pure, private loan, which had no government involvement or guarantee whatsoever.

Interviewer: So what was your own experience? Did you end up taking out a student loan for law school?

Alan: Certainly; I certainly did. It's a question of math. Ten years ago it was $52,000 a year. I think $18,500 [annually] was probably the furthest you could get with a federal loan. You had no choice but to go private to make up the difference. It was actually interesting to delve into the economics and the availability of loans in that segment because it gives you the idea of what a truly private market looks like, in comparison to the federal market. That loan was dirt cheap in terms of interest rates. One of the reasons it was dirt cheap was because I was going to be a law student, right? I know for a fact that the further that you go down in the law school peerage, the more expensive those loans get, and the more difficult they are to qualify for.

Interviewer: So what similarities, if any, do you believe exist between this situation and the subprime mortgage crisis?

Alan: There [are] a lot of similarities, to me, between this and the subprime mortgage crisis. Of course, there are a million different ways to look at the subprime mortgage crisis, as the subprime mortgage crisis is a number of different things. First and foremost, it's an asset bubble. It's a bunch of people who overpaid for an asset and also a bunch of people, who, because of their particular situation, when they overpaid for that asset, they financed almost all of the overpayments. When the thing that they purchased lost value, and the extent to which they effectively overpaid revealed itself—even if it was a relatively small decrease in value—that was sufficient enough to make it totally impossible for them to repay the debt. And also, the same time, it effectively wiped out all their wealth.

There's no more unenviable position to be in than to borrow money to buy something that ends up being worth less than face value of the loan. That is incredibly inhibiting from an economic perspective. Many people—probably half the country—wouldn't agree with me on this, but I would think redressing economic inequality would be well at the top of one list of larger policy goals. And again, if you look at the chunk of the population that is likely to be deeply under water on their student loans—their education asset—and therefore be disinhibited from moving forward as an economic matter, those are likely to be the same people who are at the bottom quartile of income or wealth distribution.

I was a middle-class 18-year-old. I'm now an upper-class adult. The structure of the student loan market served me perfectly well, tremendously well in fact. It's not those like me that [are] really hurting. I haven't spent a long time with this, but I look at the Bernie Sanders electorate, and I imagine that a large part of his base are probably recent college graduates who are deeply underwater on their education. You can understand why these people are mad as hell. You're talking about people who were doing exactly what they were told to do—that's the other thing, too. And, again, the similarities to the subprime mortgage crisis are quite pronounced. There too, people were completely underwater on an asset that we as a society, and as a government, strongly encouraged them to borrow to buy.

Alan's conclusions clearly rely on a historical economic context that prioritizes a strong consumer base that powers economic growth and prosperity. The above comments and analysis are striking in two respects: first, that the financial and economic logic of the student loan market itself is the result of several competing public policy and economic assumptions, resulting in a dysfunctional market operating under much the same logic as the periodically dysfunctional mortgage/housing market. Such a conclusion coming from the echelons of financial and political power is unsettling in and of itself.

Second, the departure from historical legal norms that the modern state of affairs represents brings us to a separate question: given that the student loan market crisis is a storm that results from competing crosscurrents of public policy (market logic/intervention, consumer-based economy, legal norms, democratic accountability of federal institutions), is there a choice to be made as to which goal should be prioritized? It would seem that attempting to maintain all four would foster yet more dysfunction. It would also seem that it would be difficult to disentangle each of those priorities given the current state of political dysfunction.

What is particularly striking is that both Goldstein and Alan pointed affirmatively to linkages and similarities between the subprime mortgage crisis and the student loan debt crisis. Both made reference to a class of ordinary people trying to stay in the middle class, and being denied access to the American Dream by any objective standard. It should be noted that both of the experts worked "on Wall Street" in the financial services sector and were able to see on a massive scale those ordinary people being, at best, misled. They were "doing everything right," as this last interviewee put it. Many of them have said as much in the context of online message boards and membership in debt resistance organizations. They also added their voices to the polls in voting for political candidates that seem to capture the essence of their discontent and sense of betrayal and alienation that would lead them to either a sense of the need for radical change or a reactionary stance against having to pay for an education at all.

The Stories of Borrower-Citizens

It is time to listen intently to the people who have come of age in a country that does not encourage their advancement. The following are interviews from former students, now debtors, who have found themselves in the situation of living with more student debt than they can afford and can "never" hope to repay. These are not composites or statistical averages; they are real people. None of them fit into a very neat archetype of how a borrower could or should appear. Not everyone who reads their stories will agree with their characterizations of their choices or the choices themselves, yet these stories are indeed representative of many of the popular perceptions of student loans, higher education, and democracy. These stories highlight the alienation from the American Dream of a generation of borrowers. In politics, however, and particularly in a democracy, the perceptions of many impact the reality of the whole. If these former students and borrowers are now citizens, they will be acting, and encouraging others to act, in a way that reflects their perceptions of their interests and the interests of society. Alternatively, they may choose not to act due to their now precarious financial status that has indebted them to large financial institutions or the federal government without any tangible asset or reasonable expectation that they will ever fully repay the balance. What is perhaps more real to them is the possibility of negative consequences if their incomes are endangered and their credit status is further downgraded.

"Paul" graduated from his undergraduate institution with a degree in communications, and after finding he had no job prospects, he pursued a master's degree in journalism. He has always had at least part-time work throughout his education (similar to 75 percent of full-time students nationally). At the time of the interview, he was in deferment, as well, but gainfully employed at a growing company. He wished to be anonymous because many employers may investigate the credit record of employees or job applicants, and he asserts that he is doing well in his current position. In his interview, he echoed the feelings of many of the borrowers, saying that he did everything he felt he was supposed to do. He has emerged with a particular viewpoint about the public conversation around student debt from political leaders, but also a different view about the distinction between public and private loan servicers.

Interviewer: Let's start with how much student loan debt you have.

Paul: I have $90,000; the number just seems like it's at the top of Mount Olympus and I'll never get there.

Interviewer: Well, let's just start with how that happened in the first place.

Paul: It had a lot to do with my parents. [They said] "you're going" and so I never really had a relationship with college that I think you need to have in order to use it efficiently, because we are borrowing money to go there. I borrowed more than what I needed because I didn't make enough through the various jobs that I had in school to support myself, so I needed extra money. I borrowed extra through my federal loans.

Interviewer: Tell me how that worked.

Paul: I would request the maximum a year through the federal loan, so I would get enough to cover all of my tuition. I would say on average a semester, I would have an additional two to three thousand, just the leftover deposited into my account to do whatever I wanted with, which, at the time, went to rent and food and gas. Not vacations or not anything like ridiculous. Because I worked the whole time I was in undergrad. I never really had a full-time job. I worked part-time at Home Depot for a while, worked part-time at Best Buy. I worked part-time on campus as a cook/host. I always borrowed more than what I needed for tuition to help me even get through those times.

Interviewer: What is your bachelor's degree in?

Paul: It's in communication studies. I really grew to be dependent on student loans. At the time, it was good because without it, I don't know what I would've done. Without it I know I would've had to either find a full-time position and school would've had to become second. Or I would've had to just ask to borrow from family more often, which I hate doing. Rent's covered, food, gas, and not really much else after that.

Interviewer: What kind of application process did you have to go through to get your loans every year?

Paul: All through FAFSA [*Free Application for Federal Student Aid*].[19] It just has the maximum amount you can request, and so I always requested it. It was usually about six to seven grand for the whole year more than what I needed. Then I would get that per semester, so I would get between two to three grand for the fall and then when I did it again for the spring, it would be the exact same process.

Interviewer: Could you talk a little about your interaction with the financial aid office?

Paul: I requested the maximum amount. They have that listed on what's called your bursar account, keeps track of all of that. I could just always log in and see what it was paid and what the refund . . . That's what it's called, a refund. "You requested this, you only needed this, you get the rest." Now I could say I wish I didn't do that. I would only say that now because of what I have to pay back now. Because when you're borrowing at the time to pay for school, it doesn't feel like you're actually taking on debt. You have no relationship with the debt. I think it has a lot to do with the stress that you're already involved in as a student, so much riding on every class you take, every test you take.

The whole time I was in school, I never made more than like thirteen grand a year with my part-time jobs, which is poverty. That's the kind of lifestyle I'm used to. Most of my twenties, that's been true. I was working with [a major global corporation] for about almost a year, and that's when I had to resign from [the major global corporation] to go back to school because they didn't have anything part-time. I still have some regrets there because I wonder now with my work ethic now, I totally could've pulled off working full-time and going to school part-time. At the time I thought that's a disaster. There's no way I'm going to go to class, because I'm working six, seven days a week usually with that job.

That was the only bright spot of my twenties where I actually made a decent income that year. I was in a really significant romantic relationship at the time. That wouldn't have continued either if I didn't go back to school because she was there to get her master's and she went to [a major university town] for a PhD, so I was sort of in this idea that an academic path is the only way out.

It's the only way out because I didn't come from wealth. We weren't born on third base, so the university is the only thing you can do, and I heard that all my life from parents and teachers. Anything that didn't require a four-year degree, it was stigmatized as a profession, which is really sad. I hope that changes at some point. We'll see. I borrowed so much to get the education I have, it's really difficult for me to think that I owe my success at my current job to that. I can't make that argument.

Interviewer: Can you talk about some of the values you carried with you in your experience, some of the influences in your decision-making process?

Paul: I feel sort of betrayed by a lot of those go-to-school slogans. I have all respect in the world for [President Obama], but when he talks about, and other members of Congress and just bigwigs talk about education is what you need, I always get mad at them, too. You're not really talking about how many other barriers there actually are that prevent someone from achieving what you can so casually put out there as easy. All you have to do is these four things and you'll be there. I've always heard that my whole life. I feel like I did what I was told mostly, I played by the rules.

Interviewer: I had heard someone mention that you thought you shouldn't have been allowed to borrow so much in student loans. Can you discuss what your feelings are on this particular subject?

Paul: There is a part of me now that thinks that shouldn't have been so easy for me and all the people like me to get extra loans, but I don't know where to go with that statement because I immediately will think of what else would I have done. Then it just becomes hypotheticals and you're not getting anywhere. I know the government does have a really important role to play in who gets to go to college because they have the money that we need to borrow to go there.

Interviewer: Do you feel like your debt has hampered your progress in some way?

Paul: It's definitely prevented me from doing a lot. Because it's the fear of garnishing wages or just coming after me. I'll never be able to buy a house or whatever because my credit's just completely [shot] from student loans. I don't know if I'll ever pay it off.

Interviewer: What kinds of loans do you have? Who are the loan servicers?

Paul: I have one private loan. That's been the worst. That's the one good thing I can say about the whole loan process, too, is that the people get it, the people that work there at the Department of Education that have to be on the phone with the millions of [people like me] that are struggling to pay back their student debt. They're the nicest people in the world.

They get it, but they are doing their job and they have to get the money from us and they want to figure out "How can we do that?" The private loan has been awful because they don't get it. They don't have to follow the same rules. They don't have the same laws protecting me from people from private financial institutions that give student loans.

Paul's odyssey through college and graduate school while negotiating the job market is the story of millions of Americans. Student loans enable people like Paul to obtain educations without looking at the cost-benefit analysis. They are dispensed in much the same way that a grant or subsidy might be, but in his case, he feels he has very little hope of actually paying back his $90,000 in student loans. He has found steady employment, and now he wishes to find a house and settle down, but is prevented from doing so by his large loan balance through multiple creditors. He became financially educated in his experience, but he was largely directed by his family about his general course of education. He is someone who has, in his own assertions, "played by the rules" and lived the values he was taught by embracing education at every turn as an avenue toward social mobility. Perhaps as a result, Paul is an example of the ambivalence graduated borrowers feel regarding their education. The surprising element of his story is the positive view he has toward the federal Department of Education. Despite the agency's policies that facilitated his loans, he feels gratitude toward the agency because it has helped him manage his debts, contrary to the private loan services with whom he also has a relationship.

Such attitudes emerging from borrowers that make a distinction between government and corporate loan servicers is worth discussing further as the direction for an eventual policy solution that requires democratic consent and popularity. Paul's experience ultimately causes him to regret and question leaders that generally align with his political beliefs, such as President Obama, by saying that they are lying to students, promising them jobs if they better themselves through education. It is fair to say Paul is alienated from the political system and higher education as a result of his experience. To confirm the commonality of Paul's experience with that of other borrowers, it is helpful to examine more of them.

This chapter continues to enter the world of student debt through the student perspective, but this time journeying with someone whose socialization and evolution as a professional is concurrent with her education. Miranda Merklein, PhD, was a published poet, labor organizer, and college professor by profession, who sadly died unexpectedly at the age of 39, before the publication of this book. Merklein exemplifies, perhaps, a generation that opted to fully adopt education as an ethic and a way of life to the detriment of their own immediate financial situation, in hopes of a long-term payoff. She had been discussing with friends a logical next step in her career trajectory and had not yet made a public decision about where she would go next. Her poetry, her family, her story, and her vocal struggle will be a lasting legacy.

Miranda's writing has appeared in many publications about her struggle to achieve her dreams and raise her children without any initial financial resources.[20] When she begins her interview, she narrates the start of her academic career when she had small children and was living on public assistance. Throughout her story, she provides a powerful window into the standpoint of an aspiring academic in the humanities "doing all the right things" with no initial well of financial stability that would enable her to continue. She alludes here to never being able to own her own home and achieve her own American Dream.

> *Merklein:* I really went into education as a way to escape poverty. I was working. It wasn't like I was lazy, or—the "welfare queen," which is not even a real thing for the most part. But I was busting my ass doing odd jobs, and you know, that was something I wanted to do. I knew that I had a lot of intellectual curiosity and that I really valued thought. I didn't really know where that was going to take me, so that's how I just entered college as a community college student.
>
> *Interviewer:* Did you begin to take out any loans at the time?

Merklein: I started to take out subsidized and unsubsidized loans because you could also get living expenses. Not enough to cover your living expenses, but you could get a disbursement back, and I think at the community college it was like a thousand dollars a semester or something like that, which was a lot of money at the time, so I could pay my rent that was a portion of—I mean, it was a public housing, like a partial payment, a voucher. And then, after I was there, I thought, hey, I don't have to stop here, I don't really see too many job opportunities—I could go on and get my BA [bachelor of arts, a four-year degree]! So, then I just went and I applied to a local—I didn't realize it at the time, but it was not necessarily like a normal school in Santa Fe, where I was, and couldn't really leave because I had two kids in shared custody. I went to the college we had in Santa Fe, a very expensive small liberal arts school.

Interviewer: What did they say when you applied without the means to pay tuition?

Merklein: They said if I did one more semester at the community college and get A's and B's, we'll let you in. Then I just went to the financial aid office, and they said yeah, okay, that we'll offer you these scholarships, now the rest you'll take out in loans, which you'll pay back later. And I understood that they were loans, and that I'd have to pay them back, and again I took out subsidized and unsubsidized loans, but I was taking out a lot of them. I had in my brain at the time the idea that I would get a job at some point and pay them back, that this was all bettering my life, getting an education. That's what I was raised with; just what people told me that was what we saw on TV, you know, education is the answer to the way to improve your life. That whole time I was getting my BA I never thought I wouldn't be able to repay them or I wouldn't get a job for a living wage with a BA. I started out as a film student, and meandered around and ended up in political science, graduated with a BA in political science. I had like $60,000 of loans at that point. My disbursement had then gone up; it was like $2,000 a semester.

Interviewer: Can you talk about your experience of getting your loan disbursement every semester?

Merklein: In a place like Santa Fe or New Mexico where poverty is so high, the need for getting your disbursement is like the bread line, you see these students standing in line and just like starving waiting for this check. I would be barely hanging on by the time I got it. I would really have to use all of my survival skills.

Eventually I thought to myself, I am way too interested in philosophy and literature to go to law school. Why don't I just keep going? I ended up going to a private liberal arts school in Santa Fe. There, my disbursements were bigger, I was getting like $5,000 a semester, I could even pay my rent. I was a freelance writer with the local paper, I got like a hundred dollars a story. I grew up in really deep poverty, and a lot of my friends went to prison or were homeless, they really weren't doing that great. New Mexico is a great place for tourists and retirees, but it's not a great place to grow up poor with no money. Everyone I know thought "you get an education, you're going to get paid more for your qualifications, especially if you're getting published," things like that.

I started getting a lot of stuff published, almost every week, some of these peer-reviewed journals. I thought, you know what, I'm gonna follow my passion. That's all I heard growing up, even on television, we'd see those infomercials, you know, "do what you love, you'll never work a day in your life."[21] So, when I got my PhD, I wasn't even necessarily that attracted to academia, since I really don't want to get a PhD in comparative literature or something where I'm going to have to write a really dry academic dissertation. I could do creative work. Since I've been speaking out about adjunctification and student loans, people would attack me and say "you should've known, you're entitled." People will say "you were just entitled, that was your problem." I didn't feel entitled. Unless entitlement is thinking that if you do the work and get qualifications, you'll get paid a real wage and have a real job, I mean if that's what entitlement is, then I guess I was.

I was at [a public university in the South] for three years. They didn't give me an assistantship the first year. They actually put me on probation the first year to see if I would make it. By the time I graduated [with my BA], I had $89,000 in debt. I knew people who graduated from there with $250,000 in debt. I still didn't think that I wasn't ever going to have a job that would allow me to repay it, so when I did my first year of nonfunded PhD, no one told me I was doing the wrong thing. Not one person in my program, not one person in my life—I never read an article, I still really firmly believed that I was on the right path, that I was a success story.

Interviewer: What about the financial aid office in any of these schools? Did they make you sign anything?

Merklein: Whenever they would advise me, they were like salespeople, they would encourage you to take out loans, they never say you should think about this. They just say you should take a little survey. I guess the surveys got more intense, but the surveys were hard to deal with, people just wanted to pass them. You had to figure out how much you will have to make by the time you graduate to answer the questions where it works out. I mean, there's no intervention as far as telling you, "You know what, you're at the danger zone. It's not likely you're going to make enough to pay them back."

Interviewer: They didn't have any kind of mandatory loan counseling in order to receive your loans?

Merklein: They call it counseling; it's really not. Financial aid people are salespeople, they're aggressive, but they also are very mean because they control the supply of the money. They control your disbursement, and so they know that students are desperate for those disbursements, so they just treat you like, "You'll get it when you get it." I would call all the time, "When is it gonna happen?" and there were always problems with the accounts. That happens a lot, so there was always a mini-crisis every semester throughout my PhD program. So, when I was granted an assistantship my second year, I was still taking out loans because by that point, I was publishing my own literary journal, I was teaching three composition classes, or two composition classes and a literature class, and actually writing this book of poetry, so I couldn't physically or mentally add another job to that or I would fail at all the other ones.

Interviewer: How did you react when you began to read those loan balances?

Merklein: I got the statements; it was very removed from my economic reality, because I just thought this was part of the process. This was part of achieving upward mobility, you know, you have to deal with this debt because I didn't come from a family with money. Other students would call their parents and get help, and I didn't have that. I didn't have a plan because I didn't know how these things worked out. No one I knew had gone through what I went through. Me and my friends were really the first generation of heavily indebted upward mobility "aspirationals."

Interviewer: What did you do after you were finished with your PhD?

Merklein: I went back to Santa Fe. I had no money. I had no disbursement anymore. I hadn't even acclimated to live outside of academia at that point. I think one person in my entire program got a job that was tenure track, and you know, it was political as much as it was merit-based in my opinion. My first job after getting my PhD was at [a large retail store chain], for ten bucks an hour. I was really depressed. I thought, "I have a PhD, I thought I was going to do something," and I thought, "Well, this is just temporary, this is just temporary," and then I started applying at the local colleges. By that point, I had $150,000 in student debt. The first [monthly] bill I got was for seven hundred bucks.

Interviewer: What did you do? Did you call the loan servicer?

Merklein: Sallie Mae at the time was really nonresponsive. I was one of those people who took out a subprime mortgage, and so we lost that house. My [student] loan was sold to someone else, and then to someone else. I would call them and they would say, "We don't own your loan anymore." The loans kept getting shuffled around; it's like debt laundering, basically.

Interviewer: Were they all federally guaranteed loans?

Merklein: Yes, I didn't have credit.

Merklein's story is one that is as fully immersed as anyone in the life of a student borrower and debtor. Her story is again one of "playing by the rules" and "doing everything right" and even upward social mobility coupled with several major successes in publishing her work and earning a PhD at a major university. She also alludes to a theme of the lack of a realized material reality of the debt. Receiving the financial statements about her debt was not sufficient to alert her about the urgency of maintaining a plan to repay her debt. Without personal mentorship in finances or education, the institutional mentorship about her long-term debt repayment plan was nonexistent, or at least insufficient to fulfill the objective of long-term financial soundness for loan recipients.

Merklein's characterization of the role of financial aid officers is also interesting, as her story gives the experience of a student perceiving her status as on the receiving end of the apparent exercise of power of financial aid officers over the loan disbursement process. Objectively, the loan officers at all institutions clearly have a process to ensure student consent, mediated partially by some questionnaires that seem to have been designed to compel students to consider fully the responsibility they were undertaking by consenting to new debt. Loan officers cannot be faulted for administrative lag times in disbursing loans. Like mortgage officers in the subprime crisis, they may have felt they were assisting people achieve upward mobility through the loan process, but safeguards such as credit checks were apparently not in place at any of the institutions Dr. Merklein attended. Someone with her potential and obvious high-energy academic achievement could certainly have avoided all of this with better counseling and more importantly, cost-free tuition at a public institution in her community. As both a teacher and a writer, Merklein exudes the kind of enthusiasm and ability that academia seems to encourage. There does not seem to be a compelling reason why such a person should have to beg for a combination of public and private loans when the public would see its subsidized investment returned tenfold over the course of her lifetime. It is a question of what type of public investment this society is intent upon making. Merklein may not have been alienated from education, simply because she took on the role of a political activist for the borrowers and contingent faculty she numbered herself among, but she is an exceptional case.

Borrowers can tend to take on the role of democratic activist as a representative of others who have gone through the same process. One such individual is Jake Virden, a writer and activist, who has used his own story of student debt accrual to organize others with similar stories. He has attended national debt organizing conferences and has encouraged others to do what is in their interest without shame or fear of reprisal. He has personally explored legal action, political action, and cultural action to address the structure of his debt, all the while questioning the legitimacy of it.

The origin of Virden's debt is very instructive and one that echoes many common themes of social mobility, explicit references to the concept of good citizenship, and the treatment of students as simultaneously one foot in and one foot out of adolescence while attending institutions of higher education. Like Paul, Jake felt pushed to earn his education by his parents, regardless of cost. Like Merklein, he did not experience the material, day-to-day reality of his debt even after he began to receive notices in the mail that he owed it to a financial institution. Like both, he had interesting experiences with the financial aid officers on his various campuses, as well.

Virden: My student loan story probably starts with my parents getting sober and wanting a better life for me. I was discouraged from looking at community college, I was encouraged more to look at private, liberal arts colleges. I had a crisis my first semester in 2004, where I saw a few too many George Bush stickers and Confederate flags, which was different than what I'm used to, what I wanted, so I transferred home.

Interviewer: What did you do then?

Virden: My next university had given me an academic scholarship package. It was kind of a rushed decision, and so the scholarship I had gotten no longer applied. I took out federal student loans and private student loans, so I'm not trying to sound like I'm making excuses. I remember really wanting to take time off, but I remember my other options were not looking sweet.

I would go back every year to the financial aid office. After the first year, I started to really feel the weight of the debt and realize that it was completely not worth it. I started to come to a different knowledge of myself. I was learning so much from this experience as a first-generation college student. I started reading and what I figured out, that what I want to do with my life is be a writer. I applied to the University of Minnesota as a transfer student. At that point, I had twenty thousand in debt, so I thought I might as well double that. The last two years I worked, too. I worked full-time at an after-school program. I needed the loans to buy books. I couldn't pay tuition, no way. My dad co-signed all of them. It's hard to even say what I graduated with. My loans got sold a couple times. Right now, I can't even keep that close a track.

Interviewer: Can you talk about how taking these loans out affected you?

Virden: I used to get these terrible stomachaches. [One servicer] telling me they sold my loans to [another loan servicer], one of those companies. People used to contact me about those too; just a dizzying array of envelopes is what I remember. Eventually, Sallie Mae ended up as the holder of my loans. I was in deferment with them. For two years, I was working full time, I was making about $30,000.

Interviewer: Was there anything you could do about your loan balance during that time? How did the envelopes stop?

Virden: I consolidated my loans with the [federal Department of Education].

Interviewer: Has your experience with that program given you more of a positive or negative feeling toward the federal government?

Virden: Honestly, it's a mixed bag, just as far as comparing the federal government as a lender to the private lenders that I've worked with, they're way easier to work with. Consolidating with the federal government was easier, and more up-front, and their terms and interest rates are lower. The way people speak to me is better, they don't harass me. They don't harass my parents, so in that sense, they're preferred. Even with the private loans that I got, and even in theory, if I had to take out money to go to school, and I had to be paying somebody back, I'd rather be paying something that I had some kind of democratic control over, something that's going to be putting something back into my community. I have a more favorable view toward federal loans than I do private loans, but it's made me feel more that the federal government and the government in general doesn't really work for working-class people or black people or Native people. People that you see who are most likely to be in student debt couldn't afford to go to school, and who really see no other options.

Interviewer: Can you talk about how you think the conversation around student debt is affecting society generally?

Virden: It strikes a nerve for the conditions of our lives, and it's frustrating for me because I feel I'm a pretty informed person, especially when it comes to student debt, I've done some research, and I've gone to college, and I kept on reading after school, and I still feel I don't even know enough about what the federal government's role has been. I do know that my Sallie Mae loans are federally backed. They provided insurance so that Sallie Mae could buy my loans knowing that I'm at high risk for default, knowing what the job market looks like, knowing that, and then the federal government tells them they're at no risk. They come buy my loans and then it's better for them if I default because they cash in both ways. The federal government's not looking out for us either.

In this first look at Virden's experience, his motivation for his later activism is obvious. He struggled to get through college, and then found that he had to struggle twice as hard after he graduated. He assigns blame for the depth, but not the totality, of his struggle to the banks and government institutions that hold his loans. The beginnings of a critique against federal government complicity, but not agency, is also apparent in his story. Like Paul, and yet more so, he felt explicitly more comfortable by the fact that his loans were held by the Department of Education. He expands his critique to one of democratic accountability of the federal government to the people, whom he further characterizes as working class. The themes of doing everything he was told to do, not by society but by his parents, like Paul, is also in evidence, as is, like Merklein, the recognition and cultivation of his creative impulses. Virden's story will be further visited in later chapters discussing the possibilities and limitations of student debt–centered debt activism. As a student and a borrower, his initial motivations are much the same as many others.

"Maggie" is a graduate with over $100,000 in student debt as of the time of her interview in 2016. She wishes to remain anonymous because she currently works in higher education as an admissions counselor, and her employer does know her history, which she prefers. Despite efforts to pay it down through public service incentives, she is currently, and for the foreseeable future, in deferment. Deferment is not the same condition as delinquency, as it is essentially getting permission from your lender to be in a state of nonrepayment of your loans due to some sort of financial hardship or mitigating life circumstance. While not as politically minded as other borrowers, Maggie has worked for the federal government in a public service position to try to mitigate her debt, and she is currently gainfully employed at a university. She also wants to make a career transition to a job with, unfortunately, more requirements for graduate coursework. In her story, there are two themes, one of someone attempting to obtain an education and the completely insurmountable nature of her debt, and of attempting to pass on individually some of the wisdom she has gained, without recourse to the political system, to the next generation.

Readers will do well to pay attention to her experience as someone who is attempting to find a passion while working through her education and early career, and how little her particular response has been political and geared toward the vocabulary of citizenship. Also take note of her positive attitude despite making reference to the possibility of regret for her education, as many of her peers apparently do.

> *Maggie:* My loan debt is $108,000 today. I transferred twice in my undergrad from a private college to a private college, both very expensive schools obviously. I earned my master's, transferred three times, and that really added up a lot too.
>
> *Interviewer:* Three transfers is a lot. Why did you transfer that much?
>
> *Maggie:* I just kept changing my mind. Right now, I'm an admissions counselor for [a for-profit university] and I make about $50,000 a year, not a lot of money when you have student loans, but as an employee I get to get my master's degree for free through them. I'm going to school at the university and working.

Interviewer: What are your degrees in?

Maggie: My undergrad degree is in psychology. I wanted to stick with something in that area but it's just too broad a subject, you're not going to get anywhere, which I found trying to look for jobs after college. I don't know, I have a lot of friends that dropped out in undergrad and they're still paying loans, so they just see it as a big waste of time. They're doing temp work.

Interviewer: How do you feel about your undergrad degree now?

Maggie: I'm really glad that I got the undergrad degree. I don't regret it. I wouldn't go back and get something else. Psychology I might have changed because it is so broad. I was looking to go into maybe a two-year degree to just start working. I work for the university now and so I work with college freshmen and seniors in high school and getting them into freshman year. You just hear these debt stories over and over so we try to offer scholarships, but it's still not enough so they have to get loans.

Interviewer: How about your story? If you could maybe talk about where you went to school, how that debt was accumulated?

Maggie: I went to a private school in downtown Chicago, so I had to live downtown, so I did [it] the sneaky way and got more loans so I could afford rent. Well, it's not very sneaky, anybody can do it, but you're asking for a lot more in loans than you actually need and I would ask for a lot more to pay rent. So, with a $16,000 tuition I would ask for $30,000 [in loans]. Now, I'm paying back money I spent on gas and food and rent, so I mean it was all worth it. I finally have a job I went to school for and—but it's going to take me until I'm 80 to pay back the loans. I know everywhere I transferred you had the exit counseling and it would say you need to make $200,000 a year to pay this back on time. You can't let it scare you. I'm deferring, actually all of them are deferred now so that's why I'm not paying anything.

Interviewer: Some people start to realize their debt when they receive notices in the mail. Did that happen to you?

Maggie: I did have this panic attack year when I first found out that it was over a hundred, and so I looked on like FinancialAid.gov and looked up different resources and ways to help bring that down. I worked for AmeriCorps for two years. I got a ten-thousand-dollar education award to use toward loans, so I have paid that toward that. It went from $108,000 to maybe $100,000 with the interest, so at that point, I told myself that I'm not taking out any more money.

Interviewer: Tell me some more about your job now at the university.

Maggie: I know at the beginning when I was telling my dad about it, it sounded more and more like a sales position, and as I worked at it I'm finding that it's not. It actually makes me a lot happier about doing it because the last thing I want to do is force a child to pay $40,000 to go to school and they don't even know what they want to do. Gen-Eds [*general education/liberal arts courses required for a bachelor's degree, usually outside of one's major*] only take up a semester at this school, so you need to know what you want to do by spring or be prepared to switch back and forth. I have a quota of every year of [a certain number of] students registered.

Interviewer: Do you talk to prospective students about financial aid or tuition or loans?

Maggie: I first ask if they're going to fill out the FAFSA in the spring. A lot of parents don't even know what that is. We actually hold financial aid workshops nights at school, so I'll talk about financial aid, how to apply, what it means if you don't get it. What are the next steps. Private loans are on the back burner: if a student can't afford to go to this school and we know it, we don't even offer that as an option.

Interviewer: You sound like you like your job. Is this something you want to do long-term?

Maggie: I really want to do addiction counseling. I've always wanted to do it. I was always too scared to get more loans out to go to school. I had enough! I should have a decent job, but I don't. I have that bachelor's degree, and in my graduate school I have never finished a degree, so it's just money that I used for nothing and now it's just sitting there and I have to pay it back.

Interviewer: Are there jobs for addiction counselors, maybe with some more security?

Maggie: There are, but when I've looked at the estimated salary of that it's less than what I make now, so it's like I don't really know. I hope so.

Maggie is certainly a hard worker who has struggled throughout her education and is now looking optimistically at the future. She is also an example of someone who attended college in preparation for a career, but now somewhat regrets the less practical aspects of her education and the loans it took to earn it. She did not end up considering any option to leave behind her education, instead transferring three times. Maggie, like millions of others, merely wishes for a rewarding career, but is stifled and stymied by her debt. Maggie's overall loan balance continues to grow despite two years in a public service loan forgiveness program. At best, her experience has made her ambivalent toward government loan policy, but not toward education, employed by a university whose goals and aims she admires. Her story is interesting not because she was in any way galvanized politically or because she blames others. She was not and she does not. Her story is interesting because it typifies what current policy is doing to people whose only aim is to do the next thing society is requiring so that they can provide for themselves, and how ensnared by public policy they become, without any stated interest in politics or government.

Notably, all four of the people we have thus far encountered have touched upon the procedure of surplus loan disbursements: the policy of allowing students to borrow cost-of-living allowances in addition to tuition. All indicated they felt they were somehow gaming the system, when in fact such practices were extremely common and easy to undertake. Borrowing more than tuition is arguably no longer a student loan, but a secured revolving credit line for which there is no credit check. As Alan, the attorney, indicated, it seemed as if society was not going to tolerate such practices, but this is belied by current student loan policy. Maggie, however, is now in a position to encounter students who are on the brink of embarking upon a similar path, but she is certainly taking steps to help students avoid those kinds of personal choices, perhaps in spite of government policy. There is more to gain from people with experience in college admissions who encounter students about to borrow hefty student loans.

Benjamin Anderson is a graduate student in a doctoral program in communications. Several years ago, after graduating with his master's degree, he found himself looking for work while figuring out the next steps in his life and career. After some time he found a position as an admissions officer at a private college. As a result of this experience, he has some profound insights into the way in which student loans are initially presented to prospective students who are attempting, like him, to "do the right thing" and earn a degree to advance their career. While his evidence is anecdotal, there is little doubt that anyone who has gone through or witnessed their child go through the college admissions process in the last decade will find all of these circumstances very familiar. What is unique is Anderson's perspective from the other side of the admissions desk, and his subsequent return to academic work. His experience demonstrates what is happening at private colleges, which, despite their nonprofit status, operate much like a business with a sales model that seeks revenue. In terms of tuition revenue, it is substantially from students who finance their education through readily available credit they do not discuss at length during the admissions process, and also creates an incentive to privilege students who can pay their full tuition over other, perhaps more deserving students who may need scholarships. Anderson also references the state of "precarity" (employment-related financial insecurity) he was experiencing at the time of his job offer, which is an increasingly common narrative among millennials and the modern working class.

> Interviewer: Can you talk about what your experience [was] as an admissions officer?
>
> Anderson: I was in the situation where I'd been searching and failing to find a living wage for a year. Finally this job came along and I applied,

and I, initially, I got a call back that I didn't get it. But apparently, I was second on the list so I ended up getting the job, and it was such a relief that I walked into it, and there's self-discipline that happens in that kind of situation where you're kind of willing to do whatever it takes to make a good first impression. I was prepared to be a "company man."

Interviewer: How was it when you got started?

Anderson: I walked in, and I had to hit the ground running because we were right on the verge of the recruitment cycle. I think I started in July or August, so right before it was time to start with the push for travel and high school visits and all this. It's kind of a crash course in learning everything about the institution, and kind of getting myself to know all of this, so not a lot of time for reflection of the process beyond my role in it.

Interviewer: What was your specific role in the process?

Anderson: A big part of it was in the early days, going to our information sessions and listening to the veteran admissions people give the presentation to visiting students, field questions and all of this. And the way that the presentation was pretty much scripted. Like everyone, there were variations, but essentially everyone followed this trajectory of promoting the school in terms of academics, location, and campus culture and then going into the nitty-gritty of the application process and the financial aid process. And in the financial aid part, almost everyone made it about: Here's how you apply, here's what people get, and the average debt, what people owed after is about $24,000. The actual implications of the cost of the place was very much downplayed. The last thing you want to do when you're selling this educational commodity is steer away your customers.

Interviewer: I'm sure it must have come up as a question, though. How did you handle it?

Anderson: There was always this bit of eggshell walking when it came to a financial aid question. I think that was uniformly the case, and a very optimistic kind of framing of that. When they were questions from parents, I would see my supervisor [or fellow admissions officer] find a way to basically redirect the question in such a way that the debt isn't a problem because we have these resources available. The people who visited, who came on an individual visit and not organized by some kind of program, those people primarily were there to get a sense of the place. These are generally the students with families with that kind of mobility to size up a place and see if it fits.

That said, pair up with just visiting the campus, and the interview definitely felt to me like one of those things that students did to get that leg up [in the admissions process]. And high school visits fall somewhere in between where I think a lot of students would come because someone recommended it. From the student perspective, generally it was about hearing about an option and sizing it up. From a parent perspective, it was a lot more instrumental; students almost never asked about cost or job prospects after, these things that we talk about so much with higher education. That's what the parents did almost across the board, which I think reveals the difference in generational culture.

Interviewer: In terms of the admission process itself, can I ask if there is any type of favor that might be shown a student if they or their family actually has some demonstrable wealth that the institution notices? In other words, are wealthy students admitted more often than similarly situated students who are not wealthy?

Anderson: If I'm reading a mid-lane application student with a very mid-lane SAT score in both of those ways, which falls toward the bottom of our averages, but I'm reading one of those mid-lane students and there's no application for financial aid, typically that's an indicator that the student doesn't intend to apply for financial aid, which is an indicator that this is a student who can pay. That does two things: it obviously limits the student's consideration for those discretionary scholarships that are often used as carrots but it also, as we talked about, often would make a questionable admission into—so instead of putting someone on the wait list it might actually bump them into admission because, well, this is a sure investment. So that was always something that irritated me.

Interviewer: How many of the students admitted actually did check the box that they needed some form of financial aid?

Anderson: Based on my memory, I want to say that, of the students, something like 75 percent were on financial aid, maybe more. I can't remember 100 percent on that, but I should say that means that 15 to 25 percent were full-pay, which is a lot of money that is pretty much in the bank at the university. The financial aid packages for most students are almost entirely federal loans and grants, so there is not a big culture of taking private loans at this institution. I can talk a little more about scholarships than I can about financial aid because the actual assessment of the need wasn't done in our office but in the financial aid office. There were a number of small- to medium-size scholarships available for students, one that dealt primarily with leadership and service or basically just extracurriculars. It was often used as a carrot for good students who aren't the best of the best. The students who are the best of the best, you know the 4.0 students who have a near perfect SAT who were student body president or have three academic publications or whatever, those students were often incentivized with a full tuition scholarship. There is only a handful of those in each class, I don't remember how many, very very few, in the single to low double digits; we're talking a very small group. And in between those there's also a couple of talent scholarships. There's a debate scholarship, there's a music scholarship, basically just little incentives to get you to check that "I accept" box. From the financial aid side of things, I don't know any more than that.

Interviewer: How did your experience influence the way you thought about higher education?

Anderson: When we are talking about an institution that costs as much as this place, and it has an endowment that isn't, you know, enviable by "[elite]" standards but is still pretty large, what we're talking about is an organization that fundraises, that gets donations, from people with really much bigger pockets than any standard alumnus. This is a big business that is considered "nonprofit" but really, that's not what universities are.

Anderson's perspectives as an aspiring academic and as a former admissions staffer and undergraduate student are instructive. His behind-the-veil experience of working for an admissions department is particularly illustrative of the profit motive of universities, even nonprofit universities, when they are faced with choices of whether to admit students who can essentially be charged more to attend. Not only does it play its part in perpetuating economic inequality by granting a kind of financial affirmative action to these students, but this profit motive also demonstrates the "rational" decision many institutions may make to garner more tuition revenue, without regard necessarily to where those funds originate, which may be from outside loans.

Further, the marketing perspective alone, the recruitment of students by "downplaying" the notion or severity of student debt is by itself disturbing. It collides with the idea that students are making informed decisions because, perhaps in part, officials from an accredited, federally recognized nonprofit institution advised them that such debt was "good" or "normal." These officials themselves are under pressure from the university administration to meet certain admission and revenue quotas, but the advice entering students are being offered in their college search is misleading at best, and at worst a systemic failure that alienates students from higher education while saddling them with debt as they enter the job market. A sales model marketing to people tasked with making a consequential and major financial decision while still in the throes of their teenage years cannot be serving any type of social interest. If it does, it is despite the malformation of this model.

The interviews in this chapter have exposed some hard truths about student debt and its relationship to the American Dream: students often are handed student loans with little or no explanation of what kind of income they will need to pay them back, or what the chances are of obtaining an income like that in the current labor market. If students transfer from one institution to another during their undergraduate education, they are often attracted to private loans, and with no credit history, they have no experience to tell them how to calculate interest rates or how to manage their debt. When students are applying from high school, admissions counselors will downplay any issues of debt in order to get students to sign on the dotted line. Experts believe these students are "doing everything right," and yet they will be graduating arguably in a worse financial position than when they entered college with no credit history and no credential. If a 22-year-old student graduates with $90,000 in debt, it is not likely they will find gainful employment in a labor market that sees over 10 percent youth unemployment and probably double that in terms of underemployment. It can cause a serious disruption in people's lives, and one that may severely hinder them financially, emotionally, and even physically.

As borrowers and experts have attested in this chapter, the student loan crisis is similar to the subprime mortgage crisis in several uncomfortable and familiar ways, but perhaps most importantly, it severely limits the ability of people to participate in the Lockean American Dream of homeownership and community. Given the historic orientation toward trust in government that is higher among homeowners, the substantial drop in the homeownership ratio is troubling. This limitation is being facilitated by federal higher education policy, the underfunding of public education, and the overreliance on no-credit loans dispensed to students without supervision or oversight until they come due after graduation or dropout. Echoes of the values of postmaterialism are also evident in many of the borrowers' narratives, which seems to have put them at a disadvantage in a higher education system that encourages them to both embrace postmaterialism in their studies while simultaneously "downplaying" the significance of the debt. This system cannot be called a public service. Private lenders have also facilitated this failure, and all institutions of higher education have become more dependent on this system of loans than they have on public subsidies, which drives up the market price of tuition.

The federal government, while being part of the problem, may also be part of the solution: several borrowers' citation of the federal government as a friendlier loan servicer that will give considerably more latitude in the repayment process is perhaps cause for further study, and is counterintuitive to the initial hypothesis of this project. Rather than loan policy and association with private banks causing animosity toward the federal government on behalf of borrowers, instead the crisis has demonstrated the capacity of public institutions to provide relief and to build goodwill toward public, democratically accountable institutions such as the Department of Education.

What's more, the political nature of student loans is demonstrated through the mobilization of activists who have gone through the process, the interaction of all of these borrowers with at least one federal government agency after their graduation, and the reference to political leaders in the same breath as their discussion of their own debt accumulation and repayment plans. What is also plain is that each of those interviewed clearly achieved a great deal in their liberal arts education and have elected to use their critical thinking and communications skills in the service of humanity, and all have a proper appreciation for the social context in which their loans exist. All, however, have lamented the extent to which this system has come about and have different degrees of thinking about whether there is a viable public policy solution. It would truly be a failure if the knowledge and ability of learned people is not harnessed for the collective good of society. The next chapter contains interviews with policy experts who have done considerable work in the very particular realm of student debt, including detailing the expansion of the debt crisis to where we have arrived today.

CHAPTER THREE

The Government's Creation and Destruction of the American University

This chapter chronicles the change in the symbiotic relationship of higher education from being a factory of idealized citizenship to a generator of profit in the form of debt payments that lead to alienation among student-borrowers. The expansion of the student base through grants and aid in the postwar period will contrast directly with the austerity-driven policy changes of recent decades that compel indebtedness today. Students who "did the right thing" and obtained an education in the past were rewarded with a degree, but students who "did the right thing" today are rewarded with debt equal to or greater than a full year of their pretax salary, if they are able to find that work immediately after graduation. The ideological narrative of the American Dream is damaged by such a disjunction when this new generation is neither able to participate in the economy nor able to participate in democracy.

The pivot point of postwar American higher education was surely the "GI Bill" or, officially, the Servicemen's Readjustment Act of 1944, under which returning veterans from World War II were now entitled to, among other benefits, the remission of college and university tuition for themselves and their dependents.[1] Given the widespread nature of military service in World War II, it was part of the informal so-called "postwar compact" that existed between American workers and employers.[2] Workers were entitled to benefits that would allow them to remain productive members of the workforce and citizens that could contribute to their community and their country. Attendance at colleges and universities began, for the first time, to approach numbers as high as the widespread nature of military service.[3] An unprecedented increase in enrollments began after the GI Bill, and further grew after the concept of student loans was created in 1958 and Pell Grants for low-income students were passed in 1965.

It is perhaps fitting that the GI Bill so reflected the political, economic, and social environment of the time and that the GI Bill of 2008 similarly parallels the current political, economic, and social environment. Called officially the Post 9/11 Veterans Educational Assistance Act, it is largely a loan package that is separate from, and can even serve as a complement to, ordinary federal student loans.[4] In effect, it has created a way to allow veterans to go further into debt than the rest of the population if they choose to further their education. Because of a strange federal loophole, in fact, for-profit colleges and universities have aggressively recruited veterans who are beneficiaries of this bill.[5]

This chapter draws upon interviews from policy experts and activists in the field of for-profit colleges and universities and federal higher education policy generally. One interview is with an administrator at a historically black college/university (HBCU), who has observed the effects of these policies on the day-to-day administration at a typical HBCU, which has a tradition of serving marginalized populations. As Goldstein explained, these populations are not as well served under a loan-focused model as they were under an aid-focused model that also prioritized public funding. They are certainly not any closer to achieving the so-called American Dream of social mobility and homeownership.

This chapter is a contextualized analysis of a collection of individual stories that inform the larger story of what higher education has become and is becoming in the United States. What has been occurring in the larger news media since the 2008 financial crisis is the story of how "irresponsible young people" have been taking out "too much money" to pay for their college education and have become saddled with debt that is crippling the economy. Adding to this story is a public policy headache about impairing consumer spending and borrowing.[6] The story that has not been heard has already been authored by the borrowers themselves. This story is told largely from the perspective of Generation X and the millennials in the United States, and how that perspective was shaped by baby boomers, and what the material consequences have been.

Millennials will be educating and socializing children and young people for the next fifty years. The millennial teachers that emerge from the socializing experience of their own education are going to have an orientation toward both the educational infrastructure and the federal government that may be completely alien to that of their parents.[7] This orientation of academics toward the government of one of the wealthiest and most politically significant nation-states in the world will inform the perceptions students and later citizens have toward education and later toward their government, with potentially global consequences.

Whom do colleges and universities serve? The common good, or the bottom line? Who is their "customer"?[8] What is the objective of education: fulfillment and enlightenment, or job training; both, or neither?[9] Is education actually an integral part of the American Dream? These questions have been asked by researchers, journalists, policy experts, as well as borrowers and their advocates. Education and the U.S. economy are now inseparable. There is $1.5 trillion in student loan debt that primarily faces the millennial generation, but also the entire U.S. economy.[10] While this debt has impacted all age groups, the under-40 age group has seen their total student debt burden increase by almost 300 percent, from $248 billion to over $642 billion, most of it now by the federal government directly.[11] The existence of this debt has begun to make itself known in cornerstones of the American economy, from buying cars to buying homes.[12] Unemployment is also high, suggesting much of this debt will never be realized in repayment.[13] It is estimated that 13.7 percent of student debt is in default, and roughly 15 percent is delinquent.[14] Of the remaining debt, less than half of those classified as "current" are in a state of repayment, while the majority are in the usually pregraduation stage of "deferment" or the temporary financial hardship status called "forbearance." Given these statistics, it is small wonder that student debt was one of the chief motivators for the Occupy movement in October 2011.[15] Even as spiraling debt has become a common rallying cry for millennials, it did not translate into a coherent agenda for the Occupy movement. However, several of the successor organizations have focused on debt forgiveness, debt avoidance, and ultimately, debt refusal.[16]

Rather than encouraging the emboldening of an intellectual and professional class through higher education policy, we have instead encouraged the shaming and juvenilization of an entire generation of borrowers. There is scant hope of ever repaying the majority of this debt, and in fact only a small minority of borrowers are even in a state of repayment to either the government or private lenders.[17] In existing literature surrounding this topic, there has not been enough focus on the long-term political consequences of such a robust debtor class that will never unshackle themselves, namely, encouraging alienation from the political system expressed through appeals to radicalism and/or reactionary politics.

Indeed, if higher education continues to devalue those who pursue careers that do not primarily seek fortune but rather seek to contribute to the larger conversation of the academy's discourse, the academy will become further vulnerable to the benchmarks of success laid out by the financial world. For example, statistics in terms of job placement, average incomes of graduates, the efficiency of content delivery, the cost of tuition, the profits to the governing board and/or executive officers of the institution will inform administrative decisions.[18] The question becomes whether the federal government, as in the case of legally mandated segregation in homeownership two generations past, will act in this crisis as the shaper of a new inequality; in turn, how will millennial citizens respond to a government that does not serve their interests? Reports by the New America Foundation, the Higher Education Research Institute at UCLA, and the National Center for Education Statistics that give context and policy history can be observed briefly in order to understand the environment of some of the following interviews in this chapter from those who have rich insights that can help us all understand how this policy nexus functions.[19]

Timeline of Federal Student Loan Policy[20]

1940—797,000 public university students, 698,000 private college students, tuition accounts for 28% of educational and general revenue, government subsidizes 30%.

1944—Servicemen's Readjustment Act (GI Bill): Subsidies for veterans, families.

1945—Wages rise commensurate with increasing productivity until 1973; borrowing affordable for consumers.

1958—First Federal Student Loan Program created.

1965—Federal Loan Guarantee Program (later FFEL) created; Pell Grants (named for Senator Claiborne Pell) for low-income students passed.

1970—6.4 million students enrolled at public colleges and universities, 2.1 million at private institutions, tuition accounts for 21% of educational and general revenue, government subsidizes 45%.

1970—75% of surveyed freshmen said it was "essential" to go to college to develop a meaningful "philosophy of life" and 39% said to "be very well-off financially."

1990—10 million students enrolled at public institutions, 3 million at private, tuition accounts for 24% of revenue, government funds for 40%.

1993—William D. Ford Direct Loans Program created.

2003—Total student debt stands at approximately $300 billion.

2008—Post-9/11 Veterans Educational Assistance Act (New GI Bill) encourages for-profit colleges (private, higher tuition) to recruit veterans, low-income students.

2008—State funding for higher education has decreased an average of 20%, or $2,000 per student, since the Great Recession. States with deepest cuts include Arizona, Pennsylvania, Michigan. Recent independent findings conclude roughly 75% of tuition increases (twice rate of inflation since 1980) can be attributed to this.

2010—Guarantee (FFEL) program eliminated; all new federal loans are direct loans ($800 million).

2014—$1.2 trillion in student loan debt and growing. New York Federal Reserve warns it may be preventing younger borrowers from buying homes, cars.

2014—14.5 million public students, 5.5 million private students, tuition 26% of higher education revenue, government subsidizes 29%.

2014—Median privately employed nonagricultural worker wages have progressed only from $19/hour to $21/hour in constant 2014 dollars since 1970. Wages for college graduates since 2000 have fallen from over $18/hour to under $17/hour.

2015—46% of surveyed freshmen said it was "very important," "essential" to develop a "meaningful philosophy of life" in college, 81% said to "be very well-off financially."

The evolution of both federal and state higher education policy has been to rely more on tuition revenue and less on public subsidies. The results of much of the last half-century of federal higher education policy on the mentality and goals of students have devalued learning in favor of financial stability. It is worth noting that as the population of students has grown significantly, there has been a shift in access to higher education. The socio-economic background of college students in the early 1960s might not reflect the same sectors of society today.

These shifts are affecting students of varied racial, gender, and class backgrounds. The growth of for-profit higher education (which relies heavily on federal subsidies), the decline of state subsidies for higher education, and the conversion of federal loans from largely a guarantee program until 2010, and thereafter a direct federal loan disbursement, all had enormous impacts on higher education. The experts interviewed here were sought for their particular expertise and perspectives in light of these changes, which they have all professionally investigated and/or worked with. Particularly, these interviewees have worked with student-borrowers or lenders themselves, and have experience with the many avenues of assistance available to borrowers, from policy creation to policy implementation, and thus have learned perspectives on how this student debt is viewed from several quarters.

Chris Hicks is a labor activist and professional organizer. He began organizing students in response to student debt while an undergraduate himself. He was soon hired by a political arm of the labor movement, Jobs with

Justice (JwJ) as the Student Labor Action Project coordinator—a joint project of JwJ and the U.S. Student Association. At the time of the interview in December 2015, he was the head of the Debt-Free Future section at JwJ. Hicks is now chief of the Higher Education Division of the American Federation of Teachers (AFT). Hicks discusses the history of how student debt has accumulated and the inequalities that both result from and are exacerbated by student loans. Student debt has affected students and members of marginalized groups in the political realm, further exacerbating inequality and alienating entire classes of people from the political system.

Interviewer: How did we get here, to this level of student debt?

Hicks: We are talking about the jump from $300 billion to $1.3 trillion in debt.[21] I would say that the answer lies mostly in the Great Recession, in two different ways. The first is the math of funding that occurred toward higher institutions. This is the type of revenue that people have come to know, but that issue has been founded by another factor of the Great Recession, which was the layoffs. This was the lack of a job, [and so] more people going to grad school or returning to secondary education to train for a specific ability. Often when we talk about the student debt crisis, the idea is limited to 20- to 30-year-olds, but when we talk about 1.3 trillion, they make up about 33 percent of that total, but those 31 to 40 also hold 33 percent of that debt, and those 41 to 50 also hold a chunk of that debt, as well. So, we saw a lot of people either go back to college because they were laid off or like people in my situation, who went to graduate school directly after their BA because there were no jobs for them to apply for. This was a time when more people than ever were going to college and the federal government was giving the least amount of money that they had in decades. Those issues in tandem with each other, as well as rapidly rising tuition costs that people hadn't counted on, was a huge factor.

Interviewer: What populations are now being most affected by the student debt crisis?

Hicks: The person most likely to default is someone who attended a for-profit [college or university], who was not able to complete their degree and dropped out, because they most likely took out a federal subsidized student loan. For-profits are pretty notorious for getting those. They have college-level debt, but they don't have college-level earning potential. This person who might have $20,000 in student loans could be working at McDonald's for minimum wage. With the relative income level, there's absolutely no way they'd be able to afford that. There are actually over 100,000 people in prison that have federal student debt. We are wasting millions of dollars in taxpayer money in trying to go after them. You could think about how civil rights plays a huge role in student debt: 42 percent of African Americans have student debt. And statistically, women borrow more and take longer to repay.

There are twenty states that will penalize you professionally if you default on a student loan, which means you're essentially fired from your job, and those professions typically targeted are health care professionals, typically nurses, and elementary school teachers.[22] And if you look at the gender makeup of those professions, that really targets women in a big way. We know every year that tens of thousands of workers are losing their ability to work because they don't have the ability to repay their debts. People like to talk about the $1.3 trillion crisis, but this is actually a public health crisis, when you're laying off nurses because they can't pay their debt.

Interviewer: Do you know anything about a provision in some state bar associations that may require attorneys to report the unethical behavior of colleagues who are defaulting on their student debt?

Hicks: I've actually had [a friend of mine] disbarred because of that. Montana actually had that law. We were able to build a coalition of Democrats and labor unions to overturn it. For-profit [colleges and universities] made a fortune off blue-collar, first-generation college students. It just compounds the issue of inequality. It has an impact on the housing market, on the car industry, and all these different changes in socioeconomic status.

It is alarming to consider that people in the "helping professions" such as nurses, attorneys, and teachers may lose their job because of delinquent student loans. Underemployed professionals easily become alienated, further weakening some of the pillars of a well-functioning democratic society. Hicks particularly notes that student debt is disproportionately held by women and African Americans, highlighting a deepening inequality because of debt. Mobilizing people for political action who might otherwise be marginalized and alienated provides one way to address the crisis in a constructive way. Many actions have been taken to combat or address student debt (which will be outlined in the next chapter), which certainly address the largest sites of culpability and misery in the ongoing crisis in terms of public funding for education, private profits from explicitly for-profit colleges and universities, and the causes and consequences of loan policy itself.

Borrowers have turned to several consumer protection centers, institutes, and organizations to find help combating predatory loan practices by financial services institutions. Professionals in such places have seen the widespread devastation student debt can wreak upon student-borrowers when their payments come due. To continue the investigation of how the crisis grew to its now-recognizable proportions, we will hear from a consumer rights attorney who was interviewed for this project.

The attorney, here named "Trudy" for reference purposes, remains anonymous, given her position. Trudy was initially asked about what kinds of practices constituted predatory practices (including that loans are nondischargeable in bankruptcy). There are many variations on those types of predatory practices, often seen at for-profit colleges and universities, that take unfair advantage of people trying to "do the right thing."

> *Interviewer:* How would you describe some of those practices that you most think of as predatory?
>
> *Trudy:* Predatory practices are not limited to schools' behavior. It sort of goes through the life of a loan. So first there's the school. In a lot of cases, we've seen, certainly, bad and abusive practices by servicers predefault. Depending on how you define predatory, I wouldn't always consider what the servicers are doing as predatory, but it certainly has a lot of harm and can be quite abusive. The collectors, that's postdefault, there's predatory behavior at that level. There's these sort of for-profit debt relief companies that a lot of borrowers, especially more recently, have been targeted by. And there's a lot of predatory behavior in that sector. And then I think you get to this a little bit, but, some of the products themselves, getting back to the loans themselves, are also what I would consider to be predatory more in the private sector. But that's another area where there were predatory practices by the lenders themselves.
>
> Some of the indicators of predatory loans are if you saw very high interest rates, very lax or nonexistent underwriting, other high fees, often very high origination fees, sometimes balloon payments. Those sorts of things we actually would see in the private loan area. And there is very little relief for borrowers who got into trouble on the loans.
>
> *Interviewer:* Could you describe some of the most common abuses or tactics that borrowers experience from lenders and collectors?
>
> *Trudy:* In the case of the institutional loans, those are really related to underwriting. But pretty clearly the loans were originated with full knowledge that a high percentage of borrowers were not going to be able to repay them. Those are all hallmarks of predatory loans. The federal loans are trickier in a way, because the terms themselves are generally not, by most definitions, what people would consider to be predatory. The interest rates are a little high, but not to the range where we were seeing in the private sector, where there are over 20 percent interest rates, or even over 30 percent interest rates. It's generally not the terms on the federal loans that could be predatory.
>
> I think what makes, arguably, the federal loan program predatory as well, is the targeting of particular populations, particularly in certain higher education sectors. There's very little gatekeeping by the federal

government in terms of which schools they allow to access the federal aid. And then those schools themselves are targeting often protected classes, like racial minorities, or low-income borrowers. I think what makes the predatory nature is that on the back ends, when those borrowers default or when they get into trouble on those loans, the collection tactics are so extreme that there's such a high percentage of borrowers that really are never able to repay. And basically, they are never even able to get out of the consequences of having those loans.

Interviewer: What else were some lenders doing in the run-up to the financial crisis?

Trudy: They were [also] doing direct-to-consumer marketing. And it was unfortunately similar to what was happening in the mortgage market with securitization kind of fueling all of this. There was very little accountability in lots of profit and lots of really, really irresponsible lending during that time period.

We've clearly seen abuses by the private collection agencies over the years in both private and federal loans. On the federal loan side, postdefault, borrowers have specific rights that they are entitled to under the Higher Education Act. That's not true in the private loan side. The collectors have given inaccurate information, have tended to push the programs that were most lucrative for them, the collectors, as opposed to comprehensively counseling borrowers on the different programs and what might be best for them. There's really been a whole range of problems in the debt collection area.

In the servicing area, which is predefault, I would say it has not been as aggressively abusive as it has been on the collection side. But the results are similar in that the servicers are often incompetent, poorly trained, give inaccurate information, or not administering or processing accounts accurately or efficiently. That's been, actually, that's a real problem for borrowers because the servicers doing their jobs are what can really prevent them from going into default and facing all the extreme consequences of that.

Interviewer: Would you say that predefault or postdefault, a borrower might describe their experience with a collector as harassment, or is that just kind of the universal experience of people who have received collection calls?

Trudy: I think that a lot of what you hear about in the collection is similar to what you hear about in other areas, sort of, unfortunately, kind of traditional or typical collector harassment. There is a really unique aspect of the student loan experience in that, unlike some other areas, like say credit cards, something like that. A federal student loan borrower has very specific rights postdefault to get out of default, to potentially get a discharge of their loan. And so the harassing behavior might be similar, but I'd say the consequences and the impact could be greater because they're harassing or because they're not giving accurate information, the borrower's not able to access these rights.

Interviewer: If there is a best policy solution you feel could exist to protect student loan borrowers, particularly, what would that look like?

Trudy: We'd like to see less reliance on loans, is kind of one of the big picture issues, because a lot of the other strategies are assuming that loans are here to stay, which they probably are. There are ways to make that experience better, but I think that we should not give up on the idea that, particularly for the lowest income people and the financially neediest people, that we should have more support for public education. We should have more targeted grants programs and that sort of thing, so people don't necessarily have to rely so much on loans in the first place.

There's a couple of reforms that I think are really important: [right now] there's no time limit on student loan collection; that they can take your earnings and tax credit; they can take portions of Social Security. None of these extreme collection powers have been around forever. They've all been created by Congress and by administrations in the last twenty, twenty-five years. They put you in a situation where if you don't succeed the first time around when you go to school (and often that's the most vulnerable students who are in that situation, but not always), that it's almost impossible to sort of dig out from under the debt, even if it's a small amount of debt, and get a fresh start. I suggest really big reforms in that area, where you restore statute of limitations; you eliminate Social Security offsets; you eliminate tax offsets. If you let people get another chance, that they may actually be able to do better in the future and pay back their loans.

I think that we have to change the current structure of who's doing the oversight. The Department of Education is the gatekeeper for the schools; they're also one of the biggest lenders in the country right now. They also supposedly are supposed to enforce borrower rights. There's too much internal conflict within that. That structure also needs to be changed to better protect borrowers.

Interviewer: About the second chances, it sounds like you're talking about bankruptcy.

Trudy: Well, bankruptcy is included in that. Not exclusively, but yes, absolutely, restoring bankruptcy rights is part of that. There's eliminating some of the most draconian collection powers themselves. And then there's also expanding the safety net so that borrowers can get relief. So, it's really both. And bankruptcy fits, I think, better into the idea of expanding or restoring the safety net.

There are many protections within the law to which borrowers are already entitled, but there are many places where borrowers are still vulnerable. The fact that bankruptcy protections do not seem to be the priority the lawyer as lawgiver would offer, but rather more straightforward borrower protections for all that would not be contingent on bankruptcy, is very much in the spirit of a collective decision that must be reached in terms of how society must deal with borrowers going forward. A piecemeal approach risks inaction, while a radical approach would likely not be sufficient. Trudy echoes other interviewers that while not everyone is "doing everything right," many think they are. Since this narrative comes from U.S. society, perhaps they should not be penalized for such a mindset. There is room for critique of the federal government's role in the process, and "less reliance on loans" would certainly be a place to start in such a spirit.

Annual federal subsidies to for-profit education conglomerates generate over one-third of student debt.[23] It is important to understanding the causes of the rapid growth in student debt from this sector, and the protection the federal government has not offered these students who Hicks sees have been exploited for their ability to borrow loans guaranteed by the federal government. One item not elsewhere covered as prominently as a feature of the student debt crisis is that as much as 10 percent of student debt at for-profit universities is held by military service members and veterans, and their families, because of these institutions' exploitation of a rule that does not count such loans as "federal." They are a revenue stream for for-profit institutions, and a debt burden for veterans. Federal policy *has* influenced the debt crisis. While Trudy has experienced the perspective of predatory lending from the perspective of student-borrowers she has worked with and given expert legal advice, another helpful perspective is that of an industry critic. A leading expert on the structural incentives and practices of for-profit educational institutions, David Halperin was sought out for this interview in order to provide background on how these institutions are connected directly with the student loan crisis. Halperin is a journalist and attorney who is a nationally recognized expert on and critic of for-profit educational institutions. He previously held a position as a fellow at the New America Foundation, he was a White House speechwriter, and he has written numerous books and articles on the growth of this industry. He reports from RepublicReport.com and has published in the *New York Times*, the *Washington Post*, and the *Nation*, among other publications.

> *Interviewer:* If you could just try to explain the business model of for-profit institutions to a lay audience, just the basic fundamentals of what they all try to do, and what some of their practices are in terms of sales, and where they get most of their income and profits.

Halperin: They're not all the same. There are good teachers and good programs within it. I'm basically talking about, if I get to generalize, I
would be talking about some of the largest companies that are like University of Phoenix, the Career Education, EDMC. Seven out of the 10
biggest for-profit [colleges and universities] are under investigation by
multiple state and federal law enforcement agencies.

    Their business model is similar to Corinthian College, which was
shut down.[24] That is, you use deceptive, misleading, sometimes coercive sales tactics. You target the most vulnerable people who are the
least sophisticated about college, which would be single parents, returning veterans, first in their family to go to college, immigrants. You are
focused almost entirely on signing them up and getting their federal aid
checks rather than making sure that they graduate or learn anything.
You get around 90 percent or even more of your revenue from federal
financial aid, but you're focused on the fact that you are required to get
at least 10 percent of your revenues from outside the Department of
Education by law, so you have to get the veterans' money.[25]

    You have to think of other tricky ways like merge with a campus in
Canada where the students are not eligible for federal aid in order to
meet your quota under that 90/10 requirement. You cut spending on
education, or you never had high spending on education. Most of your
spending is on marketing, and profit, and executive compensation. You
deal with the fact that you have high default rates, which also can lose
you eligibility, by hiring companies to convince students to not put
their loans in default, but put them into what we call forbearance,
which is a meaningless concept where the interest continues to accrue,
but you are able to claim that the students haven't defaulted on their
loans. Then you use a mandatory arbitration clause in your enrollment
agreements, which prevent students from suing you. They have to take
any dispute to arbitration. Then you hire expensive lobbyists in Washington to try to steer legislation or regulations in a way that prevents
accountability. You hire good lawyers to deal with any disputes you
might have from whistleblowers, or students, or the Department of
Education, expensive lawyers to try to prevent any court cases from
going against you. That's the basic business model.

Interviewer: Just from hearing this description, it would seem like they are
taking advantage of certain loopholes that are intended for nonprofit
traditional universities. Can you talk maybe about the evolution of how
we got here in terms of their ability to have carte blanche to just take
money however they can and not have to spend it on education?

Halperin: There is a book that came out this year by A. J. Angulo, *Diploma
Mills*.[26] It's from Johns Hopkins University Press. It does get into the
history of this. This isn't the first time that people who are mostly
focused on making money and less focused on students have gotten

into higher education. There's some cyclical nature in this, going up and down. The most recent iteration started to rev up in the 1990s. The Clinton administration got concerned and imposed limits on colleges paying their recruiters basically a sales commission to sign up students because that seemed like that was putting too much emphasis on signing up and not enough on whether the student would actually benefit from the program.

Under President Bush, though, that was rescinded pretty quickly. Also under President Bush in 2005, there had previously been a limit on federal aid for schools that were almost entirely online, and Congress passed an amendment, which got rid of that. That allowed online education to basically be treated the same way as in person. Those were a couple of the key limits that were preventing people from making even more money. When those things got swept away, the gold rush continued. Some companies became publicly traded, like EDMC has gone private/public a number of times back and forth, but Goldman Sachs in one of the transactions became a key investor. Wells Fargo became the biggest institutional owner of Corinthian Colleges.

Some of these other companies went public or were controlled by private equity firms and just became larger, like University of Phoenix. You can read a book by John Murphy, one of the former founders.[27] Their original focus was on working adults, people with jobs getting another degree to help them advance in their workplace. They basically decided to tap into the same market of low-income people that the other schools were. [For-profit colleges and universities] just took off after this money. For-profit by 2010 or so reached its peak, something like $32 billion in federal aid, 25 percent of the federal aid total with about 12 percent of the students and 50 percent of the loan defaults. That's how it really took off.

Interviewer: One of the questions that always comes up when I have discussions with people is about veterans and the 90/10 rule. [*Editor's note: For-profit institutions are only legally allowed to receive 90 percent of their tuition revenue from loans generated by the U.S. Department of Education, called "federal loans." Fully 10 percent (or more) of their revenue may come from student aid or loans granted to veterans under the new GI Bill, processed through either the U.S. Department of Veterans Affairs (VA) or the U.S. Department of Defense (DoD).*] It seems shocking that some of these veterans' loans can be exploited in this way to be a main source of their income when it only accounts for, all they can get is 10 percent of their total revenue can come from that. Can you tell me a little bit more about how veterans and military students are targeted in this way?

Halperin: The point is the fact that the VA and the DoD money is not counted as federal is just kind of ridiculous, generally, because obviously it's federal money. If the purpose of the rule is to show that it wouldn't make sense to fund a school that nobody, no student or employer would pay their own money for, then not counting the money that way undermines the purpose of the rule. In addition, it distorts the incentives and make the schools that much more desperate to recruit service members and veterans, and that hurts the service members and veterans because the most desperate schools are the worst schools.

They do things like this: the University of Phoenix last year was exposed for violating rules and recruiting on military bases, holding events as a way to get around the rule of their excessive presence on the bases, creating military challenge coins without permission. It had the University of Phoenix logo on one side and the logo of the services on the other. University of Phoenix was suspended by the DoD from recruiting service members until they lobbied and got that reversed.

There are many websites, like military.com. GIBill.com was a site that sounded like it was an official website of the government, but actually it was just run by one of the big lead generation firms, QuinStreet, to steer students to for-profit colleges. That got shut down after a bunch of state attorneys general decided to intervene. QuinStreet agreed not to do that any more, but they still work on sites like military.com and army.com, and other sites that either QuinStreet or other lead generation companies use that look like they're unbiased information and services for people in the military, and in fact they are paid lead generators for for-profit colleges like Kaplan, ITT Tech, and others. With DeVry, one of their recruiters talked about [how] they had a whole unit devoted to recruiting military involved in deceptive pitches and claiming that they worked for DoD rather than working for DeVry. It's that kind of thing, of trying to convince members that this is the official, sanctioned, approved school, and in fact it's just another way to lure service members and vets into these predatory schools.

Interviewer: It sounds like a lot of what they do is misleading. It sounds like it's all very predatory. Except for these instances where they are kind of caught red-handed, like you were mentioning, it sounds like a lot of what they do is legal.

Halperin: Well, it's arguable. The Federal Trade Commission had a whole workshop last year, which I spoke at, on lead generation [*Editor's note: for sales leads, or for college and university admissions*]. They are trying to grapple with what's legal. They came down on a lead generator the other day because you're not supposed to do something that's misleading, basically convincing people that you're one thing, and actually you're another. They are still feeling out what's legal and what's illegal. I do think that something like, for example, there's a whole bunch of websites that claim that they are job websites, but in fact all it really is a way to get people who are desperate for jobs to enter their information, and then they sell them to for-profit colleges. It's a bait-and-switch. It should be considered, to me, a deceptive business practice. It should not be legal.

Interviewer: In your professional opinion, is the idea of having for-profit colleges and universities functioning alongside nonprofits and public institutions always going to be a terribly deceptive and predatory industry, or can you have educational institutions that are run on a for-profit basis that are aboveboard and serve the students in a positive way?

Halperin: In theory it makes sense to have for-profit education, especially in career education as a way to spur innovation, create more flexibility, bring new ideas into the idea of how you train people for careers, which is a really important thing that we don't invest enough money in. In practice what has happened is the schools get money, they get rich, and then they get lobbyists. They basically use the resources the taxpayers give them to protect themselves from accountability, protect themselves from lawsuits, protect themselves from performance measurements, and protect themselves from abusive behavior. Based on the behavior of this industry in the last twenty years, I think that they have forfeited the right to do what they do.

I'm not really advocating an end to for-profit education, but I think that if the latest round of accountability measures gets watered down or defeated . . . then I would say for sure we have to get rid of this and decide that the only model for education, the only way to protect students, is through nonprofit and state institutions. We have to invest in it. We've wasted all this money giving to "crooks," but we've also cut back so much on community colleges and vocational education in high schools. We ought to be for something in addition to being against something.

Interviewer: Let me ask you about graduation rates and matriculation rates at for-profit institutions. I think in one of your recent articles you mentioned something like 4 percent for University of Phoenix online?

Halperin: Their [public relations] person complained to me that that is a calculation the Department of Education makes that only measures first-time, full-time students. When you look at other measures of non-first-time, full-time students, they do better. I thought about it, and I've mentioned that before that they've said that, but the truth is they admit full-time, first-time students. If they are going to admit that type of student, they ought to be responsible for what the graduation rate is for the students.

Interviewer: I can't remember the exact number, but you were talking about the cost per student for their educational and instructional costs.

Halperin: Eight hundred ninety-two dollars a year spending on students, according to Senator Harkin's report. I believe that's the number.

Interviewer: Then $2,400 per student on marketing? Then another $2,400 or something similar in profit?

Halperin: Yes.

Interviewer: That's amazing.

Halperin: What an amazing business. Now they're in trouble because they've been exposed as predatory.

Interviewer: You had another figure near the 4 percent. I think it was something like 16 percent.

Halperin: Sixteen percent for University of Phoenix overall, for physical campuses, plus online.

Interviewer: That's half of what community colleges graduate in two years anyway.

Halperin: Also, community colleges are much more affordable for students.

Interviewer: Absolutely. It would seem that for-profit colleges could say something similar to what community colleges do, which is, "Not all of our students are trying to graduate. They're trying to take a course for something and fill some gap in their education."

Halperin: They don't usually say that. I don't know why, but they tend to say that students are trying to get degrees. They just usually blame the students for overborrowing and blame the students for dropping out. They'll make any argument they can possibly come up with. They're always saying, "You hate people of color because you're trying to cut off their educational access." We say, "Well, we're trying to cut off their educational access to a program that's going to make them worse off than when they started." I have not heard that argument much from the for-profit colleges, but call them up and see if they're willing to make it. They'll make every other argument.

Interviewer: Is there anything that you would like to add in terms of your overarching views about for-profits?

Halperin: We could have done a lot more and should do a lot more to make sure that we are investing. In the short term we need to find places for these students. What we're doing now is we are propping up these bad institutions. Since we've been on this call, scores more people have heard deceptive pitches and enrolled in programs that will be bad for them. Those schools should be shut down, in my opinion.

    The problem is we are concerned that they are "too big to fail" and we're going to leave all these students locked out. We don't know where they're going to go. Are they just going to enroll in another bad predatory school because the good schools aren't going to accept their credits? We just need to accept that a bunch of students are going to have to start over again, and there's going to be a cost to the taxpayer, et cetera, because it's foolish to keep these institutions going. We're only making the problem worse. We're only going to need a bigger bailout like the one we required for Corinthian [*Editor's note: students who were defrauded by the for-profit Corinthian Colleges, which then went out of business, directly and successfully lobbied the Department of Education to erase their federal loan debt.*]. It's time to get serious, shut down the bad schools, impose serious rules that will hold the remaining schools to higher standards, and then take some of the money that we are going to save and invest it in better career education in more honest institutions.

Halperin's narrative and historical context surrounding for-profit colleges and universities and the "crooks" that run them is an extremely important piece of the student loan puzzle. Roughly one-third of student loans in the last decade have been taken out in order to pay tuition at institutions that only serve a much smaller fraction of the student population. His analysis is penetrating enough that he can afford to make characterizations of the behavior of these institutions that is difficult to challenge. The only difference between the analysis Halperin gives and that of the earlier consumer rights attorney is that the culprits, for Halperin, are the for-profit corporations that directly run these for-profit universities, not the lenders themselves.

It does demonstrate how powerful a business model can be that exploits the social compulsion for higher education while spending by a factor of six to one more money on advertising and profit-taking than on instruction. That business-oriented model filibusters any hope public education has of making its own compelling case in the popular media–focused mind of the potential student. Halperin's consistent outrage is directed at the owners of these institutions, which are often noneducationally focused corporations, even banking conglomerates. It is precisely for those people that he advocates, those who decided to entrust their futures to these institutions, those who are the most vulnerable and stand to be the most alienated from their own personal American Dream as a result of their inability to complete a degree at these institutions when they begin one, which is the overwhelming majority.

Student loan programs, then, are certainly subject to the shifting sands and fortunes of political alliances and coalitions. As mentioned elsewhere, there has been relatively little accomplished in the area of student debt thus far during the Trump presidency, despite several proposals being floated during the 2016 campaign and in the first two years of the new administration. Jason Rosenstock is a government affairs and financial services attorney who has represented student lenders. The interviewer is acquainted with Rosenstock personally, and asked him a question in 2015 about the chances of a proposed lifetime limit on debt forgiveness favored by the Obama administration happening. Both income-based-repayment and public service loan forgiveness are very popular when people find out about them, so such possible legislation was significant. It was never signed into law, but Rosenstock is certainly the person to ask about the viability of financial legislation. This interview also took place during the Obama administration. The federal government has made some attempts to regulate predatory practices. The Consumer Financial Protection Bureau (CFPB) is the federal agency created from legislation drafted by Elizabeth Warren in the early days of the Obama administration in the wake of the financial crisis. The CFPB has been perhaps the chief government watchdog for the consumer loan industry, making it a key player in the ongoing politics of student loans. Rosenstock, a partner at Thorn Run Partners, is the author of a weekly client newsletter and is an "aspiring pundit" whose commentary has appeared in many Washington-area news outlets.

Rosenstock provides valuable insights from the perspective of someone inside Capitol Hill and the Washington Beltway. At the policy level in Washington, we see the perceptions policymakers carry of student-borrowers, of higher education, and the relationship that both have to the financial crisis and the federal government's protections now on offer to consumers as a result. Policymakers also perceive constraints that prevent them from crafting more far-reaching solutions to the student debt crisis, along with the sympathetic view of student-borrowers as well as educational institutions themselves.

> *Interviewer:* I get the sense [the CFPB is] viewed negatively by most of the financial services industry. Is that accurate or is there more of a balanced kind of view on the part of most people working?
>
> *Rosenstock:* I think, like anything, there's a nuanced view. I think a lot of people tend to find the bureau to be a bit of a challenge to work with. The general sense is, the bureau comes out with their proposal, or with their thing and then you have this very good intellectual debate about where [it] should be, and they ultimately don't really listen to industry in any way, shape, or form. I think that's the industry's perspective, it's that the bureau has a deaf ear. And then it's just willing to add costs and build intellectually from people who think that in general that corporations are trying to rip people off. And I don't know that that's a fair assessment of the world, but that's my perspective.
>
> It's sort of interesting on the student loan front. With this transition, a lot of private issuers are getting out of the market, at least for primary loans. The bunch of companies coming in on the refinance side, like SoFi and those other folks. I don't know if at some point I suspect the bureau is going to do something there.
>
> *Interviewer:* Could you give us a read on how Republicans and Democrats generally view the income-based repayment (IBR) and public service loan forgiveness (PSLF)? I get the sense they're very popular among everyone who knows about them.

Rosenstock: As you said, they're very popular. Democrats like them because they like to think that this is part of the helping hand by getting people the opportunity to go to college or educate themselves. If they take on a ton of debt, then [they] don't actually have to go into these careers that don't necessarily, for whatever reason, allow one to repay that debt. Democrats will like that. I think Republicans find it troublesome that the federal government is subsidizing large swaths of the population. I was talking to a [reporter for the Associated Press] and he's been doing a bunch of work on student loan debt. He was saying the people who get most crushed by student loan debt, if I remember correctly, are those who do like a year or two years of college, then drop out.

Interviewer: That certainly aligns with what I've found so far, absolutely.

Rosenstock: I do think there's this belief that Democrats have, broadly, that everyone should go to college, and I don't know that that's necessarily true. I think a lot of people aren't situated for it and sort of probably the timing of it, I think a lot of people would be better if they took some time off to go work before going. Particularly, [there is a] suburban middle-class [story] of, graduate high school, go to college, graduate in four years, then go get some sort of advanced degree. I don't think it's necessarily the best policy.

Rosenstock: When we graduated [the private nonprofit institution where the interviewer and Rosenstock both attended as undergraduates], my senior year was $32,000.

Interviewer: That might have included room and board fees, too.

Rosenstock: Room and board and all of that. So that was sixteen years, seventeen years ago. And it's doubled since then. It just doesn't make sense to me. But I think in large part it's fueled by the easy credit. There's a little bit of a bubble toward it. There's no need to keep costs in check. The public universities have an external cost check to some extent, in the sense the states are peeling back the subsidies, the state subsidies. Or their investments, depending on your perspective. I think the private universities are in this arms race . . . but it's fueled in large part by, I think, cheap credit.

When I went to law school I just took out the Stafford [Loans] and I think I had, combined subsidized and unsubsidized, it was like $30,000 a year or something like that. I came out with [approximately] $120,000.

If you think about the dorms they're building now, versus the classic version, I think it's coddling the students. I get that colleges think they have to compete for students, but as I tell people all the time, you're going to go to college somewhere and you're going to be fine, you're going to get a degree. There's better networks at Princeton, maybe, than there is at [a large state university], but they have their own networks, they have jobs and there are people who will help you. I think there's a study once that [showed that] Harvard charged more, even though they didn't need to, just because people would be angry that they weren't paying the most to go to the best. So, it's interesting, the psychology of it.

Interviewer: Is there agreement about where some of the costs are in higher education?

Rosenstock: We're probably in the scenario where Republicans and Democrats bicker, where people like to point fingers. I think Republicans would point to the unions and the cost of professors. Democrats would look at administration, like why are there three deans for campus life? There is no need for this. It's interesting when people point the blame. I think collectively the answer lies in the middle. There's probably a lot of professors who are paid a lot of money for whatever reason because that's what the market will bear, but this growth tends to be on the administration side. In general, I think our education system, like many systems in our country, is very screwed up.

Interviewer: How are the kind of student loans seen in the financial services industry? Are they looked upon in any certain way or are they just kind of another product that they have to sell and trade?

Rosenstock: I don't think there's an industrywide consensus. I think that there are elements of the industry that would very much like to get back into the business, and not have to compete against the federal government. There are others who have more of a philosophical concern about the government holding so much consumer debt, and the likelihood of the ability of it ever to be repaid in any meaningful way. As you pointed out, it's the elementary conclusion [of] the popularity of loan forgiveness. Free things are always popular; the personification of that was with Bernie Sanders, and you know, his popularity among student-age or just past student-age population on this concept of free college. You look at companies like Ernest or SoFi or Common Bond, who in this techy world where they see opportunity within the student loan industry, or subindustry if you will, to innovate and come up with new products that can help people and serve a market. At the end of the day what you really want is a broad functioning market with probably some government investment.

Smarter people than I will have to figure that out, but it's going to be an issue to deal with because for a large swath of the population this [is] potentially crushing student load debt. It would be less of an issue if the economy was at a point where people were getting paid more to cover those carrying costs, but they're not. For a lot of people, we'll have reverberating effects as that generation can't buy homes.

Rosenstock's insider perspective somewhat echoes the sentiments of many analysts, but the important difference is the light shed on the political gamesmanship of Washington, D.C. Student debt is viewed in terms of market behavior that can largely be remedied with market-based solutions, which have severe limitations in terms of social salience. If he can make a casual reference to the "easy credit" of student loans, then that begs the question asked by an earlier interviewee, which is: "Why was the credit so easy when it's so difficult to get a credit card?" Given the perception of loan forgiveness as a subsidy to low- and middle-income borrowers, it will take a major change in political winds to alter the perception and create an opportunity for a more trenchant solution that involves forgiveness to a wider population than currently exists. It would only be the latest change in policy after a long history of federal policies aimed at expanding opportunities in higher education.

Finally, to take the view of how these policies are administered, we hear from an administrator who has served at several types of institutions, most recently a historically black college or university (HBCU). While HBCUs continue to serve an important role to meet a specific need, they can also be examples for all institutions with the mission of serving historically marginalized groups, which could certainly be said of at least a plurality of higher education institutions. Currently, 106 HBCUs exist in 22 states, the vast majority in the South.[28] HBCUs are a mix of private and public colleges and universities, and are a site of evolving priorities that all public institutions have experienced over the past generation. They have predominantly shifted from a model of public goods to private loans, and not because of the preferences of the institution. HBCUs and other public institutions have little choice about taking revenue from loans when states cut subsidies, and they create an educated, but indebted, graduating class that increasingly has been educated not in public service and liberal arts, but the disciplines promoted by their wealthier alumni and donors.[29]

This administrator will remain anonymous due to the penetrating nature of the insights the administrator has about HBCUs generally and the specific practices of the institution at which the administrator works, but will be referred to here as "Emily." As much as faculty organizations and unions value academic freedom, to the point where they encourage faculty to publicly criticize their own university employers, administrators are decidedly not encouraged to do so. Emily talks about the supportive culture of HBCUs, and their historical and current value to students and the public interest. What is most interesting are some of the financial practices surrounding tuition payments and funding, and how the shift away from federal funding toward private funding may have some relationship with the shift in popularity and viability of some HBCU programs. HBCUs clearly are not alone in this shift, but as institutions that were founded specifically to serve disadvantaged students (in somewhat of a similar vein as all public universities, though perhaps more so), the shift from past practices that celebrated culture and education to a culture that now prizes other departments and pursuits, it is perhaps especially a marked change.

Interviewer: Talk about, if you would, the population of HBCUs.

Emily: Forty years ago, they were the only school of choice for African American students. We're probably not that far enough from the student that would go to any one of the 106 HBCUs that are currently now in the United States. That number is dwindling, unfortunately. Some close due to accreditation issues. Others have merged, because they're struggling. Ninety percent of our students get Pell. You have a grant that was created for people who are at a very low threshold of family income, and some even in poverty. That's the grant that's getting cut. It almost makes no sense. Where do you want them to get this money? Approximately half of our students are coming from households with incomes less than $50,000. For a lot of them, we're typically their first or second choice. A large percentage of our budget comes from the state. That appropriation has been dwindling every single year. I think higher ed is just being attacked. I don't think it matters what side you're on, Republican or Democrat. I really think it's just higher education.

Interviewer: What's unique about the HBCU experience?

Emily: Our first-year retention rate is almost 80 percent, and that's because we pile it on heavy with the support services. One of the big things that students talk about is feeling really cared for, feeling like they're in a place where it's small enough and everyone knows who they are. There's accountability. There's a way they form relationships with the professors. We've had faculty take students into their homes who had nowhere to go for the whole summer. We're going to explore who you are, and what is your legacy, and the history of the legacy of exclusion in this country and what does that mean today. Over the last couple of months, you know that across the nation, a lot of students at a lot of predominantly white institutions, minority students have been rising up and protesting. I know our faculty have been able to take that and turn those into learning opportunities in their classrooms. You're going to come here, and you're going to feel a sense of belonging.

Interviewer: Let me just ask you about the fields of study at [your institution]. What would you say are the most popular majors now, the top three or four? Has it changed in the last twenty or thirty years?

Emily: Our most popular majors historically have been communications fields, like broadcasting or journalism. That always competes with criminal justice from year to year in terms of number 1 and number 2. Then, we have biology. You get into your political science and philosophy that have been dwindling down. Then, the sad story with education as well. HBCUs were actually established to train teachers to teach black children at a time when they couldn't go. That's really the foundation of HBCUs. Unfortunately, for us, over the years, education has just dwindled in terms of student interest. When you combine [economics, business, and management], that's one. You probably could slide that in as the number 4. Not too far behind that would be computer science.

Interviewer: What is the form that financial assistance usually takes?

Emily: First, we try to exhaust everything in terms of let's see everything we can give you before we have you go pick out a loan. Because, some of these students come from populations where this whole idea of taking out a loan is very daunting. They don't trust banks, or wouldn't go to one for a loan. We don't want them to show up and suddenly say to them: "Okay, just sign this promissory note. You just borrowed $25,000." We do a lot of institutional discounts where we call it different things. We have legacy scholarships, because we have a fair population coming whose parents also attended [the HBCU]. Unfortunately, because of all the things that have been reduced, it's almost inevitable that they will have to take out a loan and still do. I get the sense that both the students and their families, it's almost very abstract to them, the whole loan process. They sign [loan documents], and the next day, thousands of dollars are in their account. When everything has been paid for, and if they have $2,000 left, we turn them around and cut them a check. I've talked to freshman students who went on a shopping spree with their check. I'm not sure it's the best idea to turn around and cut any 19- or 18-year-old [a check like that].

Interviewer: If you could talk about that for a second, and about the loans themselves.

Emily: We always start with the federal stuff. That's where the lowest interest rates are. We try to help them to understand all the different types. We need to do a better job of educating the students on those kinds of loans. Some of these loans, they don't even have to demonstrate any kind of need. Now, here's the other thing that impacts some of our students in terms of the academic preparedness. When we have that one third that come in and they have to do remedial courses, that eats into their financial aid. They're coming from the [lowest-resourced school districts], and sometimes it's no fault of their own that they're coming in and they're reading at a fifth-grade level. As a last resort, you start getting into the private loans, which are just pure evil. In some cases, some of those loans, you have to be paying them back while you're in school, and they have higher interest rates.

When public universities become reliant on student tuition rather than public funding to stay afloat, the cost falls on the students. The transition from liberal arts and education to the study primarily of information technology and management and toward the business of profit is a statement of society's priorities. The fate of HBCUs is also a microcosm of what has the potential to occur when administrators are encouraging students to borrow from private institutions rather than providing them with adequate grants-in-aid, and that is to make universities dependent on students that primarily derive their tuition dollars from private borrowing. This continued practice would heavily promote the need to convert universities into business education institutions. This may teach students how to find a decent job to pay for their loans, but it also severely hampers the ability of new graduates to speak the critical language of the liberal arts and advocate for themselves and their families socially and politically.

Readers will recall how many of the borrowers in Chapter 2 reported the "sneaky" practice of pocketing their "excess checks" when borrowing money for tuition. Here, Emily expresses frustration at this policy, but is powerless to stop it. It is not clear where this policy originates, in federal or individual institutional practices, but it is clearly widespread and accounts for some unknown but likely significant percentage of overall borrowing. More research is clearly needed to see how much above-tuition money undergraduates and graduates were able to borrow in federal loans. The larger point serves to underscore how easily students are able to obtain large amounts of borrowed money with virtually no traditional lending practices being employed, such as collateral or a credit record, all the while doing so in good faith that they are "doing everything right."

Colleges and universities have gone to incredible lengths in order to keep their students enrolled, particularly the newer, for-profit institutions. They have shown a shift in focus from liberal arts to career-oriented education, the targeting of disadvantaged groups for loan disbursements that become tuition payments, and the shift in federal policy away from grants to loans. The experts agree that students are not well served by the current set of policies as they have evolved. This gives context to more students prioritizing "being well-off financially" over a "developing a meaningful philosophy of life." They have little choice in the matter once they graduate to pursue their own American Dream. The question then becomes how this picture can be changed, and how to make education meaningful again for a functioning society and a flourishing democracy.

CHAPTER FOUR

Responses to the Crisis:
The New Debtor Movements

There exists a new landscape of higher education encouraged by government policy, particularly in the realm of for-profit and online colleges. This environment has helped encourage multifaceted political actions by new debtors and their supporters. The overwhelming political narrative among the younger generation is framed by a sense of betrayal by institutions, from higher education to government itself, fueling alienation from all of these pillars of society. Political actions vary from alliances with traditionally fringe organizations to new membership in labor unions and endorsement of electoral candidates who champion the cause of student loan debtors. Stories of new debtors form the backdrop and in many cases the central motivation for activism, and provide unexpected gateways to a new political relationship with the federal government built on an adversarial, rather than a supportive, basis.

In response to record levels of consumer debt, particularly among the young, several avenues of political action have emerged in the younger generation. To begin the discussion, it seems appropriate to pay close attention to one of the originators of the federal student loan program in order to gauge the modern interpretation of the program's original intent. The late economist Milton Friedman provided a post to an online forum in 2007 that was originally intended to be an ongoing discussion by policymakers, higher education administrators, faculty, and students, but soon turned into a message board for the stories of borrowers. He added his own policy suggestions to the mix before the conversation was overtaken by standard message board behavior:

Undertaking higher education is a risky enterprise. The average returns are high but they are also variable. Moreover, some who start will not finish and will receive no return from their higher education. In short, investment in higher education is an equity investment stock in a corporation. It should in principle be treated as such, the equivalent of a stock issue not a bond issue. That would require that repayments of funds advanced for education should be linked to future earnings.[1]

Friedman clearly was of the opinion that student debt should never, ever be crippling, and indeed seemed to indicate that it ought to be forgiven if it became too much of a hindrance in a borrower's life. Elizabeth Warren, a liberal Democratic senator from Massachusetts who first came to national prominence as a Harvard Law School professor advocating for consumer rights in relation to the banking industry in the midst of the financial crisis, gives her thoughts on what the current role of the federal government is in the student debt crisis, and what it ought to be. It would seem she is much in agreement with the late Dr. Friedman:

My view is that the federal government should be working to protect borrowers. But instead, it is making things worse for these borrowers by embedding huge profits in student loan interest rates. A January GAO [Government Accountability Office] report estimates that the federal government will bring in—think about this—$66 billion in profits on just one slice of the federal loans, those made between 2007 and 2012.[2]

And finally, to make sure we know that this is a forward-facing conversation that takes the context of past policy into account, it is useful to hear from journalist Doug Henwood once again: "If education were free, as it should be, student debt wouldn't be a problem."[3] But student debt is a problem. It is an economic, a political, and even a social problem that drains the energy of citizenship from a generation and creates alienation in its place. Each of the above thinkers has diagnosed the problem and prescribed a solution to the student debt crisis. Each is speaking in the subjunctive tense of "if it were" and "should." Each recommends a course that would fundamentally address, if not necessarily put to rest, the issue of student debt. None of these recommendations are being discussed in the halls of Congress despite significant political support for each of these potential policies. Higher education and federal government action have always had a reciprocal, inextricably intertwined relationship. Unfortunately, none of the most popular and viable solutions to the crisis have risen to the level of the possible for today's policymakers: fully funding public higher education institutions to prevent future indebtedness, forgiving existing student debt on a massive scale, or at a minimum, amending the law to make federal loans dischargeable in bankruptcy, and ending federal subsidies and loans to for-profit institutions. All of these solutions would be aimed at recognizing the good faith that students had in working toward their higher education degrees, and preventing a future crisis of student loan–fueled debt.

There have been a multiplicity of responses, some of which are explored here. Responses have included the massive nationwide protests of Occupy Wall Street and later Occupy in hundreds of cities across the United States in the fall of 2011. These seemingly spontaneous protests were aimed at confronting the financial institutions that were demanding payment from consumer borrowers of various kinds, from education to housing debt, to auto loans and credit cards that had been marketed to college students. Notable outgrowths of the Occupy movement include an organization called Strike Debt, which published the "Debt Resistors' Operations Manual," offering borrowers strategies on how to legally evade their debt collections.[4] They are also the originators of the "Rolling Debt Jubilee," which buys back debt for pennies on the dollar, and then cancels the debt. Strike Debt has since evolved into the Debt Collective, and it has been instrumental in obtaining loan forgiveness for students who were defrauded by for-profit higher educational institutions owned by a company called Corinthian Colleges. The U.S. Department of Education has agreed to forgive the federal student loan debt of students who borrowed to attend these institutions, and the initial group was called by the Debt Collective the "Corinthian 15" and later the "Corinthian 100" as more former students joined their ranks in protest.

In the more traditional political realm, the liberal Democratic response has come mostly in the form of Higher Ed, Not Debt, a coalition of grassroots student and student loan groups (the U.S. Student Association and StudentDebtCrisis.org), labor unions (the National Education Association and the American Federation of Teachers [AFT], the Service Employees International Union), think tanks (the Institute for College Access & Success [TICAS], Demos, the Center for American Progress), mostly funded by large corporate foundations (the Gates Foundation and the Ford Foundation chief among them), and charities. The most vocal spokespersons for this coalition have mostly been AFT president Randi Weingarten and again, Elizabeth Warren.

The most explicit entry of student debt into the presidential campaign in 2016 was in the form of Bernie Sanders's call for a restoration of the historical status quo of tuition-free higher education at public colleges and universities, through his Senate bill, the College for All Act. The estimated cost would be under $130 billion annually, according to most recent estimates.[5] Sanders was defeated in the Democratic primaries, and nominee Hillary Clinton, rather than adopting this proposal, countered with a variation on the Obama White House proposal for free community college for students maintaining above a 2.5 grade point average (halfway between a cumulative overall grade of B and C). After the end of the primaries, Clinton altered her plan to make more of a resemblance to Sanders's, but it still stopped short of universal free tuition.[6] The other notable presidential candidate plans included that of the Green Party's Jill Stein, who called for an end and forgiveness of all student loan debt, public and private, to be paid by the Federal Reserve to private banks and the federal government, totaling $1.5 trillion. The most ideologically libertarian student debt plan was hatched by Marco Rubio, one of the earlier Republican contenders for president, who suggested matching private investors with students who wished to attend school.[7] Tom Petri of Wisconsin, a former congressman and vice chairman of the Education Committee in the House of Representatives, had long sponsored a bill (since 1983) calling for a portion of income to be devoted to repaying student loans, often called "income-share agreements" (ISAs) or "universal income-based repayment."[8]

Donald Trump, as a candidate, called for a new solution to the question of student debt. In the waning days of his campaign for president in 2016, he proposed a two-part solution: getting rid of public service loan forgiveness after ten years by replacing it with one income-based repayment program that forgave all federal undergraduate student loans after fifteen years of payments. For graduate loans, all loans could be forgiven in thirty years on an income-based repayment plan. As president, Trump has not officially proposed any aspects of this plan in legislation, executive action, or indeed, as part of a verbal commitment to action. Instead, Trump has appointed Betsy DeVos as secretary of education, who has taken no action on student loan forgiveness, even halting the existing forgiveness programs that existed under the Obama administration that forgave all federal loans borrowed to enroll at fraudulent institutions such as the Corinthian Colleges. There is media speculation about the end of public service loan forgiveness, but again, no action has been taken.[9]

There have been many popular responses to the student loan crisis. One is a cottage industry of attorneys who have devoted some or all of their practice to crusading for borrowers under self-styled names such as "The Student Loan Lawyer." One attorney hosts a radio podcast called "The Student Loan Show." Books that have been written speak to the mood of those with debt who are eager to understand or fight back against their debt: *The Student Loan Scam*, *The Student Loan Mess*, *Debt: The First 5,000 Years*, *The Student Loan Swindle*.[10]

The public concern about the crisis is high. Those most affected, millennials, see the government as a creditor, a lender, and ultimately as a collection agent. Their attitude toward government is hopeful, as many students have reported that communicating with the government about their student debt is a relatively pleasant, customer service–like experience. The government acts in cases of debt mediation, when administering programs such as income-based repayment and public service loan forgiveness, yet seems to act in the interest of the borrower.

Still, asking questions about the political economy of what benefit this state of affairs will have, and ultimately, who benefits from policies that both generate student debt and then attempt to collect on it, is a constructive first step in moving forward from this untenable problem. The generator of student debt is clearly, at its root, the political drive to invest progressively fewer government funds in higher education, making it more expensive to attend college in a wage-stagnant economy. The United States persists, however, in compelling more people to attend colleges and universities, continuing the economy's dependence on them. The political economy is forced to accept a new class of indebted citizens whose aim is not to pay off, but to live with endless debt that prevents them from attaining the American Dream paradigm of homeownership, and in many cases, retirement security.

We are even beginning to see the return of multigenerational households, people living with their parents throughout adulthood. More 18–34-year-old adults, 26 percent, live with family than before 2008.[11] Community colleges and public universities, where 80 percent of students are educated, are beginning to see declining enrollments.[12] Over 200 million Americans have debt (mortgage, auto, credit card, student loan); the median debt is roughly $65,000.[13] The mean student debt balance is about $30,000, and the median was $16,000, affecting over 45 million borrowers.[14] Between 20 and 30 percent of borrowers are on income-based repayment plans with the largest volume to private lenders: Sallie Mae, Nelnet, Great Lakes. Five million more people are in federal income-driven repayment plans. Five million more federal borrowers are delinquent in their loans.

Rather than encouraging the emboldening of an intellectual and professional class of citizens who have more bachelor's degrees than at any point in modern history through higher education policy, we have instead encouraged the shaming and juvenilization of an entire generation of borrowers. There is scant hope of ever repaying the majority of this debt, and in fact only a small minority of borrowers are even in a state of repayment to either the government or private lenders.[15] Student debt certainly seems to be here to stay, and as is noted several times in this book by interviewees, the economy is already making adjustments to their presence rather than the reverse. One important point the political system has yet to tackle is whether to protect the vast majority of borrowers from this obvious disadvantage to them or to ignore it. If financial institutions begin to calculate student debt as a regressive tax on the working class that should be forgiven or at least modified in order to free borrowers from heavy payment obligations, the economy might at least be able to sustain the large-scale borrowing necessary for the housing market to continue its ever-upward trajectory.

For nearly a century, the United States facilitated an American Dream whose centerpiece was home ownership as retirement savings and equity securitization through the mortgage interest deduction in the income tax code, and first-time homebuyer loans through the Federal Housing Administration.[16] It was debt that was central to the lives and even identity of the American middle class, so much so that homeownership dictated how people felt about education and even civil rights. Homeownership also, though encouraged, was somewhat difficult to enter, as one had to secure a large down payment and have a good credit history. Thirty-year and forty-year homeownership was supposed to translate into a relatively secure retirement plan. And if disaster struck, citizens could eventually recover their credit in a matter of several years.

Students with no credit history are able to take out the price of a house in the course of their education, and they are never able to discharge those loans, even if they default. This forms an obstacle to both short-term financial stability (difficulty in buying a car, securing an apartment, or even securing a job when employers are increasingly checking credit histories) and long-term financial stability (homeownership and retirement). Whereas for the baby boomers, debt comes with some risk and ultimately leads to equity, for millennials, debt was not assigned any risk and is now a barrier to building equity and security. It is a completely different paradigm from that of baby boomer homeownership, part of the postwar social compact that has perhaps already unraveled. Such homeownership and Horatio Alger social mobility is perhaps best communicated by many of the references that borrowers make in their stories to the "American Dream" or their "dreams" of making a living through their chosen profession.

In this chapter, the interviewees are people who have decided to fight against the new status quo. Labor organizers, students, activists, think tankers, attorneys, and legislators are all attempting to assist. In their own words, we read their approaches and some of the pitfalls they have experienced in attempting to implement a strategy that addresses, in whole or in part, the student loan crisis.

Miranda Merklein, who earlier told her story as an academic who had risen from poverty by way of accumulating student debt, now explains the course of action she has adopted to address her circumstances and those of other academics who have found themselves without full-time, traditional academic work, which are the majority. Her tactics and even overall strategy are becoming increasingly popular in higher education, and further reflect a new push for organizing what had been seen as "white-collar" workers by unions in the wider citizenry.

> *Merklein:* At one point, I read "Death of an Adjunct" about Margaret Mary Vojtko.[17] Whenever that was published, I read that, and I totally— everything just made sense to me all of a sudden: This is a scam, it's not just me, and we're not on a path, there is no path to upward mobility,

because I could look around me and see all of these people are in the same position. Here's this woman who's in her 70s, dies, and she didn't even have health insurance. At the time, I was so broke, I was back on food stamps, with a PhD, it was so depressing and I felt so horrible about myself, about everything. I was supposed to be this survivor, the person who did all the right things.

I started to have all of these thoughts that were very angry. I knew I wanted to do something. I knew that I was at war with the whole "Higher Ed Industrial Complex." This organizer showed up from AAUP [American Association of University Professors], he just showed up at the college and helped me make sense of my ideas, and start organizing. So I started organizing, and I thought I was the hero of this story, but then there was this huge backlash from the administration. I was doing this because I didn't want there to be any more Margaret Marys. Management doesn't want you to form a union, and they will do just about anything to stop you. I was getting attacked constantly while trying to teach these seven classes. My friend was fired for speaking out. I started getting invited to things, getting asked to speak at things, so I thought, "Okay, I'll be a voice for this movement."

For faculty, organizing and advocating can be especially challenging. Lack of tenure makes faculty vulnerable in such situations. Many professors, especially contingent faculty (part-time and full-time faculty without tenure protections) are overloaded with courses to meet both the demands of enrollment and to secure their own finances. Like Merklein, many academics have their own high loan balances. Merklein decided to leave higher education for advocacy work.

Merklein: I just knew that no matter what, I just couldn't do it anymore. I had all of these loans, I was in forbearance. I started applying to all of these organizer positions. I make $46,000 for this job [as an organizer for a major labor union], but $20,000 of that goes to taxes, and I live in Seattle, a very expensive city. I don't think I'll ever be able to repay my debt. I find solidarity in the fact that many people are in the same boat.

I tried to start paying [the student loans] and being a respectable citizen. Even if I got promoted and made $100,000 a year, I couldn't buy a house. I've got a high-rate loan on a used Ford Focus. I guess the economy is going to have to adjust to all of these indebted [former] students. I really value my mind, and everything I learned. I don't think the problem is with my education; the problem is with this racket we have.

Miranda Merklein, and millions of others who experienced academia as students, saw it as a desirable lifestyle and pursued it. This class would include not only higher education, but K–12 teachers, as well. They are an extremely educated, extremely indebted class of people, and there are not enough jobs to go around due to the lack of investment in education in the United States. Increasingly, business cards are being passed around at higher education conferences that label someone as a PhD but their job title is not "Assistant Professor" but rather "Organizer" for major labor unions. The majority of college and university professors now are part-time or adjunct, and they have many fewer protections than their tenured and tenure-track colleagues and are generally paid less than half the total rate for the same teaching load at the same institution. Certainly a plurality and likely a majority of those faculty have student debt, and so the college experience for new students will likely see institutions steering students away from viewing professors as examples, seeing teaching more as another support position on which they should not model their careers. That will be rather difficult, however, if students have regular contact with professors, in person or online, and they ever realize that student debt is central to the stories of people on both sides of the lectern.

One such student who opted not to enter academia after graduation was Jake Virden, whose interview regarding his own debt history was outlined in Chapter 2. Virden became a community organizer around student debt, finding that there were others receptive to this type of organizing message in his community. He describes how his involvement with the issue began as an outgrowth of his work as a local poet and musical artist in Minnesota. The interview took place in early 2016 during the primary season of the 2016 presidential campaign.

> *Virden:* It started just by speaking on it. I started speaking to other people who were coming to the same realization, facing the same reality: how are we ever going to pay this back, [against] insurmountable odds? A few of us were connected and wanted to do some organizing at this public school with high school students; a few of us were asking questions, critical questions about college and the academy, and race at the high school level. We did events and workshops; we did one called College Day where we were asking questions of high school seniors about how they felt about their options for school, and how to provide a safer space for people to really think about, well, "What is my best option?" "Is college a must?" "Must I go to college if it means I have to take on all this debt?" "And if I have to take on debt, what's the best time, what's the better time to do that?" just to have more informed decisions. We also did this thing called a "Debtors' Lounge," a happy hour. People would come out, have some drinks or some food. We had a deejay playing, we had just some readings for people to take.
>
> *Interviewer:* Have you been part of any larger statewide or nationwide organizing efforts around student debt?

Virden: I went with a group of folks to the Student Power Convergence that happened in Columbus, Ohio, in 2012. It was after Occupy, after that momentum had come to the surface. There was a group of people who called for a student movement gathering in Columbus. I got there, and it seemed discouraging. There were a lot of groups there. I think a lot of East Coast college students who were there and were the organizers. I didn't see how it translated to organizing folks at home who had debt, I didn't see a clear level of urgency, I didn't feel grounded, I didn't see how this idea of staging a student debt strike or organizing a movement didn't feel as connected with me as someone who was living through it, I didn't see how it was connected to folks at home. I just realized I had to change course and drop it for a while.

Interviewer: Where has it left your own thinking about student debt as an issue, either in organizing or for yourself?

Virden: I stopped doing public student loan debt work. I just immersed myself in racial justice work I was doing, other local organizing efforts. I still will speak about student debt; I just haven't seen anybody in organizations just working with people with debt like that. I went to that conference, I thought, [forget it], they were talking about some revolution or [something], I just need to get a plan.

I found a lawyer that does class action lawsuits, and he gave me some counsel. He said that one strategy was to push them to the point where they sue you, go all the way to default where they try to take action to collect on the entirety of the loan, and then if you get legal representation, usually then if you meet them in court, you can settle for a better term. He said, "Why don't you just settle, we could just settle right now for a lower principal?" But I'm saying right now, what are the pressures on them politically that they would be willing to offer that?

Interviewer: So, you're now at the point where you're a professional organizer, and you're having trouble seeing a constructive way forward on debt activism.

Virden: I also just believe in militant resistance, like a credit expungement kind of movement. A lot of people think: What are they really going to do? I think that kind of direct action opens the door to more progressive policy proposals. I try not to pay it, but then they call my dad eight times a day, and I can't let that happen. It was just [that] the infrastructure was not there at the policy level or the organizing level to support people that were on strike. I'm sure student debt would really resonate with people, but I haven't been able to figure that out.

Interviewer: So how do the organizing support people support an infrastructure in that instance? Let's say that there is a massive debt strike, and people stop making payments. How does the infrastructure work when the banks and the government start coming after them?

Virden: I've seen a few models. At Occupy Minneapolis, if somebody came to your house to kick you out, a text went out for people to hold the space, not violently, but to hold the space. It's not the same as legal support. I've thought about credit unions, local financial institutions. When the policy comes down that you're supposed to garnish my wages, maybe nonprofits could be organized into a noncompliance pact that says no, you can't garnish my wages.

There is as much ambiguity about how to address the issue of student debt as there is unanimity surrounding the idea that a specific and large-scale public policy is absolutely necessary to address it. There are grassroots solutions to the crisis. One is Virden's story of connecting borrowers to share stories. He was involved in the "Whose University?" campaign questioning the beneficiaries of the current university governance structure. There was the Student Power Convergence in Columbus, Ohio, that called for a student debt strike. Strike Debt, an organization encountered (and sometimes supported) by several of the activists interviewed for this book, advocates for debt refusal.

Activists, including Virden, have also found some solutions. Virden's take was simply that the Jubilee seemed impractical for the vast majority of borrowers. A collective, activist response seems to be missing in the movement. Nonviolent political action in the form of debt resistance comports with his philosophy about militant resistance spurring progressive policymaking, which is the ultimate goal. Again, from his alienation, as with Miranda Merklein, an avenue of citizen empowerment is discovered, because Jake Virden found he "did the right thing" and advanced his education to the point of becoming a writer and organizer who helps others in his own community lead political resistance to policies that negatively impact them.

In previous chapters, Alexis Goldstein, the journalist, activist, and financial services analyst who previously worked on Wall Street, discussed the relationship of the subprime mortgage crisis to the student debt crisis. Here, she discusses how she became involved and began to address the issue directly. She became involved with Occupy Wall Street and has since gone to work in the nonprofit sector.

Interviewer: Going back to Occupy, would you say that student loans were one of the top two or three reasons for that huge mobilization?

Goldstein: I don't know if I would, and if I did, I would definitely put it at position three. The Debt Collective evolved out of Strike Debt; Strike Debt evolved out of this group at Occupy called Occupy Student Debt. All of their organizing, obviously, revolved around student debt.

The thing about Occupy was, it's a hundred-tentacled monster, where it was whatever affinity group you were in. If you're asking a question about the whole thing and everybody who was there, I don't know if that was the main driver. But there was absolutely a separate affinity group, and some of the people that went on to Strike Debt and then went on to Debt Collective were a part of it.

That was obviously the central focus, and they did a lot of really interesting things: hold student debt assemblies in Washington Square Park, and encourage people to say how much debt that they were in, and confront the shame that people sometimes feel about it, and interrogate that shame, and say, "Well, why is it that we feel shame about this? Why does society want us to feel we've done something wrong? Businesses that have lots of amount of debt, people don't go around shaming them. Why is it different?" There was a lot of really amazing organizing happening simultaneous with Occupy, within Occupy, that was 100 percent about the student debt crisis.

Interviewer: It seems you got involved just from your own familiarity with Wall Street and the general malfeasance you saw going on. You've been pretty vocal about student debt since then. Could you maybe talk about the Debt Collective a little, and why you've decided to work with them as part of your activism?

Goldstein: I'm a helper when I can be, but Laura Hanna and Ann Larson are the driving force behind it and the founders of it, and deserve all of the credit. I just think that there's something particularly insulting and offensive about the way that these for-profit schools took advantage of people who were, with absolute sincerity, trying to better themselves and better their lives. These were people who very deliberately made the choice to go to school, believing everything that they had been told, and they were vocational schools. They were conned out of that and weren't able to get any kind of a job better than either the job they were able to get beforehand, or sometimes worse, because the names [of for-profit colleges and universities with low-quality reputations were] a stain on a resume to employers. Another member of the Debt Collective teamed up with an amazing lawyer who basically knew about this regulation that had been on the books for a really long time, called defense to repayment, that essentially says that if your school violates state law, you are entitled to contest your debt and apply to have your debt cancelled. You can say, "I don't have to pay these because my school broke the law, and therefore I should not be required to repay this debt because this debt is essentially illegitimate."

This beauty school had closed that targeted mainly non-English-speaking women. Together with these two volunteer programmers, they built a web app that allowed people, whatever state they were in, whatever Corinthian school they went to, to walk through this process, fill in some drop-down menus, write in their narrative, and it would pop out this defense to repayment application that included some pretty serious legal language that someone who's not a lawyer would never be able to do on their own.

Interviewer: This is one of the parallels you see between the aftermath of the 2008 crisis and the student debt crisis?

Goldstein: The [federal government] didn't help homeowners as much as they promised they would. They created all these programs that were supposed to help homeowners get loan modifications, and it just didn't work. Eventually, they just threw up their hands and essentially said, "Okay, instead of going through all these applications, we're just going to send out checks. We're going to figure out what bucket you fit in. If you were a veteran who was illegally foreclosed on, you get the biggest payout," because that's actually a crime that people can go to jail for. If it was a more minor mistake, you might have gotten a check for three hundred bucks or five hundred bucks. You don't get your house back; you get a check for $300. That's the kind of thing that happened in the wake of the financial crisis. This seemed like a more open-and-shut piece of the law that was already on the books, that didn't require action from Congress, that could potentially be used to actually get some people relief. Obviously, it's not going to give them their time back. It's not going to get them a job, but at least maybe they can move on with their life and get rid of this debt. All of that I just found incredibly motivating, and something that I wanted to try and help with as much as I could.

Student debt advocacy is part of a larger struggle against consumer debt. It is also a struggle against the political forces shifting social costs and risks from public and even corporate responsibility to the individual. There, the brunt is experienced disproportionately by consumers who cannot afford such risks, whether it be higher education or homeownership. Goldstein proves there has been work focused on practical solutions to the immediate problem of people who have suffered the consequences of taking those risks themselves under promises of a long-term payoff, and seeing their hopes dashed and their lives ruined as a result, crushing their access to the American Dream of homeownership. Our society has an ethical obligation to oppose the violence committed against ordinary people in the name of profit, whether it be their homeownership equity evaporating or their private for-profit college closing before their degree is complete and without transferable credit. In exposing and taking collective action against phenomena such as the frauds perpetrated against students and homeowners, activists like Goldstein ably articulate the vision and spirit of Occupy Wall Street.

Another person who witnessed the Occupy movement firsthand was Elizabeth Henderson. Henderson is a journalist whose work has appeared in *The Nation* and an activist who has served on the National Political Committee of the Democratic Socialists of America (DSA), the largest socialist organization in the United States. Henderson also co-chaired both DSA's national Drop Student Debt campaign in 2013–2015, and DSA's #WeNeedBernie effort in 2015–2016, which was not affiliated with the Bernie Sanders campaign, but was a base of support for his candidacy in the 2016 presidential primaries.

In her interview, Henderson stressed the fundamental draw of a public, non-election-based campaign focused on the issue of student debt, and further, the limits of such an effort.

Interviewer: You were involved in DSA already for a couple years when the student debt crisis surfaced prominently in the news. What first brought it to your attention?

Henderson: It wasn't so much I had a moment where I thought "student debt is a thing." It was more that there was already a campaign that was going on that had been voted on after the DSA national convention that I thought, "This is an issue. I have student debt. I care about this."

Interviewer: How did things with the local chapter start working in terms of the student debt issue?

Henderson: For DSA, I think the organization was recognizing that student debt is a very serious issue, and could also be a good way to tap into this community and tap into this group of young folks, or older folks who also have student debt. It would really tap into people who were demographically missing from the organization and how to engage them in a genuine way. DSA started [student debt organizing] in May 2013, that's the first date I could find, where we started doing tabling. What we were doing there is a petition, because often petitions are a very helpful tool for engaging people in discussion, hopefully moving them to action. Part of it was urging Obama to apply income-based repayment to both public and private loans. That was what the campaign was really about for a while, just collecting these signatures. It was also asking him to do this through executive order. Obama had a track record of passing executive orders in the past related to student debt, so it wasn't a completely "snowball's chance in hell" kind of situation. We did realize it probably wouldn't happen, but it was a way to engage people and start. Then we started doing a series of "Debt, Discussion, and Drinks" meetings. We would have a reading or an article or something that we would discuss, related to student debt. Even when I was out collecting signatures, there was definitely an element of shame attached to having debt. Also, just this feeling of, "oh, I somehow messed up," or indignation: "I followed the rules, I got this college degree and now Sallie Mae is just chasing me all over the place."

In January of 2014 we did a big panel. That was good, and we had about 100 people. In the spring, two major actions outside of the Board of Ed building in Philly. We also did a little skit and it was, different people play different roles. [One of our group] was wearing this graduation cap and gown saying, "I just graduated, what do I do now?" Someone played Sallie Mae and they were dressed up as Dracula.

Interviewer: This sounds amazingly theatrical.

Henderson: You did have [an] element of the theatrical and I think that does help with engaging people, which is good. This kind of setting makes it feel more engaging. Looking at our local work, for Philly, we had many members who are involved in [campaigns about student debt]. It also became a question of, wow, do we want to continue doing this work or at that point, 15 Now [*Editor's note: this was the name of the campaign for a $15/hour minimum wage.*] was really starting to take off, and we were starting to do that as well. We were kind of hitting a capacity issue in terms of doing all of those things. We had to choose between the student debt stuff and the $15 an hour stuff; we couldn't swing doing both.

Interviewer: Is it one of the strengths of trying to address the issue of student loan debt and organize around it that people don't fit into preconceived boxes? What I mean to ask is, they don't fit into blue collar or white collar very neatly, or left or right, even. Is that a strength of it? Is that a weakness? What's your take on that?

Henderson: I would say that it's probably both a strength and a weakness. I think that it's a weakness because if you look at most organizing campaigns, usually you have a very specific group of people you're organizing. I think that the people who have student debt don't all fall into the same group. It's definitely going to make it more challenging.

I would say that most of the people we were engaging were young people, majority white, and by young I mean probably under 30, 35 tops. People who were usually in jobs that they do not enjoy and many have kind of a chip on their shoulder, kind of were frustrated enough to be spurred to come to these meetings. I think it does make it trickier because you don't really have a type of person that you're organizing. There was a broad array of people. You're usually looking at a community organizing mode, going door to door and saying: "What's going on in your neighborhood?" Then coming up with a way to take care of that. It really is at the end of the day getting out there and talking to people, whether or not they're receptive, I think it does build awareness of the issue and creates the opportunities in the state to have an actual conversation.

Interviewer: I feel a lot of what you're talking about is kind of the disconnect between a national issue and organizing around it locally.

Henderson: I think that's part of it. I also think that finances and money and the debt thing, specifically, is still viewed by a lot of people as a private issue. A lot of people I talked to while we were doing this work felt like they totally owed the money, and they knew they had to pay it. Then, they automatically have this feeling of shame. Do you want to share that you borrowed this money? Most people want to pay it back and they feel bad that they can't.

Interviewer: That certainly speaks to the issue of shame and trying to get people away from the idea that it's their fault alone.

Henderson: Trying to organize people from a negative can be difficult. Especially if you're not giving a solution that really seems feasible. For us, for the national Drop Student Debt campaign, it was, "We will abolish all debt." These were things we knew were not feasible. We are the largest socialist organization in the country, but DSA was not in a position to say, "We drafted this federal law or this proposal or that proposal, and it's been very concrete. Now we have tens of thousands of people to push for this and really get organized and do a real campaign around that." We didn't have that.

I feel [Bernie Sanders's 2016 presidential campaign] really kind of sparked this feeling of "Wow, there are issues I'm confronting in my life, including student debt, including $15.00 an hour; there's this thing that I really care about that I'd like to see fixed, and no one's talking about this." For a presidential candidate to be talking about this and raising a Democratic Socialist platform, this is a game-changer for so many people. I think, specifically, the student debt issue, it was really just having somebody recognize that, "Yes, this is an issue," and also come up with a pretty solid plan that seemed very realistic. With the student debt organizing work we were doing, we never really hit a point where we were able to connect student debt in the campaign to other things in a tangible way. It was kind of like a very single-issue organizing kind of thing. With Sanders it was the vision and the plan, I think those are the two major things.

Interviewer: You're a journalist. You mentioned Sanders's plan. Did he have some kind of specific proposal or plank in his proposal that talked about specifically existing student debt? Or was he more focused on the tuition-free plan in the future?

Henderson: If I remember correctly, it was pretty much focused on making college tuition free. It was also specifically focusing on public universities and that he would do that by increasing corporate taxes. I know some other issues, including not wanting the federal government to make a profit from student loans. Also, I don't think this got a lot of attention: allowing students to refinance their loans to today's interest rates.

Interviewer: If you could kind of point the conversation or point the organization politically or socially around this issue, what are the top priorities for how to do that in the near future?

Henderson: Ideally what I'd love to see is debt forgiveness. The follow-up, of course, is, how do you manage that? How do you pay for that? I don't know, but I think debt forgiveness and I think free higher education. I also think there need to be more vocational schools and more vocational training programs. The big thing, though, which is the total debt forgiveness, I just think that that, if I got one thing, that would be it. That definitely would be amazing. Then, free higher education and expanding other educational opportunities that are similar to higher education that can get you to a similar job. Also, it's one thing to fix the college thing, it's another thing to fix the jobs thing. It would be amazing to be able to graduate from college and not have any debt! Then you get out and more and more a college degree doesn't mean what it used to mean, in terms of being competitive on the job market.

For me, it's also figuring out a way to have jobs that are well paid and offer health care and benefits, and ideally a [labor] union. Again, I have friends who have college degrees and work in coffee shops and it's not because they're trying to be ironic hipsters or something. It's because that's what they have to do right now and it's hard to find a job right now in the field that they studied in. You just find a job. I think that's the thing too, just if you get these degrees, it's great, it's a wonderful experience to even go to college and explore and learn. If you don't then have a job that respects you and you can raise and support your family, or support yourself, then it's still kind of like we really haven't fixed the entire problem. Anything that draws attention to the issue, but then you need an organized response. There are a lot of people who have a vested interest in making sure that college graduates graduate with debt. It is a debt industry, there are politics involved. I'm guessing, with all these fees and interest rates, they're not going to just give that up. It's like any kind of campaign. It's going to take a push.

Henderson returns as so many of these interviewees do to the theme of shame and the difficulty of "organizing around a negative." It seems that is her chief takeaway from her experience attempting to launch a national campaign around student debt, that many feel they owe the money and would like to pay it back. It is only when they have become involved at the activist level that many borrowers begin to link their experience to others, as in the Sanders presidential campaign. What is interesting about the DSA perspective Henderson presents is that student debt can be a decidedly "instrumental" organizing tool that may be discarded if not enough borrowers become mobilized to want to take up the issue as DSA members. It seems DSA has become one of the most enduring formal organizations to carry some of the sentiments and participation of the Occupy movement, drawing new membership from those who feel alienated from the political system.

Their messaging struck a chord—membership has skyrocketed from roughly 6,000 in 2015 to numbers approaching 50,000 in 2018. Universal loan forgiveness is favored by most borrowers, more so than bankruptcy, which carries with it a stigma and shame that is difficult to overcome. What is most insightful, perhaps, is that DSA is able to prioritize future-facing policy solutions such as tuition-free higher education without focusing as much on the immediate consequences, such as accumulated student debt, of the existing policy. It is important to note that most of the activists we have encountered, including Virden, Goldstein, and Henderson, have been struggling to advance the public conversation toward substantial public policy changes that address one of the three main policy dysfunctions that perpetuate student debt: federal loan policy to students, federal subsidies to for-profit colleges and universities, and tuition-free public higher education.

One of the chief architects of the Bernie Sanders campaign's call for tuition-free public higher education is Adolph Reed Jr., PhD, a professor of political science at the University of Pennsylvania. Reed has been an activist for decades and has previously held faculty positions at Yale University and the New School. He has most recently served as co-chair and organizer of Higher Ed for Bernie, assisted with the larger Labor for Bernie campaign, and acted as a Sanders campaign surrogate in several venues. He has served on Committee A of the American Association of University Professors, the committee explicitly tasked with advocating for academic freedom for faculty. He is a prolific public intellectual on topics as varied as the Democratic Party, race, labor unions, the state of the left in American politics, poverty, and the historical political thought of W. E. B. DuBois. In this interview, Reed gives a perspective history of the Free Higher Ed movement and its call for free tuition at public colleges and universities nationwide. He also gives a critical evaluation of current mainstream efforts to make community college tuition-free. The questions included substantive inquiries about the aforementioned areas in which Reed is an expert. His responses included evaluations about historical successes and failures of labor organizing for political ends, the polarization of wealth and income, and the struggle for de-commodified (perhaps extending the term from political sociologist Karl Polanyi) public goods, such as higher education.[18]

> *Interviewer:* We're most interested in public policy solutions to the student debt crisis. To that end, one of the more prominent organizing campaigns has been the Free Higher Ed movement that you've participated in. You've been quoted in the *Chronicle of Higher Education* and elsewhere; you've written and spoken extensively on the project. So, could you tell us something about how the Free Higher Ed movement first got off the ground?

Reed: There may be a little bit of a cautionary tale here which I think con-
nects to your question. We started the campaign as an initiative of the
Labor Party around 2000–2001. We got to a point where we had gotten
endorsements from the AFT [American Federation of Teachers]; actually, it started out with the Higher Ed division, but they pushed a reso-
lution. They, along with several of their affiliates, had already endorsed
the campaign, pushed it through the AFT, the UMass Amherst faculty
union, the MSP [Massachusetts Society of Professors], the PSC [Profes-
sional Staff Congress] of CUNY [City University of New York], the CFA
[California Faculty Association], and a few others.

Students' time horizon as undergraduates is so limited that it didn't
make sense to fight for something, or to organize them around something, that couldn't be won before they graduated. What that means is
that you shouldn't try to build a mass movement among students
around this issue.

Some in the campaign's leadership felt that we needed to go for
something more immediate and that the Free Higher Ed issue seemed
so daunting or such a big thing that what we needed to do was to break
it up into little things (you know, the kind of Alinskyite approach to
organizing). In Massachusetts, activists decided to focus on free community college in the state. And we said, okay, fine, if that's what you
want to do. What happened was, they put some effort into that. At the
same time we tried to organize a meeting of the principal union endors-
ers to try to talk about strategy and campaign building, and we had a
little bit of trouble trying to pull that off with the schedules. So anyway,
one thing led to another, and we kind of turned away from trying to do
anything with it for about a year or two, not least because the Labor
Party's resources were stretched really thin as we were running a ballot
access campaign in South Carolina.

After that, there was a students' mobilization in 2008 or 2009,
maybe in the spring of National Student Day of Action, and we just
started kind of talking about what next steps would look like if we were
to try to rekindle the Free Higher Ed initiative. Finally, we said, let's go
do it, so we went up to Massachusetts and we met with the UMass
people, and they were so chastened by the failure of the free community
college thing they tried, which, in addition to not generating enough
political support from Democrats, also failed because they got criticism
from union people when they were trying [to] organize around working-class neighborhoods. Apparently, one objection took the form of
people saying, okay, you give us free community college, the middle-
class keeps the four-year universities, right?

They were so chastened by that experience, and also having found out
that it's as tough to win something like that as it is to win the thing you
really want that they even bristled at the idea of trying to use

Massachusetts as a test case, I mean a field test for trying to organize around a national issue. We talked to the PSC and they were intrigued and on board; the CFA, which had been the most aggressively supportive in institutional terms, was on board too. So we set up a conference call among the principals that the PSC hosted, and we were in New York, and I think a couple of them were there. So that's the shaggy dog tale. Here's the cautionary part: once the unions got excited, they moved immediately to call a meeting with a number of other unions, including the AAUP at the moment the AAUP was going through some really [difficult] political stuff, and they had one meeting of the principals, and then the next thing you know they announced the launch of a new initiative called the Campaign for the Future of Higher Education, the CFHE, which is still around.

I went to their launch event in D.C. and it was full of high-tech video conferencing; they talked about having a virtual think tank, but it was and has been, and I think remains another one of those lefty moves where you get excited about getting all dressed up before you give any thought to where it is you're trying to go. So, they pushed for inclusiveness, and they're bringing in a bunch of people from other faculty unions around, and they haven't put together a program and a real agenda to fight for, so it's another one of those, you know, additive agendas, and a lot of position paper writing, and I fear, frankly, that that's what's most likely to come out of all of the after-Bernie organizing, too. So, that's kind of what happened. And that's what I would not want to see happen with whatever life the Free Higher Ed idea has after the Sanders campaign. And I think the fact that he's got this College for All Act is kind of a good thing, but I think it's also problematic, because there's a tendency, you know, that lefties have, which is to find a bill that you can organize around, and that's always a waste of time.

Interviewer: It's interesting to me to see that Hillary Clinton has been able to attack College for All from the left by saying we don't want to provide free tuition for rich kids.

Reed: I guess you saw these two economists [College of William & Mary] who apparently have been making a living at this for a few years, have been pushing now in the mainstream op-ed world what they purport to be a statistical argument that free tuition at public colleges would amount to a significant upward transfer of income. When we first started this, one of the things we thought we'd do to launch it is to get signatures from an array of academics, and we were hoping for a couple hundred of them, and you know, onto a statement, endorsing it, and [economist] Jamie Galbraith wrote a really snarky comment taking that line, basically, that in Texas, the four-year colleges are the preserves of the white middle class and so this would be a welfare program for them at the expense of the poor. And it really is a fascinating moment just throwing into relief, how in effect appeals to concentrate on the plight of the worse off can be used as a club to beat up on people pushing for egalitarianism on social policy. To be clear, I don't think that was Galbraith's intent, unlike the William & Mary economists, but intent doesn't really matter so much in this regard.

And I don't think there's any argument that can be made at this point about the good of the society as a whole. I was just saying to my son the other day that I really am feeling more and more like we've just gotten to a point where, you know that slogan from the French SDS [Students for a Democratic Society] in 1968, "Be reasonable, demand the impossible" applies. I mean, I think, you know, okay, it was clever and French then, but I think we're at a point now where that's just a literal statement of where we are.

Interviewer: Could you talk about President Obama's America's College Promise for community colleges program, which apparently has indirectly funded about $70 million for roughly 40,000 students, and some kind of grant-based competition the vice president just announced that will cost $100 million as a subsidy to some community college institutions? The stated aim of the program is to "earn a quality, affordable degree or credential that meet the demands of a competitive global economy." How do those numbers and that goal comport with the Free Higher Ed campaign?

Reed: Wow. Easy. I'd say not at all! Walter Benn Michaels and I have been talking about this and trying to work on doing something, a kind of manifesto for a fully de-commodified approach to higher education fully disconnected from human capital ideology, and fully disconnected from the labor market stuff. And obviously there are some professions for which you need to have the training and the specialized education. Liberal arts college is a great experience. My son went to Hampshire, and in four years, I don't think he ever had an in-class exam. It's always a paper, a take-home, and writing-intensive, and I mean after the fact, it was a prep school for PhD programs. I mean, yeah, it's noninstrumentalized education. And when I was coming along, it was still like that for a lot of people, that's what the idea was. You go to college to get that experience, to broaden yourself intellectually.

You could major in anything, it doesn't matter, because really, insofar as the college degree said anything about your place in the labor market, it was just that you had experience—well, two things: one is that the degree was an indication that you had, that you developed a capacity to work without direct supervision, but also it was frankly a screen in the same way that race or gender was a screen and still is. I kind of enjoy every semester seeing the look on my Penn undergraduates' faces when I have occasion to tell them well, actually it's not education that helps to lift people out of poverty; the vast majority of people would be better served by having a union at their jobs than by having a PhD.

And I'm assuming that Obama's initiative, like everything else with Clintonism, what it would amount to is a subsidy for the lenders or employers in the same way that welfare reform shifted the subsidy from poor people to employers of low-wage labor.

Interviewer: The price tag [of tuition-free public higher education], which you've said is roughly $85 billion annually, is it possible to talk about funding it through the tax loophole closing that you've talked about before without a larger conversation that involves pressuring the wealthiest taxpayers paying for public goods in a way they refuse to now? And how do we get there?

Reed: I could see when we did surveys of delegates at union conventions around the Free Higher Ed stuff, it was amazing: nowhere was the response less than 75 percent plus favorable, and most cases was over 80 percent, where the delegates thought this was a great idea, and thought it was something they wanted their unions to try to fight for. And people said anecdotally, well, if college was free, the hell with my kids, I'll do it for myself, and not necessarily connected to a job or a skills upgrade, but just because it's, you know, if I can take courses about stuff I wanted to learn more about, then I'd try to do it, right? So I think one of the things is that it's tough to figure out how to get there, but I'd like to see this develop into something or to see a campaign develop into the kind of thing that sectors of the trade union movement would pick up like they did the eight-hour day and compulsory elementary education because, speaking instrumentally, going back to the model of the post–World War II GI Bill, it's a public works program, too!

If public college becomes free, then the number of people who are going to want to go is going to increase, which means that states and the federal government will have inducement to invest, not only to compensate for all the cuts that they've made to existing public systems, but after World War II is when you saw the exponential expansion of branch campuses of public institutions in areas of states that didn't have anything like that before. And in that sense the call for free public higher education is also a call for increased public investment and the growth of the public sector. I think that feeds back into a broader struggle for de-commodified public goods. Obviously, you've got to think of something else to call it, because I shudder to see that on a bumper sticker.

I do think that there's a base, a broad base out there that can be converted without a lot of difficulty into a constituency for expansion of the public sector. And I think one of the limitations of trying to (and look, I think the Sanders campaign has been phenomenal in the way that it has used an election campaign as a platform for social movement organizing, because the two don't naturally fit together, necessarily, despite the fact that a lot of people think they do) is that you can't really have the kind of discussions it's really important to have with people at the face-to-face level and small-group level about how to restore or help to restore people's sense of confidence in the public sector. I think it can be done, it can definitely be done, but it can't be done at the level of fighting with Krugman on the op-ed pages or even in the left journals. It's got to be a popular organizing campaign; that's the only way this is going to turn.

I think the only way we can get there is to organize from other mediums. I think the upside of the sharply increasing polarization of wealth, income, and security is such that I think our potential base is a lot larger. Well, it's not a lot larger than it was objectively, but I think the subjective consciousness of that objective base is probably more open to the call to mobilize on behalf of solidaristic institutions and de-commodified public goods than has been the case in my adult life, for sure. That's why we so desperately need the involvement of the trade union movement, and that in turn is what's especially depressing, not to mention the fact that they're sacrificing their members every time they do it—to see the AFT and NEA falling in behind Obama and Clinton so quickly, and these are the forces that have been leading the attack on their members! I mean, it's amazing.

Reed's critique of the system makes it clear there is no one easy solution. Reed is primarily an activist and intellectual who is invested in attempting to prevent future student debt from accumulating, rather than a policy expert on student debt itself. His account of the social movement surrounding the drive for tuition-free public higher education in the United States is very likely the most comprehensive on record. Reprioritizing higher education as a public good would make public higher education accessible to everyone who desires it as a celebration of humanity. Idealized forms of liberal arts learning can be made available to all, strengthening the possibility of an emboldened citizenry that can engage in more robust form of democracy. As Reed suggests, public higher education has been turned toward a commodity in much the same way that health care has, in that there is an entire deconstructing of the institution that allows private interests to profit. This profit is at the expense of those who most benefit from public higher education: working and middle-class people who are attempting to achieve the American Dream of social mobility.

There is much to learn from the fight to "de-commodify" higher education in the past twenty years. Short-term, small-bore political projects make little difference in the overall, maldistributed structure of American social goods, such as the idea in Massachusetts to remove tuition from community colleges. The alternative that would have made a much greater difference to undergraduates and graduates would be removing tuition and fees from Massachusetts public universities, but the smaller goal seemed more obtainable to advocates at the time. Yet, it failed to pass the legislature. Reed's comments on this matter and indeed, on former President Obama's proposal to provide free tuition to high-achieving community college students, particularly in the sciences, indicate the relationship of the movement to reprioritize higher education as a public good to the centrist public policy community of which Obama is a capable representative. Tellingly, nothing happened in regard to Obama's proposal in the last two years of his administration.

There have been several encouraging bright spots in the movement. Several states have made community college tuition-free on an "experimental" basis, such as Tennessee, Oregon, and now California. New York State has made public universities tuition-free for students who come from families that earn less than $250,000 per year. The California State University system has opted for a tuition freeze as well, and the state legislature has increased public subsidies. Using Reed's criteria, these limited programs do not fit well into the category of universal public good. Labor activists like Reed call for the rebuilding of the American labor movement as the primary democratic political project of the modern era, but also value education as an end in itself. The presence of a labor union that may collectively bargain on their behalf may benefit more people than "a PhD." We need both to maintain a thriving democratic society with protections and social advancement for all.

Absent a national groundswell for the College for All proposal, there appears to be no possibility in the near future for public higher education that is lauded and funded as a public good and public necessity, though it may be both of those things. And amid a political climate that very nearly destroyed the financial basis for graduate education in the United States, there appears to be little support for higher education absent a purely instrumental purpose—that is, an education that is merely an instrument to achieve financial success within the current economic system, focused on business, mathematics, accounting, and high-tech skills (i.e., coding). That student debt is at its highest historical point at a time when business education is at its historical highest only adds irony. It would seem that student debt will be necessary for the foreseeable future to fund financial education being acquired to help pay down that debt. While current American workers and students are fragmented and at perhaps their lowest point of power in modern history, it is important to note what has succeeded in terms of organizing toward public policy or collective solutions, and Reed's activism in the labor movement and his championing of the classroom as a democratic space are perhaps both part of the answer.

One person who has been involved in both of those settings, but as a student first and then a professional organizer, is Chris Hicks, who is now, as mentioned in previous chapters, chief of the Higher Education Division of the American Federation of Teachers (AFT) and has appeared as a commentator on MSNBC. Hicks had several thoughts about solutions to the student debt crisis. He also addressed the question about the particular role labor unions had to play in addressing the issue, and what they have the ability to do in terms of internal organizing, contract negotiations, and institutional advocacy toward changes in public policy.

> *Interviewer:* If there was one thing that could be done currently about the student loan crisis, what would it be?
>
> *Hicks:* Frankly, I don't think there's a silver bullet. I mean, just to look at two sides of the same coin: on one side, there's the college affordability crisis. If we eliminated all $1.3 trillion today, it would just rebuild over time. We're quickly headed down a path that the Department of Education, issuing new federal student loans, if we eliminated all student debt, it's going to repopulate. And on the other side of the coin, with the $1.3 trillion, if we made college free today, we would still have 43 million people who are going to be in debt. So, just to be very up front, there is no one policy solution. Each policy response is going to benefit different parts of the population differently.
>
> *Interviewer:* I've been talking to many people about my research, and one question I've encountered is, "What do unions have to do with student loan debt?" I didn't have a great answer, so I'm hoping you can provide one.
>
> *Hicks:* If we're going to address the student debt crisis, one thing we're really going to have to address is earnings, which is part of the reason why JwJ worked so closely with unions on this. There are currently, I think, 14 million union members, and there are at least 43 million people with student debt. This could be a huge organizing opportunity for unions if they were willing to have the initiative to make this one of the leading issues, one that could make it big. You've heard of Strike Debt, the Debt Collective. I think there's a smart thing they're doing, because once you have student debt, you're not just going to have student debt; a study found that those with student debt were seven times more likely to have other types of debt. Mortgage debt, auto debt, credit card debt, that's because they're already losing a big chunk of their income when it comes time to buy a house, buy a car; anything like that, you're already less likely to have the money to do it. So debt has just become this very crippling issue in our economy, and it's always been a very prevalent issue; student debt is just the current face of it; but it's interesting that 20–40-year-olds now are the ones who are going to school.

Unions have tools to assist members with their debt by enrolling them in programs such as income-based repayment and public service loan forgiveness.

Hicks highlights the need for such programs as relief to a wide swath of the workforce who are most likely to also hold other types of debt. One organizing solution is to channel the frustration and alienation felt by the 40 million or more people with student loan debt into signing up with the labor movement in order to more collectively advocate for their interests in the form of loan forgiveness programs and other borrower protections.

While national coalitions and the American federal political structure are where the lion's share of public policy is made, several state-focused advocacy groups have begun building efforts mirroring the Higher Ed, Not Debt coalition at the state level. In Wisconsin, the effort is called One Wisconsin Now, and one of the leaders of the effort is Cory Mason, a Democratic elected official from Racine. Since this interview, Mason has left the legislature, having been elected mayor of his hometown of Racine, Wisconsin.

Mason has championed a bill that has not been able to escape the Republican-dominated committee (and legislature), a bill that would create a state-based program that refinances federal student loans. In his interview, Mason outlined the need for action on this issue, ideas behind the bill, and the challenges he has had in attempting to pass it in the legislature. He also calls attention to the culpability of public higher universities themselves, who he believes for too long acceded to cuts in funding in a political exchange that allowed them to raise student tuition and fees concomitantly.

> *Mason:* It's become crushing for people. People come and tell me stories about just how devastated they are to have this much debt. What we're proposing, we weren't saying anything near as ambitious about what Bernie has been saying, which is we should make college tuition entirely subsidized and basically free. We were just saying we let people refinance their loans at lower rates, the same way you can with a car mortgage or your credit card debt. Most people are prohibited from being able to do that in the federal rules that they're under or they don't have enough collateral to deal with the private loans they have.
>
> It's a bigger and more systemic problem than I realized. Wisconsin's about a little more than 6 million people and there are somewhere around 1.1 and 1.2 million people with student loan debt in the state of Wisconsin. It's getting to be a bigger and bigger portion of the population. What we were proposing was something between the tax deductions and the refinancing that might have saved, depending upon how much student loan debt you had, might save you two to four thousand dollars a year, but over the course of ten or twenty years, or thirty years depending on how long your loan is, that's a substantial amount of money that at least gives you a little more breathing room to try to make those loans affordable.
>
> *Interviewer:* Could you speak a bit more about what's been happening with the Finance Committee?

Mason: We've been trying to increase the grants available to incoming students so that they wouldn't have to take on as much debt as they were going through in this process of going to college. The response was just, "No more money for colleges. We want money for other things," and so it would never win Republican support. Part of crafting this legislation was trying to appeal to things that Republicans value or they say they value. First, we told them it would be letting the market work and letting people refinance in the market the way you can with any other credit transaction. The other [way] is by giving people tax deductions, which Republicans are generally supposed to like.

We have not, unfortunately, had any success getting them to buy into either of these concepts. We are seeing it moving in other states. Rhode Island's now doing it. Minnesota's now doing it. There's a number of states that are starting to allow refinancing as part of the work that they do as a state, and so it's a little bit frustrating to be the first state to propose it. I would've liked to be the first state to adopt it, but I think you're going to see more and more states begin to take on this model of addressing not only how affordable college is, but also addressing what do we do with the trillions of dollars of the student loan debt that's weighing down this economy and making it harder and harder for people to get back on their feet?

There are some legislative issues that will seem to ebb and flow or seem to wane over time. This is one where the more I talk about it, the more people have been saying, "We've got to do something."

Interviewer: It's not going away. Every year it's a higher average. I think it's up to $30,000 as the median amount that students graduate with now.

Mason: In Wisconsin they estimated it's $19 billion for the student loan debt. For a state with a $62 billion dollar GDP, that's a lot of money being tied up and not being put into the economy any given year because of student loan payments. It is a broader problem, as well, because you're taking so much money out of the economy for people to pay back their student loans.

Interviewer: What does some of the research that you've been working with say about this issue?

Mason: There's a couple things that we were able to find from the research. Number one is that we weren't able to find any people, but according to the Social Security Administration there's more than a couple of thousand people in Wisconsin who have their [Social Security checks] garnished to pay for student loans, which means as people are retiring, they're having Social Security garnished to pay for student loan debt. It's hard to believe. It screams something's inherently wrong there. There is a group called One Wisconsin Now. They've done amazing research on this. Four years ago, they actually did a survey of student loan debtors in Wisconsin. They got some ridiculous number of, I think, four or five thousand people responding to the survey, but what they asked wasn't about employment rates. They asked if you owned or rented your own house or if you were living basically with your parents. From that, and then asked people with student loan debt if they'd ever bought a new car. It's two markers of middle-class entry, but they're a bit crude.

Interviewer: That's interesting. You can feel how much it's impeding people's entry into the economy.

Mason: You were 80 percent less likely to have student loan debt and buy a new car compared to the rest of the population and you were twice as likely not to own your home compared to the general population.[19] There are these big factors of as more and more people get into this class of voters, these are people who have attained a college degree who probably have a decent middle-class childhood or normal circumstances, but because the student loan debt is so heavy on a monthly budget, they're not able to buy homes, buy new cars. One veteran featured in the report, Saul, a veteran of Iraq and Afghanistan, was talking about how he was fighting in two wars, and the student loan debt companies were garnishing his military wages for his student loan debt. His thought was, "Seriously? I'm here fighting for my country here and you're really going to take $500 a month out of my check?"

Interviewer: That doesn't really demonstrate that we value their public service.

Mason: It's also been interesting in the polling and even in the conversation, the whole refinance thing, it polls well into 80 percent approval. Such an interesting topic. I can't get Republican legislative leaders to buy in, but when you talk to voters and poll voters on it, they all just say, "Yeah, why can't I refinance my debt the way I can any other commercial loan?" It doesn't make sense. It's been a compelling issue. So [many] of the Republicans didn't adopt this package, but did very small anemic proposals to help out a couple hundred people with their student loan debt every year. They're really window-dressing proposals, but they feel they had to do something because the issue has been such a big deal.

Interviewer: I'm curious because you've really been in the trenches, if you will, with this as a leader on this issue in Wisconsin. As you said, you're the first state to really propose this particular policy solution. Can you talk about who your main political allies are on this and who, maybe somebody, the main opposition you get is or are and what kind of arguments they tend to make in the public relations fight about it?

Mason: The opposition does not engage too much in public relations on this. It is messy because you've got these private loan companies that were once government agencies that are really to blame here. It's sort of a weird mix of federal policymaking made now more than twenty years ago combined with Wall Street banks that get to hold all these. Now, if you're Wall Street and you've got a bunch of loans out there, more than a trillion dollars' worth in this country of student loan debt that can never be discharged in bankruptcy, why would you ever want to let go of that?

They don't say that and they don't want to engage it, but basically why would Wall Street banks want to give? You can lose your house through divorce or health care costs and all that other stuff and you can discharge all that debt because something horrible happens, but you can never discharge student loan debt. The Wall Street banks that were able to convince Congress to make that a policy are not going to want to be quick to give up on debt that's guaranteed until somebody dies, right?

Interviewer: Who's with you? Who are some of the main groups that are showing the most amount of effective support?

Mason: Interestingly, groups like the Dentists Association are very much for this. If you're a dentist with four hundred thousand dollars' worth of debt and you can reduce your interest payment by 2 or 3 or 5 percent, that's substantial savings in a given month, let alone a year. There have been student groups and other groups, a lot of professional groups who have loan debt for their members. They're taking a position in favor of the bill, wanting to do something to make it more affordable. Governments have been walking away from funding colleges. There was this Faustian bargain made, if you will, with the colleges and universities. State governments said: "Well, don't worry about it. You can just raise tuition and make it up there."

As Mason mentioned above, there was at least a perceived "covenant" with the middle class (which Reed contends did not really ever exist) and their American Dream of social mobility and homeownership that may have been broken with this conversion to consumer financing of higher education, and the lack of an effective public policy solution to it, leading to alienation from the political system. The political response from the activists and legislators quoted above has been to organize people around the issues and interests that matter to them that are being impeded by student debt.

It is difficult to identify a narrow swath of people who are chiefly harmed by existing student debt policy, because, as with all policies that encourage private investment, there are some who are hurt the most (those already impoverished) and some who are hurt the least (those with a low interest rate and steady income). They all saw themselves as "doing the right thing." Perhaps the existence of such a class does not necessarily or even logically translate into concerted, coherent political action on their behalf in a sustainable way.[20] This was, in the view of some analysts, the downfall of Occupy, that such a movement could only register their dissatisfaction and wait until their creditors and employers "heard" their message.[21] Unfortunately for them, the existence of their debt and the noncompetitive nature of American labor with world labor at a cut-rate wage, along with a general disillusionment about voting, gives Occupy no next step that is not fraught with danger for their future. People cannot advocate politically controversial or even socially controversial ideas because such ideas might be dangerous to their employers, or even their future employers. Most of the activists involved with Occupy were students and immediate past graduates who had no employment history and no current place in the job market. This is the same story with many modern social movements, from Tahrir Square to Kent State, and so this phenomenon of student-driven activism is not a new one or even a particularly American one. Even debt refusal does not have a sunset provision. One cannot walk away from one's student loan debt the same way one walks away from a home mortgage.

The corrupting nature of the financialization of educational instruction and consequent socialization of students is one that must be fully scrutinized. If students and their teachers are mandated to use technocratic vocabulary over the frames of art, science, and philosophy, then the mission of higher education in the United States will be one that is ineffectively preparing the next generation of citizens, rather the next generation of consumers and debtors. It will be up to activists and leaders such as those interviewed in this chapter to attempt to mobilize people who have not learned the lessons of history or the value of critical thinking. Rather than enhancing democracy, at that stage higher education will be contributing to an enfeebled citizenry.

CHAPTER FIVE

The Sin of Debt and the Hope of Forgiveness in the Twenty-First Century

Previous chapters explored the history and effect of literally banking on the success of student borrowers, and by extension, mortgage loan borrowers. The structure of these loans shares the same logic that underpins the stability of the New York Stock Exchange and the bond market: confidence in the long-term growth of the consumer-based American economy, which has as its centerpiece the American Dream of homeownership and social mobility. The government is a support mechanism in this endeavor, yet it is also the holder of most student loan notes that are hindering a generation's entry into the mortgage market. Collectively, this confidence in future performance forms the basis of the interconnected political economy of the United States.

The investor class's confidence in the American economy can be measured in the qualitative character of the types of loans that were issued to the middle class over the course of the twentieth century. Over time, mortgages were converted from a portion of the total price of a home to a small down payment with a fifteen-year repayment, to a no-down-payment, thirty-year loan with a variable interest rate.[1] Only credit cards are issued on the basis of an established credit history, and the lesser (in time or quality) the credit history, the lower the balance one can charge on plastic. A $500 balance might be given to an undergraduate or 18-year-old, who can establish a credit history while providing little if any risk to the lender. A $10,000 revolving credit card limit might be granted to a middle-income 30-year-old with a decent credit history. The higher limit is not a risk to the lender, as this person has a proven ability to pay back balances in that range. Auto loans work in a similar way, but are more analogous to mortgages. Student loans, however, are unlike any of the other three loan structures: the risk is borne almost entirely by the borrower. The lender, whether the federal government or a financial institution, allows virtually unlimited borrowing for undergraduate degrees, and higher for graduate degrees, without any credit history or regard to the field of study or the chosen institution.

In this chapter, three perspectives are offered: first, from anonymous borrowers who have posted their own stories to online message boards, and whose stories reveal how this issue is being understood by borrowers, and how those stories may be further analyzed; second, through archival research, how the federal government has in the modern era routinely exercised the legal power of forgiveness, for both financial and not strictly financial purposes; and finally, some concluding thoughts on prospects for the future of democracy in the context of the student loan crisis.

Some of the impressions of higher education are from the viewpoint of those who have become most invested, those who have either obtained PhDs or other terminal degrees that enable them to teach at the college and university level during the debt crisis. Some clarifications are necessary: (1) The word "rating," widely used in some of these testimonies, means "total loan debt" or amount the federal government claims a borrower owes. The term is meant to cast doubt on the legitimacy of whether the debt is morally or legally "owed" to the lender at all. (2) Borrowers tend to use acronyms about several repayment options that are common in this discourse, including IBR (income-based repayment) and IDR (income-driven repayment), as well as PSLF (public service loan forgiveness). (3) In many cases, borrowers have given their names, and in others they have not. To protect the identity of those who perhaps did not intend their names to be used in academic research, names have been dropped here, though they would be accessible at the original website from which the data was gathered if they left their names originally. (4) A rudimentary content analysis is undertaken in order to demonstrate the commonality of content between the three sites on which student loan debt stories are posted. (5) In order to keep the sample stories concise, they have been edited to focus on one idea and also for length.

In Table 5.1, the number of instances a word is found in the total collection of stories is tabulated in each of the three sources. The most frequent words after "loan," "debt," and "education" are words such as "never," "dream," and "American Dream."

It is now a truism that a majority of college and university faculty, and even a majority of full-time faculty do not have the job security known as tenure, which is a long-standing tradition, essentially a protection against

Table 5.1 Frequency of Words Used in Borrower Testimonials, 2011–2015[i]

Words Used in Testimonials	Crisis.org	Project	Occupy
Never	158	197	310
Default	74	78	182
Forgive	72	108	138
Dream	66	101	141
Teacher	58	131	101
Bankruptcy	38	83	111
$100,000 or 100k	33	24	60
Unemployed	30	32	128
American Dream	26	20	42
Doctoral/doctorate	13	30	24
PhD	10	25	55
Master	66	84	137
Collection	26	61	61
Poverty	23	13	31
Graduate school	20	63	65
Promise	17	27	29
Office	26	54	56
MBA	12	22	24
Cancer	10	7	15
Drop	13	35	40
Capitalized	13	12	29
With my parents	8	12	18
Reward	7	13	9
Loser	6	2	9
For-profit	5	1	15
Welfare	14	14	8
Career	53	86	89
Mortgage	43	47	58
Loan	1,202	2,173	2,457
Education	246	376	460
Debt	202	721	1041
N (approximate)	N = 200	N = 300	N = 400

[i] The stories referenced in Table 5.1 and the text of pages 122–125 are all taken from the following three websites, from left to right: http://www.studentdebtcrisis.org, http://projectonstudentdebt.org/voices_list.php, and http://occupystudentdebt-blog.tumblr.com, all accessed on March 15, 2015.

arbitrary employment termination. Without the job security of tenure and in a difficult job market, college professors are vulnerable:

> I am a first generation college graduate who finished a Ph.D. at a top research institution. . . . I have been in forbearance for most of my 3 years as a professor, because they want me to pay them 22% of my income every month, which I cannot afford. . . . I just cannot understand why the Federal Government is making it so difficult for borrowers to pay back their loans. When I decided I wanted to be an educator, I knew I was making a huge financial sacrifice in order to do so. I never knew that the Federal Government would be so callous and unyielding in their demands to their promising future educators.

This student has made explicit feelings about the federal government in particular, which has taken on the role of both loan servicer to the borrower and guarantor (enforcer) to the lender. The unintended consequence of its increasing oversight of this policy area has been reactions like this one by an entire generation of borrowers. The reality today of defunded higher education has aided the transformation from a secure professoriate to a fundamentally insecure profession. The world their parents experienced and thus encouraged them to enter is not one that they will be experiencing in academia. Another borrower decided to take out loans both for himself and his spouse, who later transferred the debt to his name during their divorce: "The government made it seem like loans were easy to repay because of good paying jobs for college graduates, but the government does not care that that script is mostly untrue. All the government wants is its money . . . with interest!"

The "script" students follow was essentially written by the federal government, and it needs a rewrite. The political implications of indebted voters who now hold credentials enough to compete at the highest educational levels and more debt than can ever be repaid is obviously problematic. The United States now has an overeducated, underemployed, highly indebted generation.

It is tempting to dismiss the concerns of the new debtor class as one of the typical American story of risks taken and not rewarded. Their common concerns and stories of private suffering provide a window into the world of an entire class of people. Many entered into a paradigm they believed would be embodied by a discourse about their chosen "passion" or field. Instead it is rife with the language of financial dependence, repercussions for transgressions, and the resultant obligatory service to their betters:

> I am enrolled in the IBR program which has lowered my payments so that I can meet my loan payments and living expenses. I am in my 40s,

gainfully employed while serving my community, and I am scraping by. I cannot buy a house, I drive a ten-year-old car with 150,000 miles, and still have to decide whether I can afford to go to a movie from time to time.

A popular idea in American political discourse has become the policy of student debt forgiveness, in whole or in part. There is nothing that student debtors would want more than this, a complete wiping clean of the slate of what former Federal Reserve chairman Alan Greenspan called the youthful "irrational exuberance" they undertook in order to obtain a college or graduate education. It would be a tremendous boon to consumer spending power, as debt payments that no longer had to be made could be channeled into higher purchasing power, mostly for millennial borrowers, but also affecting every segment of the population to varying degrees. While there have been several debt forgiveness plans and policy proposals, these plans are constantly shifting and subject to the fortunes of political leaders. Tuition-free or "debt-free" higher education can be a solution for future borrowers, but forgiveness for existing borrowers continues to be part of the conversation.

The two most prominent extant forgiveness programs are simple. The first is after that period of twenty-five years of either income-based repayment or payments of any kind, the balance of all federal subsidized loans or unsubsidized loans is forgiven. The only difficulty borrowers will face at this stage is that the loan balance will then be counted as income that year on their income taxes. Borrowers with triple-digit or high double-digit balances could see a significant tax bill of $20,000 or more, which they would likely have to finance to pay the IRS. There are currently bills in the Senate, co-sponsored by Elizabeth Warren (D-MA), Cory Booker (D-NJ), Bob Menendez (D-NJ), Debbie Stabenow (D-MI), and others, to exempt student loan forgiveness from taxable income. If this bill or similar legislation is not enacted in the next several years, pressure to do so will undoubtedly resurface as more borrowers reach the twenty-five-year mark.

The second existing forgiveness program is public service loan forgiveness. After making a cumulative ten years of payments while in the full-time employment of either a federal, state, or local government, or a nonprofit charitable organization (nonprofit groups that do not qualify include religious organizations if one's duties include religious advocacy, and a labor union or political group that explicitly engages in political advocacy), one's federal loans will be fully forgiven, and the loan balance is not subject to taxable income.

This idea of loan forgiveness comes from a long tradition in American politics of government forgiveness of either loans or misconduct. Presidents over the past fifty years have all discussed governmental forgiveness of either financial debts or debts to society. Often, the forgiveness is couched in terms of how the act of forgiveness itself is strategically useful for attaining other public policy objectives such as economic growth, disease eradication, or even foreign policy objectives. In some cases, however, the forgiveness is directly in the service of public demands for it, such as in the case of pardons for criminal activity. There have even been instances when the forgiveness is done in order to preemptively ensure that divisions do not overwhelm American society and cloud other objectives.

Every president since 1969 has discussed forgiveness either for one person, for a class of people, or for entire nations. By examining these presidential statements, we find patterns of when forgiveness can and will be adopted. It is possible for these circumstances to apply to student debt forgiveness.

Richard Nixon, a Republican from California and president from 1969 until his resignation in the famous Watergate scandal in 1974, spoke of forgiveness in technocratic terms. He saw loan forgiveness for farmers that had sustained disastrous damage as an essential part of a recovery program. In a message about disaster assistance to farmers in 1970, he outlined his specific program:

> I am proposing legislation to improve the disaster loan programs of the Small Business Administration and of the Farmers Home Administration. These loans are among our principal sources of assistance to stricken individuals. The recommended changes would provide for improved refinancing, payment deferral, and forgiveness arrangements and would assure disaster loans to older citizens. My proposed amendment would allow the FHA and SBA to provide faster service and would therefore promote speedier recovery following disasters.[2]

Although Nixon did not enact this proposal, he was prepared to use his presidential power for mass loan forgiveness. Nixon's approach to national health strategy was equally technocratic, arguably even cold. In this 1971 message to Congress, student loan forgiveness was a key part of his national health strategy to deliver medical care to areas with physician shortages:

> We should also find ways of compensating—and even rewarding—doctors and nurses who move to scarcity areas, despite disadvantages such as lower income and poorer facilities. As one important step in this direction, I am proposing that our expanding loan programs for medical students include a new forgiveness provision for graduates who practice in a scarcity area, especially those who specialize in primary care skills that are in short supply. In addition, I will request $10 million to implement the Emergency Health Personnel Act. Such funds will enable us to mobilize a new National Health Service Corps, made up largely of dedicated and public-spirited young health professionals who will serve in areas which are now plagued by critical manpower shortages.[3]

Ultimately Congress did not approve this limited loan forgiveness. Nixon was not a president inclined to forgive those with whom he had a personal or political difference, such as the Vietnam-era draft evaders. This excerpt from a 1973 news conference captures his attitude toward the opponents of the war who evaded the draft: "Those who deserted must pay their price, and the price is not a junket in the Peace Corps, or something like that, as some have suggested. The price is a criminal penalty for disobeying the laws of the United States. If they want to return to the United States they must pay the penalty. If they don't want to return, they are certainly welcome to stay in any country that welcomes them."[4] He used forgiveness for a fairly narrow purpose, as part of a way to accomplish comprehensive political relief to disaster victims, usually farmers, rather than additional government subsidies. This may be the start of a trend that exponentially grew over the next forty years of encouraging borrowing as an alternative to traditional government tax-and-spend policies.

Despite Nixon's aversion to forgiveness as a political program, he was not averse to receiving forgiveness when he resigned the presidency in disgrace. His appointed successor, Gerald Ford, pardoned the former president "for all offenses against the United States which he, Richard Nixon, has committed or may have committed or taken part in during the period from January 20, 1969 through August 9, 1974."[5] In his pardon, Ford clearly established a president's personal power while also framing his pardon unquestionably in the language of forgiveness:

> As President, my primary concern must always be the greatest good of all the people of the United States whose servant I am. As a man, my first consideration is to be true to my own convictions and my own conscience. . . . My conscience tells me clearly and certainly that I cannot prolong the bad dreams that continue to reopen a chapter that is closed. My conscience tells me that only I, as President, have the constitutional power to firmly shut and seal this book. My conscience tells me it is my duty, not merely to proclaim domestic tranquillity but to use every means that I have to insure it. I do believe that the buck stops here, that I cannot rely upon public opinion polls to tell me what is right. I do believe that right makes might and that if I am wrong, 10 angels swearing I was right would make no difference. I do believe, with all my heart and mind and spirit, that I, not as President but as a humble servant of God, will receive justice without mercy if I fail to show mercy. Finally, I feel that Richard Nixon and his loved ones have suffered enough and will continue to suffer, no matter what I do, no matter what we, as a great and good nation, can do together to make his goal of peace come true.[6]

In further contrast to his predecessor, Ford further exercised his capacity for forgiveness in attempting to pardon Vietnam-era draft evaders. He again made clear his reasons for seeking forgiveness for such a wide class of Americans:

> At the national convention of Veterans of Foreign Wars in the city of Chicago, I announced my intention to give these young people a chance to earn their return to the mainstream of American society so that they can, if they choose, contribute, even though belatedly, to the building and the betterment of our country and the world.
>
> I did this for the simple reason that for American fighting men, the long and divisive war in Vietnam has been over for more than a year, and I was determined then, as now, to do everything in my power to bind up the Nation's wounds. I promised to throw the weight of my Presidency into the scales of justice on the side of leniency and mercy, but I promised also to work within the existing system of military and civilian law and the precedents set by my predecessors who faced similar postwar situations, among them Presidents Abraham Lincoln and Harry S. Truman. . . . My objective of making future penalties fit the seriousness of each individual's offense and of mitigating punishment already meted out in a spirit of equity has proved an immensely hard and very complicated matter, even more difficult than I knew it would be.[7]

Ford was attempting a clean slate for the United States, an end to the mistakes of the past, part of what he called "A Time to Heal" (which became the title of his autobiography). Ford's opponent in the 1976 election, Georgia governor Jimmy Carter, made a campaign promise that he would pardon all Vietnam-era draft evaders, which he did with Executive Order 11803. Carter was asked a question related to the blanket pardon soon after his inauguration, and took a similar tone as Ford's public statements about the issue:

> Well, I know that my own position on granting a pardon to the violators of the Selective Service laws during the Vietnam conflict was not a popular decision for many Americans to accept. But I don't believe that the patriotism of American service men and women, now or in the future, is predicated on whether or not the pardon was granted. . . . And I believe that we can count on the full support of Americans in time of trial or time of danger to defend our country. My own son went to Vietnam. He served there voluntarily and came back home. I served in two wars. And I believe that in the future, we can count on American citizens to serve their country without any doubt. I have also a historical perspective about this question. I come from the South. I know at the end of the War Between the States, there was a sense of forgiveness for those who had been not loyal to our country in the past, and this same thing occurred after other wars as well.

In the same spirit of forgiveness, Carter later extended the review of government policy toward soldiers in favor of leniency for past violations.[8] Carter and Ford's efforts here were an attempt not to erase the past, but to allow the citizenry to move forward. The pardons offered by the presidents had the benefit of hindsight and could be taken as an apology to a generation. Soldiers and draft evaders were told through these actions that the government's action was wrong, and this apology was an act of atonement, as well as a gesture of forgiveness. Both soldiers and draft evaders believed they were "doing the right thing." Draft evaders were usually supported by emboldened student radicals; and soldiers and their families were fulfilling a part of their moral duty as Americans. The Vietnam-era youth generation was the baby boom generation. They have experienced the healing nature of an act of society-wide forgiveness, and seen the power of the democratically elected government to provide space for moving on. Ford's action was limited, but Carter seized the opportunity to offer a much wider form of the action. The forgiveness that would take place under future presidents would fall either in the Nixon "policy necessity" category or into the Ford-Carter "healing" category. Later presidents would eventually find it necessary to demonstrate that both categories were applicable when proposing forgiveness of any kind.

President Reagan seems to be the only modern president to have explicitly rejected forgiveness in his veto message of a trade bill: "I am convinced this bill will cost jobs and damage our economic growth." He claimed the bill favored "narrow special interests." Reagan referred to many provisions he believed unwise, including one provision, "A requirement to negotiate a new centralized international institution to arrange the forgiveness of billions of dollars of debt around the world—all supposedly without increasing U.S. taxes or adding to our debt."[9] Forgiving billions of dollars does not seem very narrow, but it was a goal to many Third World nations for decades before finally being achieved for a time during the Clinton administration. Reagan did support some strategic debt forgiveness for farmers on a limited basis, but only in the sense that they needed some support for their business venture rather than because of the need for agriculture as a human necessity.

There is one particular act of forgiveness for which Reagan is remembered, if, as Nixon asserted a decade earlier, amnesty is forgiveness. The Immigration Reform and Control Act of 1986 was a major presidential act, even if Reagan maintained the "illegal" nature of an entire class of people he was forgiving:

We have consistently supported a legalization program which is both generous to the alien and fair to the countless thousands of people throughout the world who seek legally to come to America. The legalization provisions in this act will go far to improve the lives of a class of individuals who now must hide in the shadows, without access to many of the benefits of a free and open society. Very soon many of these men and women will be able to step into the sunlight and, ultimately, if they choose, they may become Americans.[10]

Granting 2.7 million immigrants amnesty, this act allowed people who had to "hide in the shadows" to "step into the sunlight." It changed the lives of a generation of immigrants. Such a bold policy initiative seems impossible today. Reagan's successor, George H. W. Bush, invoked forgiveness in order to advance a foreign policy goal of moving Germany closer to unification in the immediate aftermath of the Cold War. Bush spoke about forgiveness in an explicit way in one exchange with reporters. East Germany had asked the world's forgiveness for the horrors of the Holocaust. Bush was very careful not to expect the American government to forgive anything, or the American people, only himself. It is not as sympathetic or artful as Reagan's statement, but is certainly in the "healing" category, even if for "policy necessity" reasons:

> Well, I'm one who believes in forgiveness. And for those of us who have faith, most of the teachings have ample room for forgiveness and moving on. And there's—I don't know—for our family, Easter is a very special time of year, and it's a time to take stock, and it's a time to be glad. So, I'm inclined to think we ought to forgive—not forget, necessarily, because I think you learn from history, learn . . . not to do wrong, how to conduct oneself. . . . But I'm a Christian, and I think forgiveness is something that I feel very strongly about. So, that's a personal observation. That's not a statement for our country.[11]

Bush was, however, very optimistic about the use of actual debt forgiveness for "policy necessity" when it came to foreign debt, a carrot he could offer to Egypt in exchange for its support in the Gulf War of 1991. A reporter asked him about the U.S.-Egypt relationship in view of the forthcoming war with Iraq. Bush said:

> I'm very pleased that the debt forgiveness program is of benefit to the man on the street in Egypt. I know—I don't want to put words in his mouth, but President Mubarak expressed to me, asked me to express to the American people, his thanks for this. And this is a highly significant move that gives a certain flexibility to Egypt.

Bush suggests that forgiving the Egyptian government's debts would directly and materially raise the living conditions of Egyptians. Forgiveness was meant to be healing while being part of a policy necessity.[12] In response to another reporter's question about world hunger and poverty, Bush had this to say:

I think the position that our administration has taken in debt forgiveness has been tremendously important to many of these emerging democracies in Africa and, indeed, in this hemisphere. . . . Look at the basket case that was Argentina just a while back. And working with us, they are now on the move. They've come in, they've taken a very constructive approach to their economy. They are in the debt forgiveness. We've worked out a deal, they have, with the private financial institutions just very recently to lower their debt burden. The Enterprise for the Americas Initiative and the Brady plan are meaningful. And the impoverished people in that country and in other countries in our hemisphere are beginning to get a little break here.[13]

Bush clearly believed that debt forgiveness served as a type of direct foreign aid. It is a tool he preferred to use over direct aid in order to allow the kind of bootstrap capitalism he felt the debt was restricting. However, he wielded debt forgiveness on a case-by-case basis in much the same way Ford only pardoned draft evaders or softened punishment for wounded veterans, rather than the Carter approach of a blanket amnesty of the very kind Nixon found appalling.

In comparison, Bush's successor, Bill Clinton, applied the "healing" Carter approach to debt forgiveness in Africa. Clinton invoked debt forgiveness as a victory in the political and social struggle against the AIDS epidemic. He appealed to the moralistic antipoverty grounds of a "healing" opportunity while also invoking the policy necessity of forgiveness. In another statement, President Clinton referenced Pope John Paul II's "Great Year of Jubilee," or forgiveness, for the Catholic Church. The idea of "Jubilee" comes from the classical term for the official governmental occasion on which all debts were forgiven in ancient Rome. The Clinton administration supported substantial debt reduction:

More than a year ago, His Holiness the Pope called for debt forgiveness in this, the jubilee year. With the help of countless others, this grassroots effort grew into Jubilee 2000. The United States made this issue a centerpiece of the G-7 summit in Cologne last year. We crafted a plan for creditor nations to triple the debt relief available to the world's poorest nations, provided—and this is an important "provided"— that they committed themselves to economic reform, that they channel the savings into health and education, and that they resolve to have peaceful relations with their neighbors.[14]

Following Clinton, George W. Bush sought to further bind the "healing" and "policy necessity" language of forgiveness by wedding American Dream/ homeownership rhetoric to the language of forgiveness in the run-up to the financial crisis of 2008. It's worth reading the bulk of the statement, as it liberally moves back and forth between the two frameworks, wielding the language of the individual borrower beset with unexpected circumstances, and the necessity of the government's strategic and selective intervention to salvage the greater good of the American Dream that the individual strives for, rather than a social good of a more stable housing reality for the majority of Americans:

> I'm pleased to sign a bill that will help homeowners who are struggling with rising mortgage payments. The Mortgage Forgiveness Debt Relief Act of 2007 will protect families from higher taxes when they refinance their homes. It will help hard-working Americans take steps to avoid foreclosure during a period of uncertainty in the housing market. . . . The bill I sign today will help this effort by ensuring that refinancing a mortgage does not result in a higher tax bill. Under current law, if the value of your house declines and your bank or lender forgives a portion of your mortgage, the Tax Code treats the amount forgiven as money that can be taxed. And of course, this makes a difficult situation even worse. When you're worried about making your payments, higher taxes are the last thing you need to worry about. So this bill will create a 3-year window for homeowners to refinance their mortgage and pay no taxes on any debt forgiveness that they receive. And it's a really good piece of legislation. The provision will increase the incentive for borrowers and lenders to work together to refinance loans, and it will allow American families to secure lower mortgage payments without facing higher taxes.[15]

Bush has created various tools that allow homeowners and "families" an "incentive" in granting limited debt forgiveness. He calls it "good" and homeownership itself explicitly "an essential part of the American Dream." It's very clearly an attempt to stabilize the increasingly unstable housing market, which was propped up by inflated loan packages sold between banks. A stable lending market for banks, not a social good of housing, was being protected, but Bush was able to rhetorically link policy necessity to the healing properties of mortgage debt forgiveness as a kind of universalist policy of homeownership.

In 2002, Bush supported loan forgiveness for teachers in the No Child Left Behind Act. As part of his promotion of the nationalized testing initiative in this act, Bush danced between appealing to home-schooling parents and those who wanted local control of school boards, who formed part of his party's base, and centrist Americans who looked favorably upon public school teachers and teaching:

> Parents are a child's first and most important teachers, and they provide the cornerstone of a child's early education. Quality teachers, however,

also play an important role in a child's personal and intellectual development. The No Child Left Behind Act of 2001, which I signed into law in January 2002, requires that, by the end of the 2005–06 school year, there must be a "highly qualified" teacher in every classroom. Through this new law, States and school districts will have multiple tools to help them meet the new teacher quality requirements. Key elements of this effort include providing State grants to recruit and train teachers, and recruiting high-quality individuals to become teachers, offering expanded student loan forgiveness for teachers. And we must encourage Americans to volunteer their time to serve as mentors to our young people.[16]

Bush saw debt forgiveness in this context as a strategic tool, rather than a healing opportunity. However, he did imply that debt forgiveness was a boon, a gift to teachers who must be inherently struggling. In displaying this kind of sympathy, Bush came close to a position of outright sympathy for public school teachers in much the same way Nixon and Reagan displayed sympathy for farmers, and Bush Sr. invoked the plight of the Egyptian middle class. The political reality, however, was that teachers were not in any way a constituency reachable by Republicans, being a solidly Democratic constituency. This was perhaps part of the younger Bush's "compassionate conservatism" that more than implied a moral or religious component to concepts such as forgiveness.

In another instance, Bush discusses African debt forgiveness, as Clinton did, in the context of aid that will help to heal the wounds of the struggling nations on that continent. What is most interesting, however, is how much Bush felt that blanket debt forgiveness for African nations was not applicable to strategic debt forgiveness to student loan borrowers. He signed a bill in 2007, passed by a newly elected Democratic majority in Congress, called the College Cost Reduction and Access Act, which had several important provisions, but perhaps none as potentially far-reaching as the creation of the public service loan forgiveness program, which, as noted previously, provides for the wiping clean of all federal student loans after ten years of payments while employed by the government or nonprofit sector. Not once in his statement about the College Cost Reduction and Access Act, or in any other public statements, did Bush praise the new program he signed into law. Arguably, he felt forgiveness granted by public service was not even enough of a strategic policy necessity to be worthy of praise.[17]

When pitching the idea of a $700 billion financial bailout to the American public following the 2008 market crash, Bush certainly did his best to rhetorically invoke the language not of forgiveness, but of rescue:

For more than a decade, a massive amount of money flowed into the United States from investors abroad because our country is an attractive and secure place to do business. This large influx of money to U.S. banks and financial institutions, along with low interest rates, made it easier for Americans to get credit. These developments allowed more families to borrow money for cars and homes and college tuition, some for the first time. They allowed more entrepreneurs to get loans to start new businesses and create jobs. . . . Unfortunately, there were also some serious negative consequences, particularly in the housing market. Easy credit combined with the faulty assumption that home values would continue to rise led to excesses and bad decisions. Many mortgage lenders approved loans for borrowers without carefully examining their ability to pay. Many borrowers took out loans larger than they could afford, assuming that they could sell or refinance their homes at a higher price later on.[18]

Bush's mention of "easy credit" did not extend to the student loan market, but it could just as easily have. As borrowers such as "Paul" and Miranda Merklein noted in earlier chapters, millions of young borrowers found it easier to go to college or university because they were issued loans with no investigation into their credit history. Bush here implies there is nothing to forgive, either on the part of borrowers or lenders. He merely spells out "negative consequences." He even appeals in a divisive way to those who consider themselves "responsible Americans who pay their mortgages on time, file their tax returns every April 15th, and are reluctant to pay the cost of excesses on Wall Street," signaling ambivalence toward the idea of guilt or blame, only irresponsible borrowers or irresponsible lenders. In the end, he pitches the "policy necessity" not of loan forgiveness, but a complete bailout of the financial sector:

> Under our proposal, the Federal Government would put up to $700 billion taxpayer dollars on the line to purchase troubled assets that are clogging the financial system. In the short term, this will free up banks to resume the flow of credit to American families and businesses, and this will help our economy grow.[19]

There is no morality here, and Bush is even somewhat bemoaning the lack of morality in it, emphasizing that so many "responsible Americans" have been mistreated in the financial system despite doing the right thing. Bush's call for a bailout came in the waning months of the 2008 presidential race to choose his successor. In part a result of the blame the American voters largely placed at the feet of Bush and his Republican Party, the Democratic candidate for president, Barack Obama, obtained a lead in the polls leading up to election day. While still in the Senate, Obama gave a floor speech that largely echoed the calls for bailout that Bush had made. He further emphasized the rhetoric of "rescue" rather than morality. The morality he called upon was the language of emergency:

> But while there is plenty of blame to go around and many in Washington and Wall Street who deserve it, all of us—all of us—have a responsibility to solve this crisis because it affects the financial well-being of every single American. There will be time to punish those who set this fire, but now is not the time to argue about how it got set, or whether the neighbor smoked in his bed or left the stove on. Now is the time for us to come together and to put out that fire.

Obama also apologized for the apparent immorality of the plan, promising that safeguards in the bailout package legislation would protect against further abuses, before once again emphasizing the urgency of passage:

> This is not a plan to just hand over $700 billion of taxpayer money to a few banks. If this is managed correctly—and that is an important "if"—we will hopefully get most or all of our money back, and possibly even turn a profit, on the Government's investment—every penny of which will go directly back to the American people. If we fall short, we will levy a fee on financial institutions so that they can repay us for the losses they caused. Now, let's acknowledge, even with all these taxpayer protections, this plan is not perfect. Democrats and Republicans in Congress have legitimate concerns about it. Some of my closest colleagues—people I have the greatest respect for—still have problems with it and may choose to vote against this bill, and I think we can respectfully disagree. I understand their frustrations. I also know many Americans share their concerns. But it is clear, from my perspective, that this is what we need to do right now to prevent a crisis from turning into a catastrophe.[20]

This language of "catastrophe" and "fire" are missing from Obama's later rhetoric about student loans, which, while sounding more moral, tend toward a sort of victim-blaming. In an online live chat with the website Tumblr in 2014, President Obama related to borrowers on an explicitly personal level, sharing his own story of student loans rather than the social urgency of forgiving these loans. He implies the irresponsibility of borrowers in the same way that Bush did in 2008.[21]

> I graduated from college in '83, graduated from law school in 1990. And although I went to a private school, through a combination of grants, loans, and working, I had a fairly low level of debt that I was able to pay in 1 year without getting an incredibly well-paying job. I was able to keep my

debt burden pretty low. Folks who were 10 years younger than me, they probably paid even less. And if you went to a State school at the time, typically people would come out with almost no debt whatsoever.

Today, the average debt burden, even for young people who are going to a public university, is about $30,000. And that gives you some sense of how much the cost has escalated for the average young person. Now, you mentioned earlier some people are wondering, is this a good investment? It absolutely is. The difference between a college grad and somebody with a high school diploma is about $28,000 a year in income. So it continues to be a very smart investment for you to go to college. But we have to find ways to do two things. One is, we have to lower the costs on the front end. And then, if you do have to supplement whatever you can pay with borrowing, we've got to make sure that that is a manageable debt. And about 12 months ago, maybe 16 months ago, I convened college and university presidents around the country to start working with them on how we could lower debt—or lower tuition, rather.

President Obama discusses some of the political causes of increased student debt, but does not call for the reversal of those policies. Obama is as skilled at explaining the causes of social and economic issues as Reagan is at relating humor, and at explaining what some of the main proposals for solutions are.

The main reason that tuition has gone up so much is that State legislatures stopped subsidizing public universities as much as they used to, in part because they started spending money on things like prisons and other activities that I think are less productive. And so schools then made up for the declining State support by jacking up their tuition rates. . . . What's also happened is, is that the costs of things like health care that a university community with a lot of personnel has—have to shoulder, those costs have gone up faster than wages and incomes. The combination of those things has made college tuition skyrocket faster than health care costs have.

Obama explained in this particular instance what some of his proposals were for reform, and what his administration's part in those proposals had been. Some of the proposals are very mild, including one called "Know What You Owe," which is relatively self-explanatory. His explanation of income-based repayments is also very straightforward. Obama's endorsement of this plan coupled with public service loan forgiveness is also a rather pithy defense of public service without being explicit:

It doesn't eliminate your debt. But what it does is it makes it manageable each month so that the career that you choose may not be constrained. And we then have additional programs so that if you go into one of the helping professions—public service, law enforcement, social work, teaching—then over time, that debt could actually be forgiven.

In mentioning the Nixonian plan of strategic federal loan forgiveness for physicians, Obama remarked:

I mean, right now we have some programs like this in place, but they're typically relatively small, relatively specialized. So there are some loan-forgiveness programs for primary care physicians who are going out to rural communities or inner cities or underserved communities. There are some programs that are available through the AmeriCorps program for people who are engaged in public service. They are not as broad based and widespread as I would like.

Obama's articulation typifies the difference in approach between the "policy necessity" and "healing" schools of thought on governmental forgiveness. One policy solution President Obama endorsed in his online question-and-answer session was the ability to "refinance" one's loans, that is, obtain a more favorable interest rate on the balance of one's loans with another lender, perhaps the state government, as Cory Mason has been promoting in Wisconsin. This is not forgiveness, but is a propping up of the existing loans. In the end, President Obama endorses more STEM and vocational education, and largely reflects the mainstream view that liberal arts college is somehow indulgent:

We do have to do a better job of giving young people who are interested an effective vocational education. And there are tons of opportunities out there for people—here's an interesting statistic: The average trade person in Wisconsin—and what I mean by that is an electrician, a plumber, a carpenter, a machine tool worker—the average age in Wisconsin is 59 years old, right? Now, these jobs typically pay 25, 30 bucks an hour, potentially, with benefits. You can make a really good living doing that, and there are a lot of folks who love doing it. It's really interesting work and highly skilled work. So I don't want somebody to find out about that when they're 30, after they've already . . . taken a bunch of classes and stuff that they ended up not using; now they've got a bunch of debt. I'd rather, if they got that inclination, to figure that early and be able to go straight into something that helps them get that job.

President Obama's solution was to promote income-based repayment for as many people as possible, and in the future, promote through existing financial aid structures increased vocational education and science and technology education, which, he said, makes people "better citizens." Considering that earlier interviewees both saw the idea of becoming a "respectable citizen" as synonymous with up-to-date debt payments, this seems a low bar of expectation to hope for. While one of the central programs of forgiveness is indeed targeted literally at "helping professions," this is not quite the "widespread" healing of forgiveness that the president endorses in the abstract. There was some limited forgiveness in his plan to promote social goods, including education and health care, but it is limited. Obama's actions were rather more like Nixon than Carter, more instrumental or policy necessity than healing.

Donald Trump was declared the winner of the presidency on November 8, 2016, in a stunning upset, as only a small minority of opinion polls pointed to his victory in the Electoral College. With a Republican Congress he has largely set policy according to his electoral mandate, which included a plan he released late in the campaign to address student debt directly.[22] It has also been coupled with Trump's critique of institutions of higher education, public and private. He is critical of public tuition increases, but also critical of endowments at elite private universities being tax-exempt. He also is deeply critical of public employees receiving a "deal" through the public service loan forgiveness program that is better than for those that work in the private sector.

Trump is also a private businessperson who has, among other ventures, profited from a for-profit university before it went defunct. Trump University's failure ultimately resulted in a $25 million class action lawsuit for students to recover their costs.[23] In the first two years of his presidency, his Justice Department has begun to erode protections and programs passed during the Bush and Obama administrations meant to mitigate the effects of undischargeable debt.

Bernie Sanders is on the other side. He has spent his career in public service, before that getting arrested in protests, and throughout it all, advocating for the causes of marginalized people.[24] Bernie Sanders did not create the demand for free public higher education, just as Donald Trump did not create the profit opportunities in higher education. Both, however, are the principal spokespeople for the positions of respective classes that have different goals surrounding higher education. How they prioritize public policy surrounding student debt is an excellent representation of how each class interest differs fundamentally in its orientation toward this issue. In their representations, both serve as convenient polarized archetypes for the types of approaches they champion. For Trump: cut the regulation of and public funding of higher education, believing that perhaps the sector itself, functioning as primarily private entities, will begin to reflect the priorities of investors rather than the ideals of citizenship; and for Sanders: fully fund public higher education in hopes of preserving those ideals and even strengthening them.

In a 2016 campaign speech, Trump portrays the drag on the economy caused by a generation of people being out of work and financially paralyzed:

> The share of 16- to 28-year-olds not in the labor force has increased to 45 percent during the Obama administration. . . . Students should not be asked to pay more on their loans than they can afford, and the debt should not be an albatross around their necks for the rest of their lives. . . . That is why under my student loan program, we would cap repayment to an affordable portion of a borrower's income—12.5%. And if borrowers work hard and make their full payments for 15 years, we will let them get on with their lives. Every American deserves the same deal, so we will equalize treatment so everyone can start saving for their families and retirement by the time they are 15 years out of college.

Trump had quite a bit more to say about the administration of higher education in the United States, much of it echoing rhetoric that left-leaning critics have levied at private institutions:

> In addition, I will take steps to push colleges to cut the skyrocketing cost of tuition. If the federal government is going to subsidize student loans, it has a right to expect that colleges work hard to control costs and invest their resources in their students. . . . If colleges refuse to take this responsibility seriously, they will be held accountable—including by reconsidering whether those with huge endowments deserve to keep those endowments tax-exempt. . . . . Some schools are paying more to hedge funds and private equity managers than they are spending on tuition assistance—while taxpayers are guaranteeing hundreds of billions of dollars of student loans to pay for rising tuition.

However, Trump ventures into more familiar right-wing territory when he begins to talk about "bureaucrats," administrators of federal regulations in higher education:

> Much of the skyrocketing cost of college education is due to the tremendous bloat in college administrators and bureaucrats. According to the Department of Education, the number of college administrators is up more than 60 percent since 1993—ten times the increase in tenured faculty positions. . . . Federal regulations are responsible for much of this administrative bloat. Vanderbilt University estimated that it spends $150 million per year—11 percent of the university's budget—to comply with government regulations. As president, I will immediately take steps to drive down college costs by reducing the unnecessary costs of compliance with federal regulations so that colleges can pass on the savings to students in the form of lower tuition.

Finally, Trump's call for simplicity is one that may be said to call for national healing, but insofar as his main policy objective is restoration of economic standing, student loan forgiveness is a policy necessity:

> There is a lot of room for improvement in this regard. Currently, students navigate 16 complex repayment plans, 8 forgiveness programs, and 32 deferment and forbearance options—each of these programs has their own nuances and qualifications. I will simplify this confusing maze into a single Income-Based Repayment Program, similar to those that have proved so popular in recent years. We also have to make sure that those who have graduated college and those who are soon to graduate can find a good job to start a good career when they do.

Trump follows Obama's reforms that privilege the "helping professions," Sanders's call for tuition-free public higher education, and Clinton's debt-free higher education with a call for a cheaper tuition and a better deal on loans and regulation cuts. He contends that this will lead to higher employment and economic growth, and ultimately less student debt. No doubt Trump and his advisors agreed that this was a rhetorical opening because so much discord was evident in Clinton's plan for "debt-free college" with not much to address existing student debt, at least not prominently. It also was an issue with deep resonance with millennials, who are struggling with debt as they begin their careers. The pressure from below exists to force some kind of political action, but the question is what kind of action, and what that action does to advance the common goods of democracy and education.

None of what Trump proposed in this speech on behalf of student borrowers has been realized in his administration. Instead, his secretary of education has slowed the rate at which forgiveness will be granted to students of fraudulent for-profit universities. Meanwhile, several of the activists, experts, and public officials interviewed earlier in the book have thoughts about some of the prospects, both short-term and long-term, for large-scale forgiveness, or an alternative. Several have thoughts about how student debt has affected, and will affect, American democracy.

Chris Hicks, labor and student organizer, describes the kind of direct impact student debt has on average working people he has encountered in working for labor unions and public interest organizations, and has championed programs that familiarize union members who also may be borrowers under existing government programs.

> *Interviewer:* It's plain to me that you are the person doing a huge amount of advocacy surrounding student debt in the labor movement. Can you talk about what you're doing to enroll people who are eligible in the two large debt forgiveness programs that exist?

Hicks: One of the things I spent a lot of time on in my role as the Debt-Free Future campaign organizer was developing trainings on student loan issues, particularly income-based repayment and public service loan forgiveness for union members, people who graduated from college and are now working for the government or a 501(c) (3) organization. What we know about those two programs in particular is there are twice as many people in default as are in those two programs combined. On top of that, 700,000 people are falling out every year. Even though we have terribly low numbers of people actually participating in these programs, every year about a fourth of them lose that benefit until the following year when they're able to reapply again. [Loan servicers] are getting paid very well to do this very simple task of saying here are the different repayment plans or you will lose that benefit, and you'll have to recertify eleven months later, and they're just falling down on the job. The Department of Education is not doing anything to hold these servicers accountable. And if you look at something like loan forgiveness, what we know is that there's 34 million public service workers and public service was defined by Congress as incredibly broad, as someone who works for the government, or a 501(c)(3), and a few other types of public service work, as long as you're not proselytizing. Out of 34 million actually eligible borrowers that could be enrolled in this program, there are currently less than 300,000 enrolled, less than 1 percent. It actually gets worse when you look at who's eligible and who is being recertified.

Interviewer: Can you walk us through what happens when you run one of these programs in your capacity as an organizer?

Hicks: We have an hour and a half presentation on all of the options: IBR, PSLF, we do a Q&A, we tell people different ways they can get involved, because we know that there's a relationship between how much they owe and how much they're paid. I could go out to a random worksite, all those unions that I named have public sector workers that they represent, and so we know everyone in the room with federal student debt could be taking advantage of both IBR and PSLF. They'll pay maybe a tenth of [what they were paying].

One thing that could make this even better (and this is something I've worked with a handful of people on) is workers covered by collective bargaining agreements can actually bargain for student-debt reimbursement. Just like when we contract to carry tuition reimbursement for someone who currently works for an employer and they're continuing education, they're spending up to $2,000 a year for tuition reimbursement, we've expanded that negotiation to cover previous education. One example of this is the Denver classroom teachers' associations, which has an agreement with the Denver public school systems, we actually negotiated that for the first four years you work for Denver public schools, they will give you $2,000 per year for your student debt, as long as you can show you actually have that kind of debt. It just requires that you hand them your student debt bill. There are ways to maximize those programs even further. It's a way for schools to increase some teachers' salary without having to formulate it in that way.

Hicks's program of signing people up for student debt forgiveness programs facilitated by labor union membership is a strategy with which he has enjoyed a lot of success, but that success is clearly endangered in that the programs themselves are endangered, as are public sector labor unions with the recent *Janus v. AFSCME* decision that deprives labor unions of major resources.[25] However, his strategy of seeking to incorporate widespread debt forgiveness as a potential benefit within collective bargaining agreements where high densities of borrowers exist is a potential future that seems promising.

Jake Virden, a social activist and community organizer who has provided his own background to his involvement with the student debt issue, offers an assessment of prospects for change for debtors.

> *Interviewer:* In relation to student debt, are labor unions or labor support organizations helpful around the kind of organizing you've been doing?
>
> *Virden:* I haven't really interacted with them too much on the issue, but as far as unions who actually respond to the lives of their workers, they could potentially be really useful. I wonder if teachers' unions would be. A lot of people think they are kind of bureaucratic, lined up behind standard Democratic policy positions, so I don't see them as natural allies, but maybe.
>
> *Interviewer:* What do you think of the public policy solution of making bankruptcy available at all to people with student loans?
>
> *Virden:* Would bankruptcy help? I'm for it. Bankruptcy still puts the fault on the students. Most of us were 18, 19, 20 years old. Most of us were not on equal terms with the people we were negotiating with, so bankruptcy seems like a crumb, so it doesn't satisfy my issue, but I would definitely take it.

Virden seems at least somewhat in favor of action by labor unions and the idea of bankruptcy for some borrowers who need it. In the context of bankruptcy as a solution, he also reminds the reader of the age at which many borrowers began to consider the prospect of student loans, the same age at which other costs increase like housing and auto insurance. This all falls short, however, of his ultimate demand of widespread debt forgiveness, which again seems as radical as it seems necessary to those who are demanding it.

Other organizers interviewed here have much the same orientation, and they are listening to the needs of those they organize.

Alexis Goldstein gives some closing commentary on the need to make up some of the democracy deficit that has occurred over the course of the last political generation. Goldstein charitably answers a tough interview question by calling attention to some of the practical facts and prospects in the current political moment.

Interviewer: Why is fully funding public higher education a solution to the student debt crisis?

Goldstein: We are in the position that we are in because of ongoing disinvestment in education. I think it's part of a larger cultural shift and media narrative that's been happening, probably since Ronald Reagan, that government is, not only not a force for good, but is a force for evil. That's the sort of right-wing position. The left-wing position is okay, well, let's defund government, but we'll do it a little bit softer, and a little bit slower, and a little bit gentler, but the private market knows best. First of all, I disagree with that. I think that government can be a force for good. I think higher education is something we should provide the citizens and residents of this country with.

> The Federal Reserve has warned about the size of the outstanding student debt and has said that it's a risk to the economy. These are the people whose job it is to make sure that the economy continues to move and function.

> I do think that how we fix it going back in time is a trickier question. There are certainly people that either have examined, or are examining what would it take, what would a complete jubilee look like? I have tended to focus in on more of the microcosm of Corinthian because it's not really about does it make sense or not make sense from a fiscal perspective? The law is the law.

Interviewer: There's a couple of articles that I've seen on this that people have actually written pretty recently.

Goldstein: I do think the prospective solution is not as expensive as people think, especially when you take into account how much money we're currently spending on for-profit schools. Now, it's not a one-for-one. If we ended all of the federal funding and federal loans going to for-profit schools, we wouldn't have enough right away to fund all two- and four-year public institutions. It's something like $8.6 billion, if I recall correctly. It's in the range of $8–$9 billion that we are, essentially, just handing over to for-profit schools. Strike Debt has this whole proposal called How Far to Free; it's based on the work of Bob Samuels, who has a whole book about this.[26] Essentially, what they did in their white paper is get rid of the tax incentives that exist, right? Right now, you can write off the credit interest on your student loans, and they thought: What if we get rid of that? Let's get rid of any grants to for-profit schools. Then reallocate it to free public higher education, and then you're basically $15 billion a year short, so it's just a matter of raising that.

Goldstein's assessment that tuition-free higher education is the most constructive, future-facing solution to the debt crisis that we currently have available, and that it is not without historical precedent, must certainly be good news for those interviewed here such as Adolph Reed that have long campaigned for it. As far as existing debt, in addition to the income-based repayment programs, there is also the refinancing solution that Cory Mason has proposed in Wisconsin. Mason was able to directly address a question about how student debt may have an impact, positive or negative, on American democracy overall.

> *Mason:* I would look at democracy very broadly in terms of how democracy has worked in this country for a couple hundred years. I think [the student loan crisis] threatens democracy and political action in a couple different ways, and you sort of see it playing out in the tone of the presidential race. We've had so many people in the middle class who work hard and play by the rules but still can't make ends meet economically. It has an effect that people start to lose faith in the system, and you see aberrations like a Trump candidacy appear with all of this jingoism and anti-Muslim, anti-immigrant rhetoric. I think when you have that much student loan debt it really has a deforming effect on our economy, and by extension, our democracy. I think part of the reason our democracy has worked so well for so long is because we've had at least two really strong institutions that helped hold it up and expanded, and that's a strong middle class and access to higher education, where the Enlightenment principles that helped found this country were built into the DNA of this country. Colleges and universities would help bring reason and wisdom to public dialogue. When access to that higher education community becomes so much more expensive and so much more inaccessible, I think that, too, has a negative impact on our democracy. I think if you threaten either of those, I think it threatens democracy. To threaten them both in the long-term, I think the consequences would be disastrous.

The current state of affairs seems to have a negative impact on democracy. Limited choices will severely impact citizens' political attitudes and actions, and ultimately what they convey to future generations of citizens. President Trump's program will not include public service loan forgiveness, and his administration may move to eliminate the program. This would certainly produce more alienation from the political system as well as the economic system in the years to come, if this particular social contract is breached on such a large scale.

If Trump's earlier pledge to eliminate the Department of Education and get the government "out of the student loan business" is fulfilled, students may need to take out private loans to attend universities to achieve their educational goals. If a democratically elected legislature is not distributing collected government tax revenues and directing them to public higher education and Pell Grants, then it is an open question who will finance our socially compulsory higher education, which presidents have endorsed an expansion of vocational education to help solve.

California, which educates 25 percent of American community college students, has seen most class enrollments rise to between 40 and 50 students per section, and there is a major push to shift many courses to online course delivery, particularly since the passage of an online-only, statewide community college that the faculty opposed.[27] If the prospect of high-risk debt with no public assistance contributes to a decline in demand for higher education, there will be further budget cuts and a professoriate squeezed and cowed by the prospect of dismissal from institutions that fear the presence of social critics that could cost them tuition dollars. Higher education will have no impact on citizenship at all. At the moment, the prospect of large-scale debt forgiveness of the $1.5 trillion of student loan debt held by Americans seems a distant hope, overshadowed instead by the $1.5 trillion tax cut passed by Congress in December 2017.[28]

If no effective plan or program emerges as a result of a deadlock between Congress and the presidency, there could be greater default rates, especially in future recessions that yield high unemployment. It could be a facet of a Greece or Spain scenario, with 50 percent youth unemployment rates coupled with high national debts and internationally mandated austerity programs.[29] Trump alluded to a statistic that sounds similar to this, asserting that 45 percent of youth are not in the labor force.[30]

If not even a minimal bankruptcy reform occurs, then the political economy of the United States does not adequately account for a generation of future employment and growth prospects. The political power of the generation is sufficiently fragmented to be able to play upon as many divisions as is traditionally the case, but the future may not be bright if attention is not paid to their material interests. A bare minimum of policy solutions must address the prospect of widespread indebtedness that has the legal power to forgive all debt, the crisis of public higher education funding, and the subsidies to for-profit institutions. Attempts to "do the right thing" in work toward a higher education degree comes with a high price. The generation of voters who see their concerns addressed adequately and convincingly by a party leader will support that party at the polls. The party that fails to do so will be stuck in the political wilderness. If no party addresses their concerns, this could result in a long-term pattern of declining voting, mass alienation, and a failed democracy with a political system unresponsive to the majority of voters.

The American Dream of homeownership and social mobility is a fading ideology, but the betrayal and abandonment of a generation assuredly will not be forgotten. Massive alienation has staying power. It is incumbent upon political analysis to realize the meaning and the importance of how student debt feeds that existing power dynamic. Now is the opportunity for real change with assistance from democratically elected political structures, institutions, and focused popular demand.

Notes

Introduction

1. http://www.carolhanisch.org/CHwritings/PIP.html, accessed July 17, 2018.

2. https://www.cnbc.com/2018/02/15/heres-how-much-the-average-student -loan-borrower-owes-when-they-graduate.html, accessed January 2, 2019.

3. https://www.newyorkfed.org/medialibrary/media/press/PressBriefing-Ho usehold-Student-Debt-April32017.pdf, accessed August 20, 2018.

4. An important recent work of history is Cornell University historian Louis Hyman's *Temp: How American Work, American Business, and the American Dream Became Temporary* (Penguin Publishing Group, 2018). Hyman focuses on the economy-wide transition to contingent labor since the 1970s, but in doing so, confronts and defines the idea of the "American Dream."

5. https://www.ed.gov/stem, accessed July 31, 2018.

6. https://www.americanprogress.org/issues/education-k-12/reports/2018 /02/21/446857/state-civics-education/, accessed July 31, 2018.

7. https://www.jacobinmag.com/2015/11/case-deaton-study-death-rate-health -care/, accessed July 31, 2018.

8. https://www.commondreams.org/views/2016/08/11/battle-over-trumps -taj-mahal-battle-us-all, accessed July 31, 2018. Author Adolph Reed character- izing the forces of reaction, the motivation behind the destruction of the welfare state and the safety net: "it stems from a desire to eliminate any organized expressions of workers' power, to clear the way to realizing the other objective: creation of a world in which we would have no alternative other than to accept work on whatever terms employers choose to offer it. That, of course, would be employers' utopia and workers' hell."

9. https://www.forbes.com/sites/jeffreydorfman/2018/05/10/student-loan -debt-hits-record-high-and-thats-good/#52c0f0f91bf9, accessed July 31, 2018.

10. Joel Best and Eric Best, *The Student Loan Mess: How Good Intentions Created a Trillion-Dollar Problem* (Berkeley: University of California Press, 2014); Alan Collinge, *The Student Loan Scam: The Most Oppressive Debt in U.S. History, and How We Can Fight Back* (Boston: Beacon Press, 2009); Bill Zimmerman, *The*

Student Loan Swindle: Why It Happened—Who Is to Blame—How the Victims Can Be Saved (Seattle: CreateSpace Publishing, 2014).

11. https://ticas.org/sites/default/files/pub_files/cdr_nr_sept_27.pdf, accessed October 11, 2017.

12. Further, this author is not even the first to reference the song in relation to the current crisis, as noted publications from British standard newspaper *The Guardian* (https://www.theguardian.com/money/us-money-blog/2013/mar/19/studen-loan-debt-providers-soul, accessed October 1, 2017) to the Phi Beta Kappa honor society publication *The American Scholar* (https://theamerican scholar.org/federal-student-loan-sharks/, accessed October 1, 2017), among other less significant online publications, have made editorial references to the song's concept as a metaphor and even guide to understanding the student loan debt crisis. There is not a much better barometer of modern popular culture than online Wikipedia entries. While it is perhaps not a scholarly resource per se, here is a sampling, thanks to Wikipedia (http://en.wikipedia.org/wiki/Sixteen _Tons, accessed March 27, 2015), of those who have covered the song "Sixteen Tons" as a symbol of downtrodden American workers generally: Dennis Kucinich, Tom Morello, Rockapella, B.B. King, LeAnn Rimes, Johnny Cash, ZZ Top. It has also been featured on the iconic television shows *The Simpsons, The Wire, The Big Bang Theory, Mad Men*, and the Tom Hanks film *Joe Versus the Volcano*, all as a reference to laborious workplace drudgery. Another author that has apparently used this metaphor is noted sociologist Tressie McMillan Cottom on her blog, wherein she also makes reference to the work of Douglas Edwards: https://tressiemc.com/uncategorized/marxism-student-loan-debt-and -alienation-of-labor/, accessed October 1, 2017. McMillan Cottom also authored a primary text on for-profit universities, *Lower Ed: The Troubling Rise of For-Profit Colleges in the New Economy* (New York: New Press, 2017). An excellent interview in which McMillan Cottom outlines the argument of her work can be found here: https://www.npr.org/2017/03/27/521371034/how-for-profit-colleges -sell-risky-education-to-the-most-vulnerable, accessed August 20, 2018.

13. In the early '50's, Tennessee Ernie Ford made a hit out of "Sixteen Tons," a song that was a pure economic determinist account of the reality of coal mining life, but nobody took it seriously. At that point in time, American song hits were generally written for someone else to sing and not sung by the man who wrote them." Ralph J. Gleason, "The Greater Sound" in The Drama Review: TDR Vol. 13, No. 4, Politics and Performance (Summer, 1969), pp. 160–166.

14. One exchange on Doug Henwood's blog (https://lbo-news.com/2012 /11/15/the-debt-obsession/, accessed October 1, 2017) by a commenter with the pseudonym "Anarcissie" makes the point while discussing David Graeber's Occupy-era book on debt: "We could all read Graeber's Debt (again?) and remember how central it has been to our way of conducting our political and social lives. I take it buying up and canceling debts is meant to remind us of the buying and freeing of slaves, one by one, before the Civil War, and I fear it will be about as effective. But someone has to do something. Too many people owe their souls to the company store."

15. Price V. Fishback's tome on the subject, *Soft Coal, Hard Choices: The Economic Welfare of Bituminous Coal Miners, 1890-1930* (Oxford: Oxford University Press, 1992) is worth mentioning here for its thorough treatment of the truck system.

16. https://fred.stlouisfed.org/series/SLOAS, accessed October 11, 2017.

17. https://www.nytimes.com/2017/05/17/business/dealbook/household-debt-united-states.html?_r=0, accessed October 11, 2017; http://www.pewresearch.org/fact-tank/2017/08/17/5-facts-about-the-national-debt-what-you-should-know/, accessed October 11, 2017.

18. https://www.newyorkfed.org/studentloandebt/index.html, accessed October 11, 2017; https://ticas.org/sites/default/files/pub_files/cdr_nr_sept_27.pdf, accessed October 11, 2017.

19. http://www.pewresearch.org/fact-tank/2017/08/24/5-facts-about-student-loans/, accessed October 11, 2017.

20. https://www.fool.com/retirement/2017/06/25/the-average-american-has-this-much-student-loan-de.aspx, accessed October 11, 2017.

21. https://www.usatoday.com/story/money/personalfinance/2017/04/28/average-student-loan-debt-every-state/100893668/, accessed October 11, 2017.

22. http://www.pewresearch.org/fact-tank/2015/03/19/how-millennials-compare-with-their-grandparents/, accessed October 11, 2017; https://www.usatoday.com/story/money/personalfinance/2017/04/28/average-student-loan-debt-every-state/100893668/, accessed October 11, 2017.

23. https://www.usnews.com/news/articles/2014/08/07/having-high-levels-of-student-loan-debt-can-hurt-your-health-too, accessed October 11, 2017; https://www.nar.realtor/sites/default/files/documents/2017-student-loan-debt-and-housing-09-26-2017.pdf, accessed January 1, 2019; https://www.cnbc.com/2017/10/10/americans-are-more-terrified-of-student-debt-than-north-koreas-kim-jong-un.html, accessed October 11, 2017; https://www.axios.com/millennials-debt-biggest-daily-concern-poll-274c0573-180e-471b-9639-d47605ded341.html.

24. https://www.theatlantic.com/business/archive/2015/06/millennials-student-loan-debt-money/396275/, accessed October 11, 2017.

25. http://www.ajc.com/business/consumer-advice/more-americans-want-forgive-trillion-dollar-student-loan-debt-than-want-repaid/wI5xkXb3sgjANCuhEzg6hO/, accessed October 11, 2017.

26. https://www.cnbc.com/2014/07/06/student-loan-forgiveness-may-be-coming-in-the-future.html?view=story&percent24DEVICEpercent24=native-android-tablet, accessed October 11, 2017.

27. http://www.npr.org/sections/ed/2017/07/16/536488351/teachers-with-student-debt-the-struggle-the-causes-and-what-comes-next, accessed October 11, 2017.

28. http://rollingjubilee.org/, accessed October 11, 2017.

29. http://www.businessinsider.com/millennials-regret-student-loans-2016-4, accessed October 11, 2017.

30. https://www.huffingtonpost.com/roger-hickey/student-debt-jubilee_b_913 4632.html, accessed October 11, 2017; https://www.huffingtonpost.com/maria -mayo/forgive-us-our-student-loan-debts_b_1564098.html, accessed October 11, 2017.

31. http://www.apa.org/gradpsych/2013/01/debt.aspx, accessed October 11, 2017.

32. http://www.uscourts.gov/services-forms/bankruptcy/bankruptcy-basics /discharge-bankruptcy-bankruptcy-basics, accessed July 4, 2017.

33. http://www.studentloanborrowerassistance.org/bankruptcy/,   accessed July 4, 2017.

34. To the extent it is happening in state legislatures, here is a synopsis of the various refinancing programs being proposed: http://www.ncsl.org/blog/2015 /11/09/states-moving-to-help-refinance-student-loans.aspx; Congress also has a number of bills that have been proposed that have seen no action taken. See the legislative database page here in a search on "student loan" conducted on and accessed July 4, 2017: https://www.congress.gov/search?searchResultViewType =expanded&q={percent22congresspercent22:percent22115percent22,percent 22sourcepercent22:percent22legislationpercent22,percent22searchpercent22: percent22\percent22student+loan\percent22percent22,percent22bill-statusperc ent22:percent22floorpercent22}.

35. For a succinct summary of his life and work, visit https://www.britannica .com/biography/Thomas-Malthus, accessed July 4, 2017.

36. For the evolution of thinking about federal representation in the United States, see the official version of history at https://history.house.gov/Historical -Highlights/1901-1950/The-Permanent-Apportionment-Act-of-1929/, accessed January 1, 2019.

37. See campaign finance scholar's latest work at http://digitalcommons.law .utulsa.edu/cgi/viewcontent.cgi?article=3072&context=tlr for a summary of the current state of campaign finance regulation, accessed July 4, 2017. For an exploration of the impact of campaign finance on the electoral cycle, here is a good summary of some recent research: https://www.nytimes.com/roomfordebate/2016 /02/25/does-money-really-matter-in-politics/campaign-fund-raising-is-an-arms -race-with-limited-impact, accessed October 11, 2017.

38. Isaac William Martin, *The Permanent Tax Revolt: How the Property Tax Transformed American Politics* (Stanford: Stanford University Press, 2008).

39. http://fusion.net/story/291271/student-debt-arrests-houston/,   accessed July 4, 2017.

40. Timothy Bewes, *Reification or the Anxiety of Late Capitalism* (London and New York: Verso Books, 2002).

41. Adam Seth Levine, *American Insecurity: Why Our Economic Fears Lead to Political Inaction* (Princeton: Princeton University Press, 2015).

42. https://www.cnbc.com/2018/07/20/1-in-3-millennial-homeowners-get -money-to-buy-from-retirement-funds.html, accessed July 24, 2018.

43. David A. Graeber, *Debt: The First 5,000 Years* (New York: Melville House, 2012).

44. https://www.newamerica.org/education-policy/policy-explainers/higher
-ed-workforce/federal-student-aid/federal-student-loans/federal-student-loan
-history/, accessed July 11, 2017.

45. https://www.brookings.edu/blog/brown-center-chalkboard/2017
/01/11/how-much-do-for-profit-colleges-rely-on-federal-funds/, accessed July 11,
2017.

46. http://www.epi.org/publication/manufacturing-job-loss-trade-not-produc
tivity-is-the-culprit/, accessed July 11, 2017.

47. http://www.epi.org/press/6-4-million-americans-are-working-involuntarily
-part-time-employers-are-shifting-toward-part-time-work-as-a-new-normal/,
accessed July 11, 2017. Also see https://www.theatlantic.com/business/archive
/2015/05/the-new-normal-for-young-workers/393560/, accessed July 11, 2017, and
https://www.newyorkfed.org/medialibrary/media/research/current_issues/ci20-1
.pdf, accessed July 11, 2017.

48. Arne L. Kalleberg, *Good Jobs, Bad Jobs: The Rise of Polarized and Precarious
Employment Systems in the United States, 1970s to 2000s* (New York: Russell Sage,
2011).

49. https://cew.georgetown.edu/wp-content/uploads/2014/11/Recovery2020
.ES_.Web_.pdf, accessed July 11, 2017.

50. https://www.chronicle.com/article/The-Day-the-Purpose-of-College/151
359?key=JGcpOdN1K0OGKPwPgpF9yOfqN7ILfTlMdoCfM-GQIa0DMf_6W
-RtaNV4lhs_0OhoMW85TXNwQkZNNDRXM1M4emFQekhnbXFMMmx4NX
QzalVpOHF4QlZKMTFIMA, accessed July 30, 2018.

51. https://www.washingtonpost.com/news/answer-sheet/wp/2018/03/21/uni
versity-of-wisconsin-campus-pushes-plan-to-drop-13-majors-including-english-
history-and-philosophy/?noredirect=on&utm_term=.db923ab6abbf, accessed July
24, 2018.

52. https://www.insidehighered.com/news/2014/01/31/obama-becomes-latest
-politician-criticize-liberal-arts-discipline, accessed February 23, 2019.

53. http://www.politico.com/story/2014/02/president-obama-apologizes-to-art
-history-professor-103626, accessed July 12, 2017; https://www.nytimes.com/2015
/02/16/opinion/save-the-wisconsin-idea.html, accessed July 12, 2017.

54. http://news.stanford.edu/2015/03/06/higher-ed-hoxby-030615/, accessed
July 12, 2017. For a good representation of the kind of vocabulary being increasingly utilized on campus (such as "ROI"), read Larry Goldstein, *College & University Budgeting: An Introduction for Faculty and Academic Administrators* (4th ed.)
(New York: National Association of College & University Business Officers,
2012). In this book, Goldstein, himself a former officer of his publisher's association, is informing and thus influencing novice administrators and faculty department chairs to speak the language of business, rather than the reverse. It is a
widely popular title, and Goldstein himself is a widely hired consultant whose
job is to help institutions implement this very framework.

55. http://www.reuters.com/article/us-column-weston-enrollment-idUSKCN0
HV1AE20141006, accessed July 12, 2017; http://money.cnn.com/2017/05/11/pf
/college/tennessee-free-community-college/index.html, accessed July 12, 2017;

https://www.washingtonpost.com/news/grade-point/wp/2016/07/12/a-year
-after-sweet-briar-was-saved-from-closing-school-leaders-celebrate-fundraising
-growth/?utm_term=.75385b2c5e33, accesssed July 12, 2017; https://www.inside
highered.com/news/2017/04/10/new-york-state-reaches-deal-provide-free
-tuition-suny-and-cuny-students, accessed July 12, 2017.

56. http://fortune.com/2015/09/22/utica-college-tuition-cut/, accessed July
12, 2017; http://www.businessinsider.com/congrats-you-got-into-the-school-of
-your-dreams-now-its-time-to-think-about-how-to-pay-for-it-2015-4, accessed
July 12, 2017; http://www.kiplinger.com/slideshow/college/T014-S003-colleges
-that-won-t-make-you-take-student-loans/index.html, accessed July 12, 2017.

57. http://libertystreeteconomics.newyorkfed.org/2017/04/diplomas-to
-doorsteps-education-student-debt-and-homeownership.html, accessed July 12,
2017.

58. https://www.federalreserve.gov/econresdata/feds/2016/files/2016010pap
.pdf, accessed July 12, 2017.

59. The Institute on College Access & Success Project on Student Debt.

60. https://lbo-news.com/2012/01/29/reflections-on-the-current-disorder/,
accessed July 12, 2017.

61. http://www.businessinsider.com/millennial-homeownership-lower-2017-6,
accessed July 12, 2017. One recent conference specifically addressing this point
is explained here: http://www.deansatdepauw.com/2017/04/depauw-university
-liberal-arts-and-global-citizenship-conference-a-portal-to-the-world-in-green
castle/, accessed July 12, 2017.

62. https://www.bostonglobe.com/opinion/2014/02/25/popping-higher-edu
cation-bubble/VrtQjf8cilYd1tvKfoN4CO/story.html, accessed July 12, 2017.

63. See Jeffrey M. Hornstein, *A Nation of Realtors: A Cultural History of the
Twentieth Century American Middle Class* (Durham, NC: Duke University Press,
2005) for a recounting of Richard T. Ely's explicit introduction of John Locke's
political theory of property into the shaping of federal homeownership policy in
the early 1900s.

64. https://www.theguardian.com/commentisfree/2013/sep/23/freshers-failed
-experiment-higher-education, accessed July 12, 2017.

65. https://www.bizjournals.com/phoenix/blog/business/2015/03/living-under
water-phoenix-arizona-among-worst-in.html, accessed July 12, 2017.

66. https://www.aaup.org/sites/default/files/files/2014%20salary%20report/zre
port_0.pdf, accessed January 1, 2019. According to https://www.heri.ucla.edu
/monographs/TheAmericanFreshman2016.pdf, accessed July 12, 2017, 48 percent of first-year students agree that developing that meaningful philosophy of life
is a priority, but 82 percent consider being very well-off financially the priority. In
1967, one of the first years of this survey, the reverse was true: 40 percent of first-
year students at coeducational nonsectarian institutions (and, it should be
said, roughly the same percentage in every category of college or university) considered being very well-off financially a primary consideration, and 87 percent
considered developing a meaningful philosophy of life a priority (and it was
90 percent in some categories of colleges): https://www.heri.ucla.edu/PDFs/pubs

/TFS/Norms/Monographs/NationalNormsForEnteringCollegeFreshmen1967.pdf, accessed July 12, 2017.

67. https://www.psychologytoday.com/us/blog/hide-and-seek/201205/our-hierarchy-needs, accessed July 24, 2018.

68. http://washingtonmonthly.com/magazine/septoct-2014/why-are-harvard-grads-still-flocking-to-wall-street/, accessed July 12, 2017, and https://www.thenation.com/article/universities-are-becoming-billion-dollar-hedge-funds-with-schools-attached/, accessed July 12, 2017.

69. http://www.aacsb.edu/knowledge/resources/indexes/donors, accessed July 13, 2017.

70. http://www.latimes.com/local/education/la-essential-education-updates-southern-uc-regents-approve-first-ever-limit-on-1495123220-htmlstory.html, accessed July 13, 2017.

71. https://www.forbes.com/sites/nickmorrison/2016/08/09/if-theres-one-thing-millennials-regret-its-going-to-college/#6925aff13536, accessed July 13, 2017.

72. https://www.moodys.com/research/Moodys-downgrades-University-of-California-to-Aa2-and-assigns-Aa2--PR_294817, accessed July 13, 2017.

73. https://www.washingtonpost.com/news/grade-point/wp/2016/09/01/moodys-warns-that-graduate-student-unions-could-hurt-private-universities-but-not-the-ones-you-might-think/?utm_term=.1df9708e02d0, accessed July 13, 2017.

74. For example, there is the Student Loan Lawyer at http://thestudentloanlawyer.com/ and the Boston Student Loan Lawyer at http://bostonstudentloanlawyer.com/, both accessed July 13, 2017. Also see the National Consumer Law Center's Student Loan Borrower Assistance program at http://www.studentloanborrowerassistance.org/, accessed July 13, 2017.

75. For official information from the Department of Education, https://studentaid.ed.gov/sa/repay-loans/forgiveness-cancellation/public-service, accessed July 13, 2017, and https://studentaid.ed.gov/sa/repay-loans/understand/plans/income-driven, also accessed July 13, 2017.

76. http://www.slate.com/articles/business/moneybox/2014/04/income_share_agreements_instead_of_taking_out_loans_students_sell_stock.html, accessed July 13, 2017. A critique from the American Association of University Professors can be found here: https://academeblog.org/2014/04/22/a-new-far-right-proposal-for-financing-college-innovatively-or-how-to-graduate-from-college-as-an-indentured-corporate-servant/, accessed July 13, 2017.

77. https://www.insidehighered.com/blogs/just-visiting/battle-liu-brooklyn-whose-university-it-anyway is one faculty member's analysis of the situation, accessed July 13, 2017.

78. http://www.huffingtonpost.com/davidhalperin/a-dubious-benefit-big-emp_b_10185936.html, accessed July 13, 2017.

79. https://lendedu.com/blog/june-student-loan-political-survey/, accessed July 13, 2017.

80. Some media outlets are beginning to ask this question, such as CNBC: http://www.cnbc.com/2015/12/08/the-long-term-consequences-of-student-loans.html, accessed July 13, 2017, and US News: https://www.usnews.com

/education/blogs/student-loan-ranger/articles/2016-01-20/study-student-loan
-borrowers-delaying-other-life-decisions, accessed July 13, 2017.

81. https://www.washingtonpost.com/news/grade-point/wp/2016/12/20/the
-disturbing-trend-of-people-losing-social-security-benefits-to-student-debt
/?utm_term=.8433f4d0e413, accessed July 13, 2017.

82. https://www.forbes.com/sites/robertfarrington/2014/07/14/parents-stop-tak
ing-out-loans-for-your-childs-college-education/#4503889b60a6, accessed July 13,
2017.

83. http://time.com/10577/student-loans-are-ruining-your-life-now-theyre-ruin
ing-the-economy-too/, accessed July 13, 2017.

84. http://debtorsanonymous.org/about-da/, accessed July 13, 2017, and https://
www.consumerfinance.gov/ask-cfpb/category-student-loans/, accessed July 13, 2017.

85. http://strikedebt.org/, accessed July 13, 2017, and the Debt Collective is at
https://debtcollective.org/, accessed July 13, 2017.

86. https://higherednotdebt.org/, accessed July 13, 2017.

87. From Elizabeth Warren, her statement on student loans as government
revenue: https://www.warren.senate.gov/?p=press_release&id=454, accessed
July 13, 2017.

88. For this point, see David Halperin's exhaustive reporting on the subject in
his book, *Stealing America's Future: How For-Profit Colleges Scam Taxpayers and
Ruin Students' Lives* (Washington, DC: Republicreport.org, 2014).

89. Actually, one is a textbook that has at least two editions: Peregrine
Schwartz-Shea and Dvora Yanow, *Interpretive Research Design Concepts and Pro-
cesses* (New York: Routledge, 2012); the other is a reader, drawing together work
on various aspects of interpretive research design from a diverse array of scholars: Dvora Yanow and Peregrine Schwartz-Shea, *Interpretation and Method:
Empirical Research Methods and the Interpretive Turn* (M. E. Sharpe, 2006; Pro-
Quest Ebook Central).

90. The story behind their Methods Cafe, practiced annually at both the
Western Political Science Association and American Political Science Association annual meetings, is chronicled here: D. Yanow and P. Schwartz-Shea, "The
Methods Cafe: An Innovative Idea for Methods Teaching at Conference Meetings," *PS: Political Science Politics* 40, no. 2 (2007): 383–386.

91. Schwartz-Shea, Peregrine, and Samantha Majic. "Introduction." *PS: Politi-
cal Science & Politics* 50, no. 1 (2017): 97–102. The title of the symposium is
"Ethnography and Participant Observation: Political Science Research in this
'Late Methodological Moment.'"

92. Yanow and Schwartz-Shea, *Interpretation and Method.*

93. James M. Curry, "In-Depth Qualitative Research and the Study of American Political Institutions," *PS: Political Science & Politics* 50, no. 1 (2017): 114–20.

94. Matthew Lange, *Comparative-Historical Methods* (Los Angeles: SAGE,
2013), 14–20.

95. Joe Soss et al., *Disciplining the Poor: Neoliberal Paternalism and the Persistent
Power of Race* (University of Chicago Press, 2011).

96. John Joseph Brady, *The Craft of Interviewing* (Cincinnati: Writer's Digest), 72–6.

97. See the 2016 campaign of Green Party candidate Jill Stein, at http://www .jill2016.com/platform, accessed July 13, 2017, and the activist groups such as Popular Resistance found here: https://popularresistance.org/category/resistance -report/, accessed July 13, 2017. Rolling Jubilee (rollingjubilee.org, accessed July 13, 2017), Strike Debt, and the Debt Collective are also advocates of debt aboli- tion/forgiveness, as well as this piece by stakeholders from the progressive action group Campaign for America's Future and the National Student Debt Jubilee Project: http://www.huffingtonpost.com/rj-eskow/liberate-41-million-ameri_b _6547510.html, accessed July 13, 2017.

98. http://houseofdebt.org/2014/05/18/debt-forgiveness-in-history.html, ac- cessed July 13, 2017.

99. Notably Maurizio Lazzarato, in his book *Governing by Debt* (South Pasa- dena, CA: semiotext(e), 2015). Lazzarato also refers to institutions of higher edu- cation as "factories" of debt, similar to Randy L. Martin naming such institutions "engines of debt" here: Randy Martin, "What Has Become of the Professional Managerial Class?" in Leo Panitch and Greg Albo (eds.), *Socialist Register: Trans- forming Classes 2015* (London: Merlin Press): "higher education continues to expand even as it shifts emphasis and effective consequence from an engine of mobility to one of debt. The class question posed by the [professional-managerial class] then becomes how to understand the social conditions of these massive aggregations of debt, which, if taken as a source of expansive revenue streams suggest a rethinking of the relations between labour and capital."

100. http://money.cnn.com/2017/05/18/pf/college/betsy-devos-public-service -loan-forgiveness/index.html, accessed July 14, 2017.

101. http://www.marketwatch.com/story/5-ways-the-trump-administration -is-undoing-obamas-student-loan-legacy-2017-07-12, accessed July 13, 2017.

102. https://www.nytimes.com/2017/06/22/business/consumer-agency-cond emns-abuses-in-loan-forgiveness-program.html, accessed July 13, 2017.

103. http://www.consumerreports.org/student-loans/what-to-do-if-you-face -trouble-repaying-a-student-loan/, accessed July 13, 2017.

104. https://www.nytimes.com/2017/07/06/business/dealbook/massachusetts -betsy-devos-lawsuit.html, accessed October 1, 2017.

105. Here is the link anyway: http://mappingstudentdebt.org/#/map-2-race, accessed July 13, 2017.

106. Gary C. Jacobson, *How Presidents Shape Their Party's Reputation and Pros- pects: New Evidence* (2014). APSA 2014 Annual Meeting Paper. Available at SSRN: https://ssrn.com/abstract=2454911

107. http://fortune.com/global500/list, accessed July 13, 2017.

108. http://blogs.findlaw.com/greedy_associates/2015/04/defaulting-on-a-stu dent-loan-can-cost-you-your-law-license.html, accessed July 4, 2017. http://www .businessinsider.com/you-could-lose-your-drivers-license-for-missing-student -loan-payments-2015-10, accessed July 4, 2017.

109. http://law.emory.edu/ebdj/content/volume-32/issue-1/comments/non-dis chargeability-private-student-loans-looming-crisis.html, accessed July 4, 2017.

Chapter 1: The American Debtor as Worker, Consumer, and Citizen

1. For an expanded version of this thesis about nationalism, all should read the latest edition of Benedict Anderson, *Imagined Communities: Reflections on the Origins and Spread of Nationalism* (London and New York: Verso, 2016).

2. Jeffrey J. Williams's well-received essay in 2009, http://www.alternet.org /story/121955/are_students_the_new_indentured_servants, accessed July 26, 2017, gives a lucid treatment of this usage, but his later essay incorporating borrower testimonies is particularly illustrative: Jeffrey J. Williams, "The Remediation of Higher Education and the Harm of Student Debt," *Comparative Literature* 66, no. 1 (2014): 43–51. Williams culls stories from studentloanjustice.org, an aggregation website for borrower testimonials. There are several heartwrenching anecdotes, but there are millions more where they came from.

3. Writing in 1845, Karl Marx and Friedrich Engels concluded, "The class which is the ruling *material* force of society, is at the same time its ruling *intellectual* force," in *The German Ideology* (New York: International Publishers, 1970), 64. They elaborated: "The class which has the means of material production at its disposal, has control at the same time over the means of mental production, so that thereby, generally speaking, the ideas of those who lack the means of mental production are subject to it. The ruling ideas are nothing more than the ideal expression of the dominant material relationships, the dominant material relationships grasped as ideas." This insight is straightforward and should be clear enough to anyone not in thrall to the various academic and other discourses that have taken shape around the project of rendering capitalism invisible and obfuscating its class dynamics. Writing in the modern day, Adolph Reed translates this critical conclusion in the following way: "Being a progressive is now more a matter of how one thinks about oneself than what one stands for or does in the world. The best that can be said for that perspective is that it registers acquiescence in defeat. It amounts to an effort to salvage an idea of a left by reformulating it as a sensibility *within* neoliberalism rather than a challenge to it.

"The power of ideology as a mechanism that harmonizes the principles one likes to believe one holds with what advances one's material interests; they also attest to the fact that the transmutation of leftism into pure self-image exponentially increases the potential power of that function of ideology." http://nonsite .org/feature/django-unchained-or-the-help-how-cultural-politics-is-worse-than -no-politics-at-all-and-why#foot_src_20-5381

4. There are other classic definitions of ideology, found in a qualitative comparison in John Gerring's methods textbook, *Social Science Methodology: A Criterial Framework* (Cambridge and New York: Cambridge University Press, 2001); all quotes are on page 72 of Gerring's book:

"An organization of opinions, attitudes, and values—a way of thinking about man and society. We may speak of an individual's total ideology or of his ideology with respect to different areas of social life; politics, economics, religion, minority groups, and so forth," Theodor Adorno et al. in 1950.

"Maps of problematic social reality and matrices for the creation of collective conscience," Clifford Geertz in 1964/1973.

"A typically dogmatic, i.e. rigid and impermeable, approach to politics," Giovanni Sartori in 1972.

None of these are inconsistent, but it is the Adorno definition that speaks to the politically weaponized version of ideology for the ruling class. Geertz's, however, is, as Gerring asserts, "useful for some types of work (particularly of the interpretive variety)," of which this work is one.

5. Thomas Piketty and Arthur Goldhammer, *Capital in the Twenty-First Century* (Cambridge, MA: Belknap Press of Harvard University Press, 2014). http://search.ebscohost.com/login.aspx?direct=true&scope=site&db=nlebk&AN =663460; Thomas Piketty and Gabriel Zucman, *Wealth and Inheritance in the Long Run*, http://piketty.pse.ens.fr/files/PikettyZucman2014HID.pdf, (2014), accessed August 20, 2018.

6. One indicator that this is still an ongoing debate is the post on a prominent university business school's online blog: https://insight.kellogg.northwestern .edu/article/is_the_sunk_cost_fallacy_actually_smart_business, accessed July 27, 2017.

7. As Bridget Terry Long of Harvard University explains: "With regard to recessions and the business cycle, as earnings decrease and unemployment becomes more likely, theory suggests that individuals will be more likely to attend college." Her most persuasive finding: "Using the Current Population Survey from 1968 to 1988, which includes four US recessions, they find that a 1 percentage point increase in the unemployment rates is associated with a 2 percent increase in college enrollment." http://www.nber.org/chapters/c12862 .pdf, accessed July 27, 2017.

8. http://thefederalist.com/2014/04/23/why-inequality-doesnt-matter/, accessed August 1, 2017; https://www.cnbc.com/2015/06/15/why-wealth-inequality-isnt-a -bad-thing-commentary.html, accessed August 1, 2017; https://www.forbes.com /sites/jeffreydorfman/2014/05/08/dispelling-myths-about-income-inequality /#73de77a67c77, accessed August 1, 2017.

9. https://www.cnbc.com/2017/04/28/companies-are-holding-trillions-in-cash -overseas.html, accessed August 8, 2017; https://www.cnbc.com/2014/09/22/bil lionaires-are-hoarding-piles-of-cash.html, accessed August 8, 2017.

10. Luke Winslow, "Doing More with Less: Modeling Neoliberal Labor Relations in *Undercover Boss*," *Journal of Popular Culture* 49, no. 6 (2016).

11. Thomas Frank, *Listen Liberal: Or, What Ever Happened to the Party of the People?* (New York: Metropolitan Books, 2016). For a diagnosis of just how the political economy arrived at this state of affairs, no less an authority than Cornell University professor Louis Hyman, scholar of such works as *Borrow: The American*

Way of Debt (2012) and *Debtor Nation: The History of America in Red Ink*, summed it up thusly in his brief article, "The Politics of Consumer Debt: U.S. State Policy and the Rise of Investment in Consumer Credit, 1920–2008," *Annals of the American Academy of Political and Social Science* 644 (2012): 40–49. On page 49, his conclusion: "Whereas in the postwar period, the 1 percent paid the 99 percent in wages, after 1970 the 1 percent increasingly just lent the 99 percent money. Mortgage-backed securities and then other forms of asset-backed securities channeled capital from the top to the borrowers at the bottom. [. . .] But unlike in the postwar economy, these borrowers, with their stagnant incomes, had no way to repay the loans. Only through rising house values, which further increased demand for mortgages, were borrowers able to repay their debt. [. . .] Even now as we consider remedies to the financial crisis, we should be considering not just what the state can restrict but what it can do, using the lessons of history to guide our choices, recognizing that personal debt is anything but individual."

12. https://cew.georgetown.edu/wp-content/uploads/Press-release-Working Learners__FINAL.pdf, accessed August 1, 2017.

13. https://www.cnbc.com/2017/06/28/veterinarian-on-death-sex-and-money -owes-517000-in-student-loans.html, accessed August 2, 2017; https://www .nytimes.com/2017/05/26/your-money/student-loan-repayments.html, accessed August 2, 2017.

14. https://www.washingtonpost.com/news/wonk/wp/2013/04/04/u-s-tax -code-isnt-as-progressive-as-you-think/?utm_term=.d5b8d05dd04b, accessed August 2, 2017; https://www.nytimes.com/2017/05/20/opinion/sunday/student-de bts-economy-loans.html, accessed August 2, 2017; https://www.wsj.com/articles /loan-binge-by-graduate-students-fans-debt-worries-1439951900.

15. https://www.wsj.com/articles/more-than-40-of-student-borrowers-arent -making-payments-1459971348, accessed August 2, 2017.

16. http://time.com/money/4586201/income-based-repayment-student-loan -forgiveness-cost/, accessed August 2, 2017.

17. https://www.navient.com/loan-customers/payment-plans/plans-based-on -your-income/, accessed August 2, 2017; https://www.mygreatlakes.org/educate /knowledge-center/income-driven-repayment.html; http://www.aessuccess.org /manage/repaying_your_loan/repayment_plans.shtml; https://www.nelnet.com /income-driven-repayment-plans.

18. Anne Moore and Michael Moore, *Capitalism: A Love Story* (2015).

19. https://www.marxists.org/archive/marx/works/1867-c1/ch25.htm, accessed October 1, 2017.

20. Johann Wolfgang von Goethe, Howard Brenton, and Christa Weismann, *Faust: Parts I & II* (2014), http://public.eblib.com/choice/publicfullrecord.aspx ?p=1903732.

21. https://www.youtube.com/watch?v=9GorqroigqM&vl=en.

22. "The Story of Stuff," https://www.youtube.com/watch?v=9GorqroigqM, accessed February 23, 2019.

23. The author's upbringing included viewing an old Disney film, a modern, family-friendly repackaging of *Faust* called *The Devil and Max Devlin* (1981). The plot revolved around the Devil allowing Devlin to go free only if he lures three innocent souls into a slum that serves as a gateway to the netherworld. Walt Disney Company, *The Devil and Max Devlin* (Burbank, CA: Walt Disney Home Video, 2006).

24. https://finance.yahoo.com/news/most-borrowers-dont-think-trump-1400 00367.html, accessed August 9, 2017.

25. Charles E. Lindblom, *The Market System: What It Is, How It Works, and What to Make of It* (New Haven: Yale University Press, 2002). The earlier article was Charles E. Lindblom, 1982. "The Market as Prison," *Journal of Politics* 44, no. 2 (1982): 324–336.

26. https://www.aaup.org/article/critical-thinking-and-liberal-arts#.WYJGxI grKUl.

27. "We must present a vision of a world outside of the constraints of neoliberalism. Neoliberalism is all about commodification and the inescapable dictatorship of the market over all of human activity. This movement must work to decommoditize the public and civic spheres by asserting the values of public goods and the public sphere in healthcare, education, housing, etc." Mark Dudzic and Adolph Reed Jr., "The Crisis of Labour and the Left in the United States" in Leo Panitch and Gregory Albo. *Transforming Classes. Socialist Register 2015* (London: Merlin Press).

28. https://washingtonmonthly.com/magazine/septoct-2014/why-are-harvard -grads-still-flocking-to-wall-street/, accessed July 31, 2018.

29. For example, Wells Fargo can boast of the following: the Wells Fargo professorships in Finance and Management and Business Administration in Georgia and Alabama, respectively (http://www.provost.gatech.edu/endowed-chairs -and-professorships, accessed January 2, 2019); https://www.uab.edu/news/peo ple/item/720-klock-appointed-wells-fargo-endowed-chair-in-business-adminis tration, accessed January 2, 2019); the Wells Fargo Room at a prominent California business school (http://www.haas.berkeley.edu/facilities/rooms/wellsfargo .html, accessed January 2, 2019); the Wells Fargo endowed scholarship in North Carolina (https://www.ncat.edu/admissions/financial-aid/pdf/endow-schl/end owment-app-wells-fargo-ug-1617.pdf, accessed January 2, 2019); and the Wells Fargo Faculty Award for Excellence in Virginia (http://store.darden.virginia .edu/uva-darden-school-announces-annual-wells-fargo-award-recipients, accessed January 2, 2019).

30. https://www.thenation.com/article/universities-are-becoming-billion-dol lar-hedge-funds-with-schools-attached/, accessed July 31, 2018.

31. https://harpers.org/archive/2016/03/save-our-public-universities/, accessed October 1, 2017.

32. https://www.amazon.com/Guide-College-University-Budgeting-Institutional -ebook/dp/B0093QKWQO/ref=cm_wl_huc_item, accessed August 9, 2017.

33. https://www.insidehighered.com/blogs/confessions-community-college-de an/exchange-concessions-management, accessed August 9, 2017: "Creditors are different [from donors]. Legally, they're entitled to repayment [and] unlike both donors and employees, they're almost entirely indifferent to the long-term health, or even survival, of the college. As long as they get paid, they're happy. If that means firing half of the employees or selling off entire campuses, then so be it." The two pieces Matthew Reed references are here: https://www.insidehighered .com/blogs/confessions-community-college-dean/corporate-governance-and -shared-governance, accessed August 2, 2017; https://www.insidehighered.com /news/2015/02/23/colleges-debt-troubles-are-making-new-promises-investors, accessed August 9, 2017.

Chapter 2: The Ideology of Homeowner Democracy and Trust in Government

1. https://www.newyorkfed.org/microeconomics/hhdc.html and https://www .newyorkfed.org/newsevents/news/research/2018/rp180517, accessed August 1, 2018. At the time of this writing, the latest report on consumer debt by the New York Federal Reserve was based on data from the first quarter of 2018, when student debt officially stood at $1.41 trillion, and nonhousing consumer debt at $3.84 trillion.

2. Mortgage debt in the same report stood at $8.94 trillion.

3. Jeffrey M. Hornstein, *A Nation of Realtors: A Cultural History of the Twentieth-Century American Middle Class* (Durham: Duke University Press, 2005).

4. Stuart Murray and James McCabe, *Norman Rockwell's Four Freedoms: Images That Inspire a Nation* (Stockbridge, MA: Berkshire House, 1993).

5. The American National Election Studies (www.electionstudies.org) TIME SERIES CUMULATIVE DATA FILE [dataset]. Stanford University and the University of Michigan [producers and distributors], 2010. Of those respondents that generally show trust in government, 68 percent have been homeowners, but of those that generally do not trust the government, 62 percent are homeowners.

6. http://portal.hud.gov/hudportal/HUD?src=/program_offices/housing/fhahis tory, accessed August 1, 2018.

7. http://blog.credit.com/2015/08/80-of-americans-are-in-debt-122255/, accessed October 1, 2017.

8. https://libertystreeteconomics.newyorkfed.org/2013/02/just-released-press -briefing-on-household-debt-and-credit.html, accessed January 2, 2019.

9. https://fred.stlouisfed.org/series/AHETPI, accessed January 2, 2019, demonstrates the increase in nominal average wages; however, the inflation calculator at https://www.bls.gov/data/inflation_calculator.htm, accessed August 1, 2018, demonstrates that this increase is very little in constant dollars. In other words, this is a visual representation of wage stagnation in the United States.

10. http://www.epi.org/publication/raising-americas-pay/, accessed September 15, 2016.

11. Gary C. Jacobson, "How Presidents Shape Their Party's Reputation and Prospects: New Evidence." Prepared for delivery at the 2014 Annual Meeting of the American Political Science Association, August 28–31, 2014, pp. 28–29. http://papers.ssrn.com/sol3/papers.cfm?abstract_id=2454911. "People entering the electorate during the New Deal remain disproportionately Democratic. Each age cohort is increasingly Republican through the Eisenhower years; that trend is reversed with the onset of the Kennedy-Johnson years, culminating with predominantly Democratic cohorts among those coming of age during the Nixon-Ford administrations. A swing back toward Republicans appears among the Reagan-GHW Bush cohorts, but since then succeeding cohorts are decisively Democratic by either measure. This pattern reflects Clinton's success and Bush's failure in delivering peace and prosperity, but it also reflects strong demographic trends and the Republican Party's adoption of resolutely conservative stands on social issues that are unattractive to most young voters. [. . .] Younger cohorts are much more likely to initially declare themselves independents, but a substantial majority of them lean toward one of the parties; proportion of pure independents is actually lower among the youngest cohorts than among their slightly older contemporaries."

12. One report compiles a differentiated list regarding the attitudes of the British public toward public social welfare spending by generation, including baby boomers, Generation X, and "Generation Y" (millennials). Though the report is compiled from the British Social Attitudes Survey, the findings are nonetheless valid and relevant to attitudes in the United States. On the baby boomers: "The Baby boomers felt let down by the system they have contributed to over time. This was something felt particularly acutely by those receiving low levels of out-of-work benefits, which they thought of as unfair given the amount they have contributed. They thought that the welfare system does not do enough to support people (back) into appropriate work."

On millennials: "Generation Y tended to think that the welfare system does not reward responsible behaviour, for example, not adequately supporting graduates who have tried to improve their skills, by helping them to find appropriate work. Additionally, they had little faith that the system would provide social insurance across a person's life, seeing it simply as a means of redistribution."

These quotes are from the summarized report "Attitudes of Different Generations to the Welfare System," https://www.jrf.org.uk/report/attitudes-different-generations-welfare-system, accessed January 2, 2019. The full report, "Generational Strains," by Bobby Duffy, Suzanne Hall, Duncan O'Leary, and Sarah Pope, is available here: https://www.demos.co.uk/files/Demos_Ipsos_Generation_Strains_web.pdf, accessed January 2, 2019.

13. For information about the Public Service Loan Forgiveness program, which compels borrowers to work for a certified public institution or private institution with 501(c) (3) charitable nonprofit status (which explicitly excludes work for labor unions) while making 10 years' worth of payments toward forgiveness of the balance of the loan, see the government's own fact sheet, *Federal Student Aid Public Service Loan Forgiveness Program Fact Sheet*, https://studentaid.ed.gov/sa/repay

-loans/forgiveness-cancellation/public-service, accessed January 2, 2019, on who and what loans are eligible. As is clear from many complaints on many of the Stories sites providing the data for this project, many who believe themselves eligible for the spirit of the program find themselves unable to take advantage of it because they began repayment before the program was created in 2007.

14. The endorsement of homeownership as synonymous with wealth creation is articulated as the root of twentieth-century racial discrimination in a recent piece by Mark Dudzic and Adolph Reed Jr., "The Crisis of Labour and the Left in the United States," in Leo Panitch and Greg Albo (eds.), *Socialist Register: Transforming Classes 2015* (London: Merlin Press): "housing policy materially reinforced racial and other starkly clear hierarchies because the privatized system of real estate valuation assigned a premium to white exclusivity in neighborhourhoods, and federally subsidized mortgage financing adopted the industry's valuation framework. The real estate market was therefore structured on a racially discriminatory basis that all but denied minorities, especially but not only blacks, access to that important tier of the semiprivate welfare state. Worse, the threat that non-white 'encroachment' on a neighbourhood would ensue in reduction in residential market value gave material force to racial bigotry and exclusion, which occasionally erupted in violence against non-whites perceived as interlopers. In addition to direct disadvantage with respect to access to desirable housing, the pattern of discrimination and exclusion had intergenerational effects inasmuch as home equity was a primary source."

15. To fully explain this phenomenon, there is perhaps no better source than Ronald Inglehart himself, who was tasked with authoring the Encyclopedia Britannica entry on Postmaterialism, last updated January 18, 2015, at http://www.britannica.com/EBchecked/topic/1286234/postmaterialism: "The term *postmaterialism* was first coined by American social scientist Ronald Inglehart in *The Silent Revolution: Changing Values and Political Styles Among Western Publics* (1977):

"Until the 1970s, it was nearly universal for individuals to prioritize so-called materialist values such as economic growth and maintaining order; on the other hand, postmaterialists give top priority to such goals as environmental protection, freedom of speech, and gender equality.

. . . "By the turn of the 21st century, however, materialists and postmaterialists had become equally numerous in many Western countries.

. . . "For example, at the turn of the 21st century, materialists outnumbered postmaterialists in Pakistan by more than 50 to 1 and in Russia by nearly 30 to 1. But, in prosperous and stable countries such as the United States and Sweden, postmaterialists outnumbered materialists by 2 to 1 and 5 to 1, respectively.

. . . "For example, postmaterialists and the young are markedly more tolerant of homosexuality than are materialists and the elderly, and they are far more permissive than materialists in their attitudes toward abortion, divorce, extramarital affairs, prostitution, and euthanasia. There is also a gradual shift in job motivations, from maximizing one's income and job security toward a growing insistence on interesting and meaningful work. Economic accumulation for the sake of economic security was the central goal of industrial society. Ironically, their attainment set in motion a process of gradual cultural change that has made these goals less central, bringing about a rejection of the hierarchical institutions that helped attain them."

16. Noted in Jacobson, "How Presidents Shape Their Party's Reputation."

17. https://www.bostonglobe.com/metro/2016/04/14/duxbury-father-wins-student-loan-relief-seeks-more-change/fcaiQWEjrhRd7EdDDsHWsL/story.html, https://www.leagle.com/decision/inadvbco140903000865, accessed September 5, 2017.

18. https://www.consumerfinance.gov/data-research/research-reports/2017-college-credit-card-agreements/, accessed October 16, 2018.

19. https://fafsa.ed.gov/, accessed August 20, 2018.

20. In *Academe*, the monthly magazine of the American Association of University Professors at https://www.aaup.org/article/organizing-advocacy#.W3sGZ-gzqUk, accessed August 20, 2018. From the well-known *The Professor Is In* blog: https://theprofessorisin.com/2016/01/11/building-solidarity-across-the-profession-a-guest-post/, accessed August 20, 2018. An interview by *Inside Higher Ed*, https://www.insidehighered.com/advice/2014/03/07/two-adjuncts-discuss-their-career-realities, accessed August 20, 2018. Her dissertation of fifty-seven poems is here: https://aquila.usm.edu/dissertations/988/, accessed August 20, 2018. A sampling of her published poetry work is in the *Santa Fe Literary Review*: https://issuu.com/sfcc_pubs/docs/sflr2014v2web/268, accessed August 20, 2018.

21. An important exploration of this topic began with academic Miya Tokumitsu in *Jacobin*, available here: https://www.jacobinmag.com/2014/01/in-the-name-of-love/, accessed August 20, 2018. Tokumitsu developed this concept into a book (Verso).

Chapter 3: The Government's Creation and Destruction of the American University

1. Suzanne Mettler, *Degrees of Inequality: How the Politics of Higher Education Sabotaged the American Dream* (Ebooks, 2014). http://cmich.idm.oclc.org/login?url=http://lib.myilibrary.com/detail.asp?ID=574596.

2. Thomas K. McCraw and William R. Childs, *American Business since 1920: How It Worked* (New York: John Wiley & Sons, 2018).

3. Nearly: Total fall enrollment in degree-granting postsecondary institutions, by control and level of institution: 1970 through 2014, http://nces.ed.gov/programs/digest/d15/tables/dt15_303.25.asp, accessed November 4, 2016. For military numbers: https://www.nationalww2museum.org/students-teachers/student-resources/research-starters/research-starters-us-military-numbers, accessed July 30, 2018.

4. Mettler, *Degrees of Inequality*.

5. https://www.businessinsider.com/for-profit-colleges-target-military-veterans -2017-12, accessed July 30, 2018.

6. For an analysis of data from the New York Federal Reserve on this subject, see a column by Doug Henwood, "The Economic Consequences of Student Debt," published on his blog, *LBO News with Doug Henwood,* April 17, 2013, http://lbo-news.com/2013/04/17/the-economic-consequences-of-student-debt/.

7. David Rankin does a nice job articulating the difference in political perception between millennials and baby boomers in his book based on his research teaching American government to students at SUNY Fredonia, *U.S. Politics and Generation Y* (Boulder and London: Lynne Rienne Press, 2013).

8. Joel Thomas Tierno writes "How Many Ways Must We Say It?: A Tired Meme That Just Won't Die" about the destructive nature of the student-as-customer model and vocabulary in a recent issue of *Academe* (November-December 2014), http://www.aaup.org/article/how-many-ways-must-we-say-it#.VRSeG 454q6l.

9. The famous perennial UCLA study by John H. Pryor, Sylvia Hurtado, Victor B. Saenz, Jose Luis Santos, and William S. Korn, *The American Freshman: Forty-Year Trends* (Los Angeles: Cooperative Institutional Research Program, 2006), http://heri.ucla.edu/PDFs/40TrendsManuscript.pdf was best at demonstrating the contrasting trendlines between 1965 and 2006 that asked incoming first-year college students whether they sought "to develop a meaningful philosophy of life" versus "be very well-off financially" as the goal of their education. Philosophy went from 85 percent of freshmen in 1965 to 40 percent in 1990 (and plateaued through to the present), and finance increased from 45 to 70 percent (also plateaued). No doubt this is somewhat of a proxy for the increasing universality of public higher education during this era, but it is still of some note to document the changing cultural nature of higher education as a whole.

10. This is a readily accessible factoid, so here is one source that is somewhat helpful to borrowers (and purposefully so): http://www.finaid.org/loans/student loandebtclock.phtml.

11. The New York Federal Reserve has interesting data on student debt, and from 2005 to 2012, the burden reflected above is shown in "Student Loan Debt by Age Group" (March 29, 2013) here: http://www.newyorkfed.org/student loandebt/ (accessed March 27, 2015). The overall debt held to the federal government itself is quite striking, having risen astronomically during the 2008 financial crisis: "Financing Postsecondary Education in the United States" (National Center for Education Statistics, May 2013). Figure 4, "Total Outstanding Balance of Student Loans Owned by the Federal Government, in Constant 2011 Dollars: October 2000 through October 2012," shows a rise from $124 billion in 2000 to $516 billion in 2012. https://nces.ed.gov/programs/coe/indicator_tua.asp

12. Henwood, "The Economic Consequences of Student Debt."

13. "Graph: Why Student Loan Delinquency Is Still So High," published by the Century Foundation (August 27, 2013) at http://www.tcf.org/work/educa tion/detail/graph-why-student-loan-delinquency-is-still-so-high essentially lays

the blame with unemployment itself, but shows the delinquency rate still at a high of roughly 12 percent.

14. Nick Anderson, "National Student Loan Default Rate Dips to 13.7 Percent; Still 'Too High,' Official Says," *Washington Post* (September 24, 2014), http://www .washingtonpost.com/local/education/national-student-loan-default-rate -declines-to-137-percent/2014/09/24/d280c8bc-43ee-11e4-b437-1a7368204 804_story.html.

15. Petra Cahill, "Another Idea for Student Loan Debt: Make It Go Away: As Anger Builds over Deep Pool of Red Ink, Some Advocate Forgiveness or Mass Payment Stoppage" on msnbc.com, October 26, 2011, at http://web.archive.org /web/20120511192206/http://www.msnbc.msn.com/id/45040659/ns/us_news -life/t/another-idea-student-loan-debt-make-it-go-away/ (accessed March 27, 2015).

16. Debt refusal has been discussed chiefly by the Occupy group Strike Debt!, but its chief academic advocate seems to be Andrew Ross at New York University. His book *Creditocracy: And the Case for Debt Refusal* (New York and London: OR Books, 2013) has been very widely read, and it begins with an understanding that student loans simply should not be a source of debt for the average person. He somewhat echoes David Graeber and his 2011 Occupy-era book *Debt: The First Five Thousand Years* (Brooklyn: Melville House, 2011). Graeber summarizes his book in response to a characterization by popular economist Doug Henwood on Henwood's blog: "My book actually relies on an explicitly Marxist analysis of two cycles of postwar capitalism inspired mainly by the Midnight Notes Collective, and combines it with an equally explicit challenge to mainstream Marxist theory by noting that the money forms (including central banking system, stock markets, etc.) typical of capitalism, which are indeed new, emerged prior to factories or even the widespread use of wage labor but rather as a way of handling the profits of militaristic colonial ventures which involved extraction of labor value largely through slavery, debt peonage, and other coercive means. I then point out that both unfree labor, and the connection between military power and forms of money creation, have never disappeared and in some ways [have] been coming back stronger than ever in the current neoliberal form of capitalism" (November 16, 2012). In essence, debt throughout history has been a source of political control by the ruling military class, and this pattern has seemed to recur in the current era.

17. One particularly insightful piece of information is from the Liberty Street Economics blog hosted at the New York Federal Reserve Bank. It declares that 37 percent of borrowers are currently in repayment. The piece is entitled: "Payback Time? Measuring Progress on Student Debt Repayment" by Meta Brown, Andrew Haughwout, Donghoon Lee, Joelle Scally, and Wilbert van der Klaauw (February 20, 2015), at http://libertystreeteconomics.newyorkfed.org/2015/02/payback_time _measuring_progress_on_student_debt_repayment.html#.VRhpPY54q6k (accessed March 29, 2015).

18. "But what seems to now be emerging is an attributional notion of class where professionals are securitized through circulating attributes of their labour in which performance outcomes matter more than expertise. The doctor, lawyer,

professor, finance engineer are assessed by metrics of productivity, customer satisfaction, portfolio contributions, rather than by measures of their expertise or knowledge per se. This is the predicament of a professional subsumed to a managerialism that ranks their performance on a pricing model that does not recognize intrinsic value and refuses translation of specific knowledge in favour of measures of worth added to the portfolio of the enterprise." Randy Martin, "What Has Become of the Professional Managerial Class?" In Leo Panitch and Gregory Albo, *Transforming Classes. Socialist Register* (London: 2015).

Author's note: "precarity" is a term in vogue among critical academics, in the social sciences particularly, to convey in language the precarious nature of modern work and subsistence under neoliberal-style capitalism.

19. Graphs of the changing goals of students who enter higher education, drawn from data obtained in both other literature and government documents: http://www.heri.ucla.edu/monographs/50YearTrendsMonograph2016.pdf, accessed October 1, 2017.

20. Bankruptcy law, Sallie Mae, Navient, Freddie Mac, New G.I. Bill, banking, campaign finance, profits from loans (New America Foundation: https://www.newamerica.org/education-policy/policy-explainers/higher-ed-workforce/federal-student-aid/federal-student-loans/federal-student-loan-history/).

Total fall enrollment in degree-granting postsecondary institutions, by control and level of institution: 1970 through 2014, http://nces.ed.gov/programs/digest/d15/tables/dt15_303.25.asp, accessed November 4, 2016.

21. https://www.federalreserve.gov/releases/g19/current/, accessed July 28, 2018.

22. https://www.nytimes.com/2017/11/18/business/student-loans-licenses.html, accessed August 20, 2018. You can see the tracking of which states repealed these laws at the top of this blog: http://www.jwj.org/in-22-states-your-student-debt-could-cost-you-your-job, accessed August 20, 2018.

23. https://www.theatlantic.com/business/archive/2015/09/the-failure-of-for-profit-colleges/405301/, accessed August 20, 2018. http://forprofitu.org/fact-sheet/, accessed August 20, 2018.

24. https://www.usnews.com/news/articles/2015/04/27/for-profit-corinthian-colleges-shuts-down-all-remaining-campuses, accessed August 20, 2018.

25. https://www.nytimes.com/2011/09/22/opinion/for-profit-colleges-vulnerable-gis.html, accessed August 20, 2018.

26. A. J. Angulo, *Diploma Mills: How for-Profit Colleges Stiff Students, Taxpayers, and the American Dream* (Baltimore: Johns Hopkins University Press, 2016).

27. Halperin refers to a highly critical account of the "rise" of the University of Phoenix: John D. Murphy, *Mission Forsaken: The University of Phoenix Affair with Wall Street* (Cambridge, MA: Proving Ground Education, 2013).

28. https://www.niche.com/blog/list-of-hbcu-schools-in-america-2/, accessed February 23, 2019.

29. A recent important study of HBCUs in a political science journal is Clyde Wilcox, JoVita Wells, Georges Haddad, and Judith K. Wilcox, "The Changing Democratic Functions of Historically Black Colleges and Universities," *New*

Political Science 36, no. 4 (2014): 556–572. *Academic Search Complete*, EBSCOhost (accessed August 1, 2018).

Chapter 4: Responses to the Crisis: The New Debtor Movements

1. "Recent Stories" from the Project on Student Debt: An Initiative of the Institute for College Access & Success, http://projectonstudentdebt.org/voices _list.php, accessed March 19, 2015.

2. https://docplayer.net/18032335-Remarks-as-prepared-for-delivery-by-sen ator-elizabeth-warren-student-loan-symposium-march-12-2014.html, accessed August 21, 2018.

3. https://lbo-news.com/2013/09/24/situating-finance/, accessed August 21, 2018.

4. http://strikedebt.org/The-Debt-Resistors-Operations-Manual.pdf, accessed August 20, 2018.

5. http://college.usatoday.com/2017/04/17/heres-how-much-bernie-sanders -free-college-for-all-plan-would-cost/, accessed August 20, 2018. The most credible, thorough proposal, advanced by Robert Samuels of the University of California–Santa Barbara, president of the University of California union for faculty and librarians, can be found here, with a similar estimate: https://ucaft.org /content/making-all-public-higher-education-free-bob-samuels, accessed August 21, 2018. His book of roughly the same time, based on the paper, is *Why Public Higher Education Should Be Free: How to Decrease Cost and Increase Quality at American Universities* (New Brunswick: Rutgers University, 2013). His most recent book includes the most recent iteration of his proposal in addition to an overall look at higher education politics: *Educating Inequality: Beyond the Political Myths of Higher Education and the Job Market* (New York and London: Routledge, 2018).

6. https://www.hillaryclinton.com/issues/college/, accessed August 20, 2018.

7. https://www.rubio.senate.gov/public/index.cfm/2017/3/rubio-warner-intro duce-legislation-to-ease-burden-of-student-loan-debt, accessed August 20, 2018.

8. http://www.slate.com/articles/business/moneybox/2014/06/elizabeth_war ren_student_debt_crisis_it_s_actually_tom_petri_who_has_the.html, accessed August 20, 2018.

9. https://www.thenation.com/article/sick-with-worry-gop-bill-to-eliminate -public-service-loan-forgiveness-threatens-social-work-sector/, accessed August 20, 2018.

10. Joel Best and Eric Best, *The Student Loan Mess: How Good Intentions Created a Trillion-Dollar Problem* (Berkeley, Los Angeles, London: University of California Press, 2014); Alan Collinge, *The Student Loan Scam: The Most Oppressive Debt in U.S. History, and How We Can Fight Back* (Boston, MA: Beacon Press, 2009); David Graeber, *Debt: The First 5,000 Years* (Brooklyn: Melville House, 2014); Bill Zimmerman, *The Student Loan Swindle* (Seattle: Amazon, 2014). The Student Loan Lawyer can be found at https://thestudentloanlawyer.com/, accessed February 23, 2019.

11. http://www.pewsocialtrends.org/2015/07/29/more-millennials-living-with -family-despite-improved-job-market/, accessed August 20, 2018.

12. https://www.insidehighered.com/news/2018/06/21/community-college -enrollment-rates-expected-keep-falling, accessed August 20, 2018.

13. https://www.newyorkfed.org/microeconomics/hhdc.html, accessed August 20, 2018.

14. https://studentloanhero.com/student-loan-debt-statistics/, accessed August 20, 2018.

15. One particularly insightful piece of information is from the *Liberty Street Economics* blog hosted at the New York Federal Reserve Bank. It declares that 37 percent of borrowers are currently in repayment. The piece is entitled "Payback Time? Measuring Progress on Student Debt Repayment" by Meta Brown, Andrew Haughwout, Donghoon Lee, Joelle Scally, and Wilbert van der Klaauw (February 20, 2015), http://libertystreeteconomics.newyorkfed.org/2015/02/payback_time _measuring_progress_on_student_debt_repayment.html#.VRhpPY54q6k (accessed March 29, 2015).

16. The endorsement of homeownership as synonymous with wealth creation is articulated as the root of twentieth-century racial discrimination in a recent piece by Mark Dudzic and Adolph Reed Jr., "The Crisis of Labour and the Left in the United States," in Leo Panitch and Greg Albo (eds.), *Socialist Register: Trans-forming Classes 2015* (London: Merlin Press): "housing policy materially rein-forced racial and other starkly clear hierarchies because the privatized system of real estate valuation assigned a premium to white exclusivity in neighborhour-hoods, and federally subsidized mortgage financing adopted the industry's valu-ation framework. The real estate market was therefore structured on a racially discriminatory basis that all but denied minorities, especially but not only blacks, access to that important tier of the semiprivate welfare state. Worse, the threat that non-white 'encroachment' on a neighbourhood would ensue in reduc-tion in residential market value gave material force to racial bigotry and exclu-sion, which occasionally erupted in violence against non-whites perceived as interlopers. In addition to direct disadvantage with respect to access to desirable housing, the pattern of discrimination and exclusion had intergenerational effects inasmuch as home equity was a primary source."

17. http://www.post-gazette.com/opinion/Op-Ed/2013/09/18/Death-of-an-ad junct/stories/201309180224, accessed August 20, 2018.

18. Reed's 2015 essay with Mark Dudzic outlined a similar argument: https:// www.commondreams.org/sites/default/files/dudzic_and_reed_the_crisis_of _labour_and_the_left_in_the_united_states_sr_2015.pdf, accessed August 20, 2018.

19. https://onewisconsinnow.org/press/new-poll-finds-overwhelming-biparti san-support-among-wisconsin-voters-for-allowing-student-loan-refinancing/, accessed August 1, 2018.

20. Adam Seth Levine, *American Insecurity: Why Our Economic Fears Lead to Political Inaction* (Princeton: Princeton University Press, 2015).

21. Henwood's blog, *LBO News*, has featured regular posts by Henwood that are generally skeptical of the ability to organize around debt at all, let alone in the Occupy-style manner that would seek a "debt strike." Some of his pieces include "Rolling Where?" (November 13, 2012); "The Debt Obsession" (November 12, 2012); "The Economic Consequences of Student Debt" (April 13, 2013); and "Situating Finance" (September 24, 2013). In the post "Responding to Mike Konczal's Response" (November 15, 2012), Henwood asserts in response to generalized debt relief jubilee from an Occupy-style organization: "even if the relieved debtors knew about their liberation, which they well might not, it would be viewed more as a *deus ex machina* than a political act." The site is *LBO News from Doug Henwood: Insta-Punditry on Political Economy* at lbo-news.com (accessed March 2, 2015).

Chapter 5: The Sin of Debt and the Hope of Forgiveness in the Twenty-First Century

1. Jeffrey M. Hornstein, *A Nation of Realtors: A Cultural History of the Twentieth-Century American Middle Class* (Durham: Duke University Press, 2005).

2. Richard Nixon, "Special Message to the Congress on Federal Disaster Assistance," April 22, 1970. Online by Gerhard Peters and John T. Woolley, *The American Presidency Project*, http://www.presidency.ucsb.edu/ws/?pid=2479. Nixon also later proposed loan forgiveness for farmers and small businesses in another disaster circumstance in 1972, in the aftermath of Hurricane Agnes, found at Richard Nixon, "Message to the Congress Proposing Additional Disaster Relief Measures Following Tropical Storm Agnes," July 17, 1972. Online by Gerhard Peters and John T. Woolley, *The American Presidency Project*, http://www.presidency.ucsb.edu/ws/?pid=3498, accessed March 11, 2019.

3. Richard Nixon, "Special Message to the Congress Proposing a National Health Strategy," February 18, 1971. Online by Gerhard Peters and John T. Woolley, *The American Presidency Project*, http://www.presidency.ucsb.edu/ws/?pid=3311, accessed March 11, 2019.

4. Richard Nixon, "The President's News Conference," January 31, 1973. Online by Gerhard Peters and John T. Woolley, *The American Presidency Project*, http://www.presidency.ucsb.edu/ws/?pid=3930, accessed March 11, 2019.

5. Gerald R. Ford, "Remarks on Signing a Proclamation Granting Pardon to Richard Nixon," September 8, 1974. Online by Gerhard Peters and John T. Woolley, *The American Presidency Project*, http://www.presidency.ucsb.edu/ws/?pid=4695, accessed March 11, 2019

6. Ford, "Remarks on Signing a Proclamation Granting Pardon to Richard Nixon."

7. Gerald R. Ford, "Remarks Announcing a Program for the Return of Vietnam Era Draft Evaders and Military Deserters.," September 16, 1974. Online by Gerhard Peters and John T. Woolley, *The American Presidency Project*, http://www.presidency.ucsb.edu/ws/?pid=4713, accessed March 11, 2019.

8. Jimmy Carter, "Veterans Benefits Statement on Signing S. 1307 into Law," October 8, 1977. Online by Gerhard Peters and John T. Woolley, *The American Presidency Project*, http://www.presidency.ucsb.edu/ws/?pid=6771, accessed March 11, 2019.

9. "Message to the House of Representatives Returning Without Approval the Omnibus Trade and Competitiveness Act of 1988," May 24, 1988. Online by Gerhard Peters and John T. Woolley, *The American Presidency Project*, http://www.presidency.ucsb.edu/ws/?pid=35873, accessed March 11, 2019.

10. Ronald Reagan, "Statement on Signing the Immigration Reform and Control Act of 1986," November 6, 1986. Online by Gerhard Peters and John T. Woolley, *The American Presidency Project*, http://www.presidency.ucsb.edu/ws/?pid=36699, accessed December 20, 2017.

11. George Bush, "Exchange with Reporters Aboard Air Force One," April 13, 1990. Online by Gerhard Peters and John T. Woolley, *The American Presidency Project*, http://www.presidency.ucsb.edu/ws/?pid=18355, accessed March 11, 2019.

12. The full exchange ensues when a reporter asked Bush what role the U.S. relationship with Egypt was playing in the lead-up to the war with Iraq. Found in George Bush, "Remarks and a Question-and-Answer Session with Reporters Following Discussions with President Mohammed Hosni Mubarak in Cairo, Egypt," November 23, 1990. Online by Gerhard Peters and John T. Woolley, *The American Presidency Project*, http://www.presidency.ucsb.edu/ws/?pid=19090, accessed March 11, 2019.

13. George Bush, "Remarks to the American Society of Newspaper Editors," April 9, 1992. Online by Gerhard Peters and John T. Woolley, *The American Presidency Project*, http://www.presidency.ucsb.edu/ws/?pid=20825, accessed March 11, 2019.

14. The full statement is found at William J. Clinton, "Remarks on Funding to Provide Debt Relief for Poor Nations," November 6, 2000. Online by Gerhard Peters and John T. Woolley, *The American Presidency Project*, http://www.presidency.ucsb.edu/ws/?pid=1058, accessed March 11, 2019.

15. George W. Bush: "Remarks on Signing the Mortgage Forgiveness Debt Relief Act of 2007," December 20, 2007. Online by Gerhard Peters and John T. Woolley, *The American Presidency Project*.

16. George W. Bush, "Proclamation 7534—Education and Sharing Day, U.S.A., 2002," March 21, 2002. Online by Gerhard Peters and John T. Woolley, *The American Presidency Project*, http://www.presidency.ucsb.edu/ws/?pid=61831, accessed March 11, 2019.

17. George W. Bush, "Remarks on Signing the College Cost Reduction and Access Act," September 27, 2007. Online by Gerhard Peters and John T. Woolley, *The American Presidency Project*, http://www.presidency.ucsb.edu/ws/?pid=75821, accessed March 11, 2019.

18. George W. Bush, "Address to the Nation on the National Economy," September 24, 2008. Online by Gerhard Peters and John T. Woolley, *The American Presidency Project*, http://www.presidency.ucsb.edu/ws/?pid=84355, accessed March 11, 2019.

19. Bush, "Address to the Nation on the National Economy."

20. Congressional Record, Proceedings and Debates of the 110th Congress, Second Session S10189, Vol. 154. Washington, Wednesday, October 1, 2008, No. 159, October 1, 2008. https://congress.gov/crec/2008/10/01/CREC-2008-10-01-pt1-PgS10189-7.pdf, accessed March 11, 2019.

21. Rather than footnote each quotation from President Obama in this online forum, the citation will be listed here and will be the citation of record for all quotations going forward quotations until another one is cited: Barack Obama, "Remarks at a Question-and-Answer Session on Student Loan Debt and College Affordability with Tumblr Participants," June 10, 2014. Online by Gerhard Peters and John T. Woolley, *The American Presidency Project*, http://www.presidency.ucsb.edu/ws/?pid=105256, accessed March 11, 2019.

22. The quotations that follow are all from one public appearance, cited here: Donald J. Trump, "Remarks at the Renaissance Hotel in Columbus, Ohio," October 13, 2016. Online by Gerhard Peters and John T. Woolley, *The American Presidency Project*, http://www.presidency.ucsb.edu/ws/?pid=119173, accessed January 2, 2019.

23. https://www.cnn.com/2018/04/10/politics/trump-university-settlement-finalized-trnd/index.html, accessed February 23, 2019.

24. https://www.jacobinmag.com/2018/06/bernie-sanders-civil-rights-movement-activism, accessed February 23, 2019.

25. https://www.nytimes.com/2018/06/27/us/politics/supreme-court-unions-organized-labor.html, accessed August 21, 2018.

26. https://ucaft.org/content/making-all-public-higher-education-free-bob-samuels, accessed January 2, 2019.

27. https://edsource.org/2018/as-gov-brown-urges-work-on-new-online-college-community-college-faculty-drop-their-opposition/600256, accessed August 21, 2018.

28. https://www.nytimes.com/2017/12/22/us/politics/trump-tax-bill.html, accessed August 21, 2018.

29. https://tradingeconomics.com/spain/youth-unemployment-rate, accessed August 21, 2018. Yanis Varoufakis alludes to mandated austerity in his most recent book: Yanis Varoufakis, *Adults in the Room: My Battle with Europe's Deep Establishment* [S.l.] (Vintage, 2018).

30. http://www.presidency.ucsb.edu/ws/?pid=105256, accessed August 21, 2018.

Index

Activism: of Adolph Reed Jr., 107–112;
of Alexis Goldstein, 100–102; of
Chris Hicks, 113–115; debt strikes,
99, 100; of Elizabeth Henderson,
102–106; of Jack Virden, 98–100;
lack of employment after education,
96–98; Occupy movement, 69,
93, 100–102, 119; in Wisconsin,
115–118
Admissions, 52–53, 59, 62, 63
Admissions officers, 57–63
Adults living at home, 95
Affirmative action, financial, 63
Affordable Care Act, 9
Africa, 131, 133
African Americans, 73
"Alan," 41–45
Alienation: from civic effectiveness,
22; from debt, 47–48, 72, 136–137;
default and, 7, 145; delinquency
as basis for, 73; Democratic
Socialists of America and, 106–107;
partisanship about, 145–146;
from pillars of society, 6, 124;
shaping society, 69–70; Trump and,
144–145. See also Democracy
American Dream: death of, 1;
education as commodity and,

111–113; as foundation of U.S.
system, 4; homeownership as part
of, 11, 35–36, 38, 95–96; loans
coming due and, 26; military
members, 117; Reed on, 117, 118;
tropes about, 23–24
America's College Promise, 110–111
Amnesty for immigrants, 129–130
Anderson, Benjamin, 60–63
Angulo, A. J., 78–79
Attorneys, 13, 73, 94

Baby boomers, 38, 96
Bailouts, 41, 133–135
Bankruptcy. See Nondischargeable
debt
Banks. See Financial institutions
Binder, Amy, 31
Brady, John, 18
Bureaucratic organizations, 139
Bush, George H. W., 130–131
Bush, George W., 79, 131–134

California, 113, 145
Campaign for the Future of Higher
Education (CFHE), 109
Capitalism, 28, 36
Capitalism: A Love Story, 27

CARD Act (Credit Card Accountability Responsibility and Disclosure Act), 43
Career choices limited by debt, 59
Carter, Jimmy, 128
CFHE (Campaign for the Future of Higher Education), 109
CFPC (Consumer Financial Protection Bureau), 14, 84
Chopra, Rohit, 39
Citizenship, 14, 23, 29–30
Civic education, 1–2, 10. *See also* Liberal arts education
Class structure and mobility, 24, 26, 44–45, 55. *See also* American Dream
Clay, Henry, 16
Clinton, Hillary, 93–94
Clinton administration, 79, 131
Coal mining, 24–25
Collective action, difficulty with, 7–8
Collectors, 74–75, 76
College Cost Reduction and Access Act of 2007, 133
College for All Act, 93, 109
College professors, 96–98, 122–124
Colleges. *See* For-profit colleges and universities; Institutions of higher education; Public college and universities
Community colleges, 82, 113
Company stores, 25, 30–33
Company towns, 5, 25
Consolidated debt, 56
Consumer debt, 5, 35, 43, 121–122. *See also* Mortgages
Consumer Financial Protection Bureau (CFPC), 14, 84
Consumerism, 27–29
Consumers, debtors as, 27–29
Corinthian Colleges, 79, 83, 93
Cost-benefit analysis, 42, 49
Counseling about loans, 52–53, 54

Courts of law versus courts of equity, 43–44
Credit Card Accountability Responsibility and Disclosure Act (CARD Act), 43
Credit cards, 43, 121–122
Curry, James M., 16

"Death of an Adjunct," 96–97
Debt: amount of, 95; consumer debt, 5, 35; credit cards, 43, 121–122; student debt leading to other debt, 114; to support consumerism, 28; trust in government and, 38; types of, 121–122. *See also* Mortgages; Student debt
Debt bondage, company towns as, 5
Debt Collective, 93, 101
Debt relief companies, 74
Debt Resistors' Operations Manual, 93
Debt strikes, 99, 100
Deceptive business practices, 80–81
Default: alienation and, 7, 145; forbearance compared, 78; number of, 27; private versus federal loans, 75; professional licensure loss, 73; for-profit colleges and universities and, 72–73
Defense to repayment, 101–102
Deferment, 57
Delinquency, 57, 69, 73, 95
Democracy: harmed by student debt, 3, 144; home ownership and, 36; liberal arts education as foundation of, 1–2, 10; Locke on, 35, 36; political participation, 2, 8, 21–22, 28, 30; representation and, 7. *See also* Alienation
Democratic Socialists of America (DSA), 102–106
Department of Education, 21, 76
Department of Housing and Urban Development (HUD), 37

Deriesewiecz, William, 31
DeVos, Betsy, 21, 94
DeVry, 80
Diploma Mills (Angulo), 78–79
Disaster assistance to farmers, 127
Disbursements above tuition cost:
as common, 60; historically black
colleges/universities and, 89;
risks of, 90; unreality of debt and,
47–48; uses of, 51, 58
Dischargability. *See* Nondischargeable
debt
Discrimination, 39–40
Draft evaders, 127–128, 129
Drop Student Debt, 105
DSA (Democratic Socialists of
America), 102–106

East Germany, 130
Economy, student debt impacting, 69,
95, 116, 143
EDMC, 79
Education, 48, 49, 51. *See also* Free
education
Egypt, 130–131
Election of 2016: forgiveness
programs, 94; Sanders and, 93,
105, 107, 109, 111–112; student
debt and, 20; turnout, 2
"Emily," 87–89
Endowments and hedge funds, 31
Equity, 43–44
Ethnography, 15–18
Excellent Sheep (Deriesewiecz), 31
Executive Order 11803, 128

Faculty, 96–98, 122–124
Farmers, disaster assistance to, 127
Federal government: acting as
company store, 25; alienation from,
6, 124; interaction with and political
participation, 21–22; as lender, 41;
as loan servicer, 64; role of, 3; tax
system, 15

Federal loans, default protections
and, 75
15 Now, 104
Financial affirmative action, 63
Financial institutions: alienation
from, 6; bailout of, 133–135;
elite universities' relationship
with, 12, 30–33; for-profit
colleges and universities and, 15,
79; view of student loan system
by, 86
Follow-up questions, 18
Forbearance, 78
Ford, Ernie, 5
Ford, Gerald, 127–128, 129
Foreign debt forgiveness, 129–131,
133
Forgiveness: Barack Obama and,
134–135, 137–138; Bill Clinton
and, 131; George H. W. Bush
and, 130–131; George W. Bush
and, 131–134; Gerald Ford and,
127–128; Jimmy Carter and, 128;
Richard Nixon and, 126–127;
Ronald Reagan and, 129–130
Forgiveness programs: election of
2016 and, 94; Henderson on,
106; need for, 6; policy issues,
125–126; under Trump, 21; Trump
and, 94; types of, 125. *See also*
Income-based repayment (IBR);
Public service loan forgiveness
(PSLF)
For-profit colleges and universities:
amount of debt, 77; business model
of, 78, 83; default and, 72–73;
discrimination by, 40; financial
institutions and, 15; graduation
rate, 14; role of, 3; subprime
mortgage crisis and, 39; taking
advantage of people, 73, 77–83;
as too big to fail, 82–83; veterans
sought by, 68, 77, 79–80
Freedom of Speech painting, 36–37

Free education: Clinton on, 93–94; de-commodifying public goods, 111–113; Henwood on, 92; for-profit colleges and universities and, 143–144; public support for, 111; Reed on, 107–112
Free Higher Ed movement, 107–112
Friedman, Milton, 10, 91–92
Future debt payments as unreal, 47–48, 72, 136–137

Galbraith, Jamie, 109–110
Garnishment of Social Security, 116
Generational differences, 38
Generation X, 38
GI Bill (Post 9/11 Veterans Educational Assistance Act of 2008), 68
GI Bill (Servicemen's Readjustment Act of 1944), 67–68
Goldman Sachs, 79
Goldstein, Alexis, 100–102, 143–144
Graduation rate, 14, 81–82
Graeber, David, 9
Great Recession, 72, 132, 133–135
Greece, 145

Haley, Alex, 18
Halperin, David, 77–83
Harassment, 75–76
HBCU (historically black colleges/ universities), 68, 87–90
Health policy, 126–127
Hedge funds, elite universities' relationship with, 12, 30–31
Henderson, Elizabeth, 102–106
Henwood, Doug, 35, 36, 92
Hicks, Chris, 71–73, 113–115, 140–142
Higher Ed, Not Debt, 14, 93
Higher Education Act, 75
Higher education policy. *See* Policy issues

Historically black colleges/universities (HBCU), 68, 87–90
Homeownership: class structure and, 11; mortgage debt and, 95–96; student debt making impossible, 37–38, 49, 64; trust in government and, 35–38. *See also* American Dream
Hornstein, Jeffrey, 36
How Far to Free, 143–144
HUD (Department of Housing and Urban Development), 37

Immigration Reform and Control Act of 1986, 129–130
Income-based repayment (IBR): default and, 27; Friedman on, 92; Hicks on, 141; partisanship about, 84–85; as policy, 13; testimonial about, 124–125; Trump on, 140
Income gap, 112
Income-share agreements (ISAs), 13, 94
Inequality, 25–26, 72–73
Institutions of higher education, 6, 10, 32–33, 62–63. *See also* For-profit colleges and universities; Private colleges and universities; Public college and universities
Interest rates, 74, 92
Interpretive research, 15–18
Interview questions, 18
ISAs (income-share agreements), 13, 94

Janus v. AFSCME, 142
Job market: alienation from, 6; career choices limited by debt, 59; degree needed to access, 9; difficulty with, 64; Great Recession and, 72; manufacturing jobs disappearing in, 9; unemployment, 69, 72, 145
John Paul II (Pope), 131
Jubilees, 93, 100, 131

"Know What You Owe," 136–137
Koch, Charles, 12

Labor costs, consumerism and, 28
Labor unions, 25, 114–115, 142
Lange, Matthew, 17
Layoffs, 72
Lead generation companies, 80
Lebow, Victor, 27–28
Leonard, Annie, 27
Liberal arts education: citizenship
    and, 1–2, 10, 30; elite universities
    and, 31–32; historically black
    colleges/universities and, 88–90;
    incentive to obtain as gone, 11, 12,
    110–111
Lindblom, Charles, 29
Loan counseling, 52–53, 54
Loan to value ratio, 42, 49
Locke, John, 35, 36
Low income people, 88. *See also* Class
    structure and mobility

"Maggie," 57–60
Majic, Samantha, 16
Manufacturing jobs, decrease in, 9
The Market System (Lindblom), 29
Mason, Cory, 115–118, 137, 144
Merklein, Miranda, 50–54, 96–98
Methods Cafe, 15
Military members, 68, 77, 79–80, 117
Millennials, 38, 68–69, 96
Minimum wage, 104
Moody's, 12–13
Moore, Michael, 27
Mortgage Forgiveness Debt Relief Act
    of 2007, 132
Mortgages: American Dream based
    on, 95–96; amount of, 37, 121;
    limitations imposed by having, 35,
    36; subprime mortgage crisis, 11,
    39–46, 64, 102

New York State, 113

90/10 requirements, 78, 79–80
Nixon, Richard, 126–127
No Child Left Behind Act of 2001,
    132–133
Nondischargable debt: banks
    wanting to keep, 118; equity and,
    43–44; morality and, 22, 42;
    need to change policy about, 10,
    76; securitization and, 22; undue
    hardship and, 41; Virden on, 142

Obama, Barack, 10, 103, 110–111,
    113, 134–138
Occupy movement, 69, 93, 100–102,
    119
One Wisconsin Now, 115–118
Online education, 79, 145
Oregon, 113
Organizing, difficulty with, 104–105

Pardon, of Nixon, 127
"Paul," 46–49
Pell Grants, creation of, 68
Petri, Tom, 94
Piketty, Thomas, 24
Policy issues: consumer protection,
    84; forgiveness programs, 84–85;
    Friedman on, 91–92; historically
    black colleges/universities
    and, 87–90; inequality, 72–73;
    inequality resulting from, 72–73;
    predatory lending and, 74–76;
    for-profit colleges and universities
    and, 77–83; reform suggestions,
    76, 92–93; timeline of, 70–71. *See
    also* Forgiveness programs; Free
    education
Political ethnography, 15–18
Political participation: debt as
    limiting, 8; interaction with
    federal government and, 21–22;
    voter turnout, 2, 28, 30. *See also*
    Democracy
Political powerlessness, 28

Post 9/11 Veterans Educational Assistance Act of 2008 (GI Bill), 68
Postmaterialism, 38, 64
Predatory lending, 74–76
Private colleges and universities, 9, 12, 30–33, 60
Private versus public loans, 49–50, 56, 75
Professional licensure loss, 73
Public college and universities, 11, 12
Public service loan forgiveness (PSLF): Hicks on, 141; partisanship about, 84–85; as policy, 13, 125; under Trump, 21

Questions during interviews, 18
QuinStreet, 80
Quotas for admissions officers, 59, 63

Racial discrimination, 39–40
Rating, 122
Reagan, Ronald, 129–130
Reed, Adolph, Jr., 107–112
Refinance of student loans, 115–118, 137, 144
Refunds on student loans. *See* Disbursements above tuition cost
Regulations, 139
Reification, 8
Renters, trust in government and, 37
Retention rate, 88
Return on investment, 10
Risk allotment, 121–122
Robinson, Marilynne, 31–32
Rockwell, Norman, 36–37
Rolling Debt Jubilee, 93, 100
Rosenstock, Jason, 83–87
Rubio, Marco, 94

Salesperson attitude about financial aid, 52–53, 59, 63, 80
Sallie Mae, 56
Samuels, Bob, 143–144

Sanders, Bernie, 93, 105, 107, 109, 111–112, 138
"Saving Our Public Universities" (Robinson), 31–32
Scholarships, use of by schools, 62–63
Schwartz-Shea, Peregrine, 15–16
Securitization, 40
Servicemen's Readjustment Act of 1944 (GI Bill), 67–68
Servicers, 74, 75
Servitude, citizenship compared, 23
Shame, 101, 103, 105
Sixteen Tons, 5
Social mobility. *See* American Dream; Class structure and mobility
Social Security garnishment, 116
Soss, Joe, 17–18
Spain, 145
State legislatures, role of, 3
Stein, Jill, 94
The Story of Stuff, 27
Strike Debt, 93, 100, 143–144. *See also* Debt Collective
Student debt: amount of, 1, 5, 29, 37, 95; changes in structure of system, 9; default, 27; as easy to obtain, 52–53, 87; economy and, 69, 95, 116, 143; as half of consumer debt, 35; households with, 30; impacts of, 2–3, 5–6, 114, 144; lack of information about, 63–64; need for less reliance on, 76–77; not anticipating consequences from, 28–29, 53–54, 57; other types of loans compared, 42–43; for-profit versus other schools, 77, 83; as rational decision in circumstances, 2; refinance of, 115–118; status of, 69
Student debt crisis: causes of, 39–41; policy solutions to, 76, 92–93; subprime mortgage crisis compared, 11, 39–46, 64, 102

Student-debt reimbursement, 141–142
Student loans, creation of, 68
Student Power Convergence, 99, 100
Subprime mortgage crisis: racial discrimination and, 39–40; student debt crisis compared, 11, 39–46, 64, 102
Sunk-cost fallacy, 25

Tax system, 15, 125, 145
Taylor, Astra, 31
Teachers, loan forgiveness for, 132–133
Tennessee, 113
Tenure, 122–124
Testimonials, words used in, 122–123
Timeline of student loan policy, 70–71
Too big to fail attitude, 82–83
"Trudy," 74–76
Trump administration, 21, 83, 94, 138–140, 144–145
Trump University, 138
Trust in government, home ownership and, 35–38
Tuition increases, 71, 89, 136
2016 election. *See* Election of 2016

UMW (United Mine Workers), 25
Undue hardship, 41
Unemployment, 69, 72, 145
Unions, 25, 114–115, 142
United Mine Workers (UMW), 25

Universal income-based repayment. *See* Income-share agreements (ISAs)
Universities. *See* For-profit colleges and universities; Institutions of higher education; Public college and universities
University Inc. (Washburn), 31
University of Phoenix, 80, 81–82

Veterans, 68, 77, 79–80
Vietnam War draft evaders, 127–128, 129
Virden, Jake, 54–57, 98–100, 142
Vocational training, 30, 137
Vojtko, Margaret Mary, 96–97
Voter turnout, 2, 28, 30

Wage stagnation, 9–10, 37, 104
Walker, Scott, 10
Warren, Elizabeth, 92, 93
Washburn, Jennifer, 31
Wealth gap, 112
Weingarten, Randi, 93
Wells Fargo, 39–40, 79
"Why Are Harvard Grads Still Flocking to Wall Street?" (Binder), 31
Women, 73
Worker productivity, 26, 37
Workers, debtors as, 24–27
Workplace exploitation, 5, 27, 28
Workplaces, alienation from, 6

Yanow, Dvora, 15–16

About the Author

Daniel T. Kirsch, PhD, earned his doctorate in political science from the University of Massachusetts Amherst and now teaches at California State University, Sacramento. He is a proud member of the American Association of University Professors and the California Faculty Association. His work includes his dissertation, "Southie versus Roxbury: Crime, Welfare, and the Racialization of Massachusetts Gubernatorial Elections in the Post–Civil Rights Era," and contributions to the *Encyclopedia of American Political Parties and Elections* and the *Encyclopedia of Greater Philadelphia*. He resides in Woodland, California with his family. This is his first book.